IMAGES
of America

BRIDGEPORT

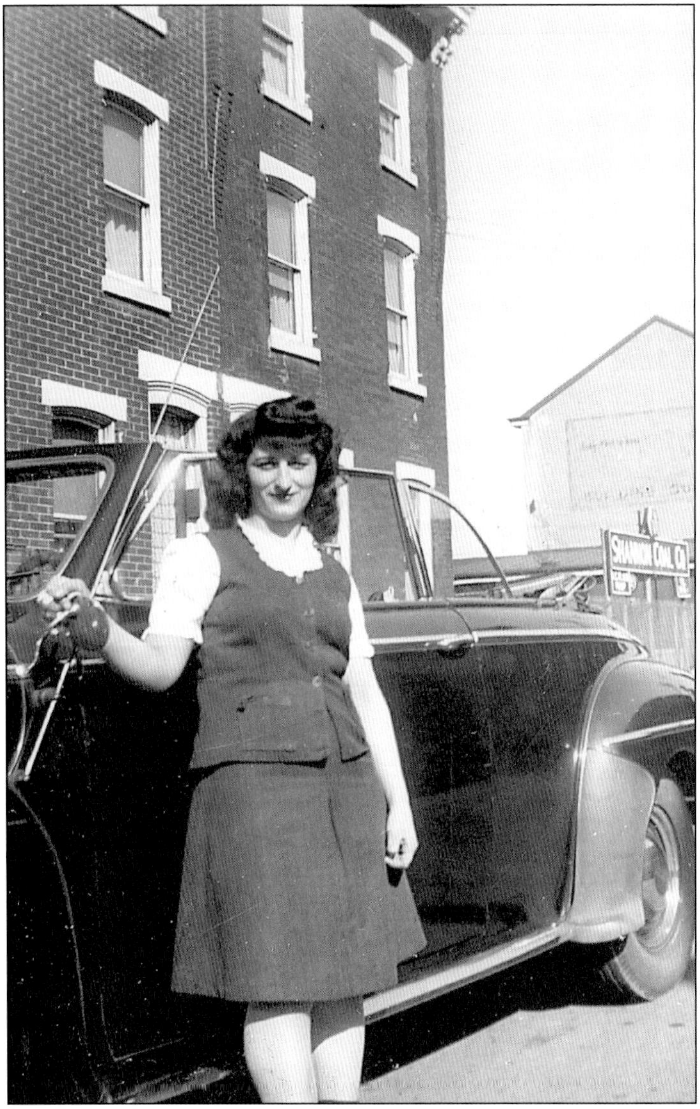

Margaret Pizza Roberto poses with a convertible car back in 1945 on West Fourth Street. The sign at the right is for Shannon Coal Company, which was located where Armond Aquatech Pools is currently located. Roberto was working at Bridgeport Luggage Company, located in the same building as the Bridgeport Pants Factory. In 1945, Roberto could buy gas for 15¢ per gallon at any one of five Bridgeport gas stations, including Differ Brothers located at 100 Dekalb Street, George Jacobs at 114 Dekalb Street, George Loving at 1069 Dekalb Street, Bernardo Marinelli at 1070 Dekalb Street, or Pure Oil Company at 437 Ford Street. (Phil Johns.)

On the cover: This rare classroom photograph taken at Bridgeport High School back in 1925 shows students working in a chemistry lab. It is interesting that all the students are wearing neckties or bow ties, including the lone female third from left. Bridgeport's first school was built in 1842, before the borough was incorporated and was still a part of Upper Merion Township. At the height of the borough's population peak in the mid-1940s, Bridgeport had four public schools, including the high school and two parochial schools. In 1966, Bridgeport School District merged with Upper Merion Township School District. (Bridgeport Hall of Fame.)

IMAGES
of America

BRIDGEPORT

Jack Coll

ARCADIA
PUBLISHING

ISBN 978-0-7385-5505-8

Published by Arcadia Publishing
Charleston SC, Chicago IL, Portsmouth NH, San Francisco CA

Printed in the United States of America

Library of Congress Catalog Card Number: 2007928793

For all general information contact Arcadia Publishing at:
Telephone 843-853-2070
Fax 843-853-0044
E-mail sales@arcadiapublishing.com
For customer service and orders:
Toll-Free 1-888-313-2665

Visit us on the Internet at www.arcadiapublishing.com

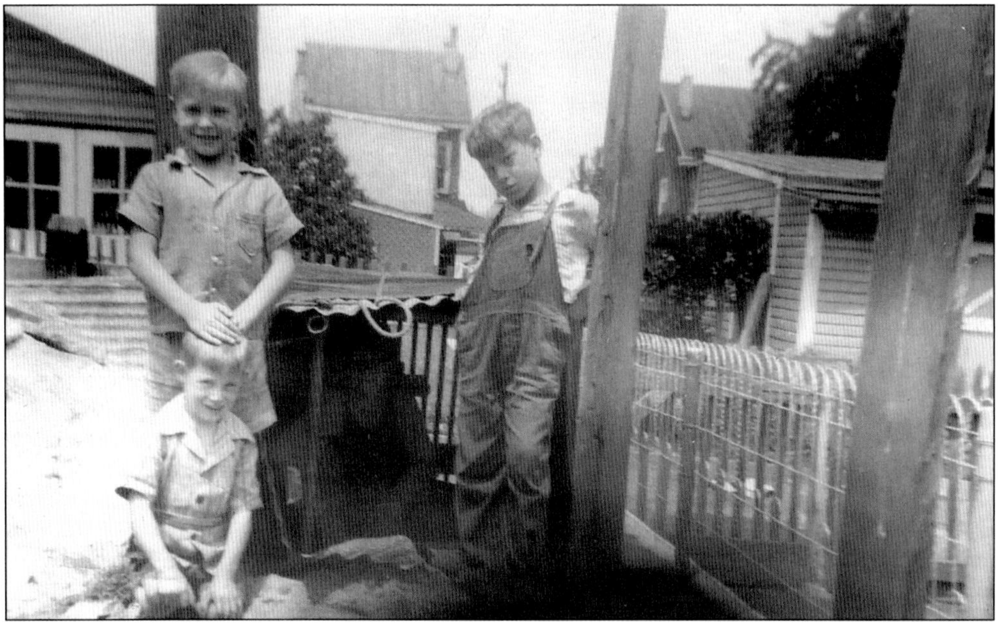

Three children playing in the backyard at 441 Bush Street in the summer of 1941 include, from left to right, Andrew Yakscoe (standing), Alex "Jake" Hall, and Nicholas Valerio. Bridgeport had three public elementary schools in 1941 and two parochial elementary schools. More than 1,300 students enjoyed Bridgeport's schools in 1941, with more than 700 of them in the Bridgeport High School. The easy times in the port would not last, however, as World War II loomed and many of Bridgeport's sons and daughters would participate on behalf of the United States. (Alex Hall.)

Contents

Acknowledgments

Bridgeport is made up of 422 acres with some of Montgomery County's best-kept secrets in the borough. When I think of Bridgeport, I think of Franzones Pizza, Suzy-Jo Donuts, Mount Carmel's Feast, and a long line of great athletes who have come from the borough over the years.

When I think of Bridgeport, I think of a young marine named John Todd III who was killed while serving his country in Iraq, and I pray for him and his parents, John and Carol, almost everyday. Bridgeport has offered up its best to serve in all wars, and they take great pride in doing so.

When I think of Bridgeport, it takes me back to my childhood when I participated in St. Augustine's Boy Scouts. I also think about playing pool at a place called Puco's. And I often think about a guy named Al Donofrio, a Bridgeport High School graduate who worked at the Conshohocken Fellowship House until his death in 1976.

Arcadia Publishing insists that all of the images in this book are a quality product, and I would like to thank the following people who contributed to *Bridgeport*. Nobody knows Bridgeport like Nick Rotondo, and Nick was a big help offering up the images in the Bridgeport Hall of Fame. Thanks also to Doris Frymoyer of Bridgeport Fire Company No. 1 for her assistance and Philip O'Brien of the Goodwill Fire Company.

Once again, thanks to Dave Wingeron at Main Street Photo, who has gained recognition as Norristown's premiere film-processing center for his efforts on all four Arcadia publications I have been involved with.

Thanks to the Historical Society of Montgomery County for offering up information dating back a couple hundred years. The society can be contacted at 610-272-0297 or at www.hsmcpa.org.

Other information for this book was obtained from *Montgomery County: the Second Hundred Years*, *Boyd's Directory*, the *Norristown Times Herald* newspaper, and *Centennial Edition, History of Bridgeport* by Edward Pinkowski. Thanks to Colleen Popewicz and St. Augustine's Church, Maureen McQuaid at Our Lady of Mount Carmel Church, and Linda Brady at the *Norristown Times Herald*, to me simply called "De Witt."

Not mentioned in my credit line is Johnny Nicola, who in fact was responsible for many of the photographs shown. Nicola was a longtime photographer and writer for the *Norristown Times Herald*, and many of his photographs can be seen at the Bridgeport Hall of Fame.

Thanks to the many businesses and residents in Bridgeport for supporting this project.

INTRODUCTION

The Borough of Bridgeport was incorporated on February 27, 1851. The borough's geographic territory lies between Upper Merion Township and the borough of Norristown.

At the beginning Bridgeport grew to become a paramount industrial region, a blue-collar, blue-chip community and employed more than its listed residential population. Its industry was diverse and financially lucrative.

The name Bridgeport was established in 1829. A port by the bridge. The name was embraced by early settlers that included the Swedish and Welsh immigrants who settled in 1723. Irish immigrants settled more than a century later in 1860, and Italian immigrants settled in the 1890s. The middle of the 19th century saw the Slovaks, Ukrainians, and Poles also immigrate to Bridgeport. All came because of the mills along the Schuylkill River. In 1851, there were 550 residents, and a century later, in the 1950s, the borough had 5,827 residents. Today there are 4,250 people living in the borough.

The immigrants who settled in the borough later formed clubs to gather with friends. The social fraternities also played an important part in promoting sports. The Catholic Community Club, Italian Citizens Club, and Triple "S" Club (St. Salvatore Society), just to name a few, still meet today. The year 1944 saw the formation of the Bridgeport Community Park as a recreation center for youth.

The borough of Bridgeport peaked in population in the 1950s with 5,800 residents and had four public schools, including one high school and three parochial schools. Inclusive enrollment neared 800 students. The public schools enrollment of kindergarten through grade 12 was 900 students. Bridgeport High School had three varsity sports for boys and two for girls in the 1950s. In 1937, Bridgeport School systems had 1,250 students, in 1966, the Bridgeport public schools consolidated with Upper Merion Area School District, leaving the borough with one public elementary school.

The memories that will last forever in Bridgeport include a whistle stop on a train to Bridgeport in 1948 that helped get Harry Truman elected as president of the United States. The appearance by John F. Kennedy in Bridgeport in October 1960 helped him get elected to the office of president of the United States as well. Vice Pres. Al Gore visited the doll factory in the industrial park in August 2000 as a presidential candidate. These are just a few of the political memories residents have enjoyed over the years.

The Bridgeport Hall of Fame houses all of the Bridgeport artifacts and history in the municipal hall located on Fourth Street; the hall of fame was founded in 1972. The hall of fame has entertained a number of reunions over the years and has enjoyed contributing to Arcadia Publishing's *Bridgeport* publication.

Today Bridgeport and its residents enjoy a strong sense of community; the borough is still home to working-class citizens, much as it was more than a century and a half ago. Not only is Bridgeport a great place in America to work, worship, play, and live, but residents stay busy with community events year round, including church festivals, the annual car show, Christmas tree–lighting ceremonies, youth leagues, and a strong recreation center. These components make for a strong family-oriented community, and in a nutshell, that would be Bridgeport, Pennsylvania.

—Nick "Chief" Rotondo
Bridgeport Hall of Fame Founder and Curator

One

Buildings and Industry

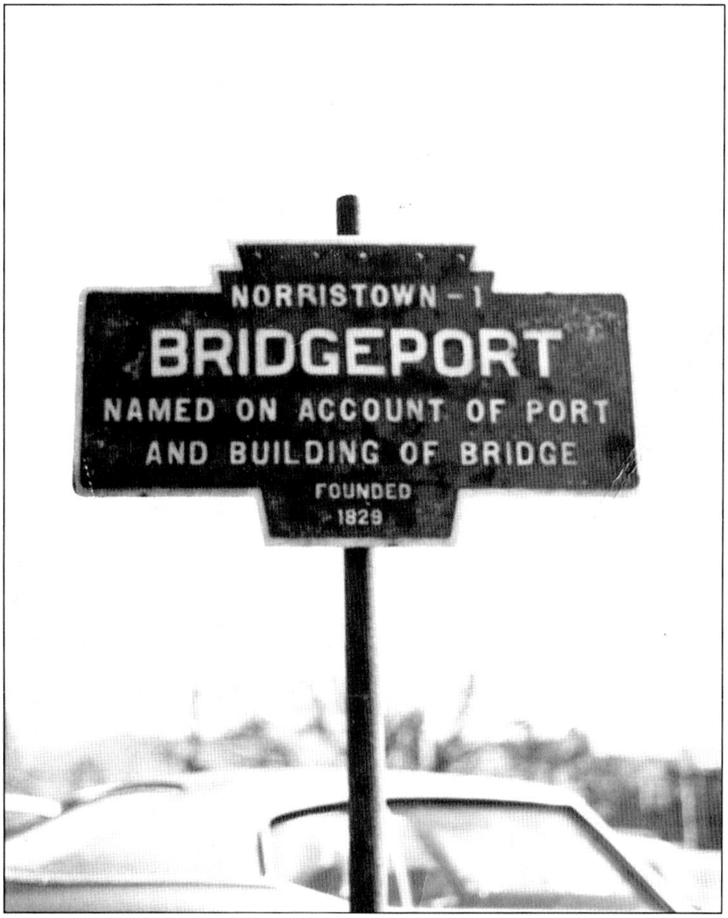

Signs at the entrance to Bridgeport state that Bridgeport was named on account of being a port and the building of a bridge. The village of Bridgeport was founded in 1829 but was not incorporated until 1851. Bridgeport had a canal running through the industry belt as early as 1825, and although it was called the Norristown Canal, the borough of Norristown really never had a canal.

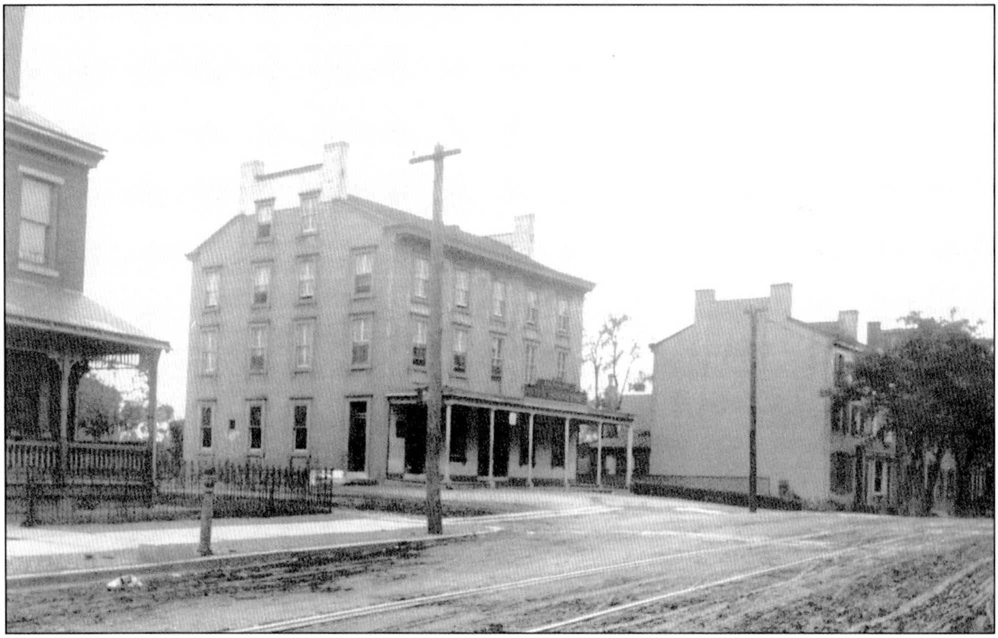

Hotels played an important part in Bridgeport's growth in the early years. In the early days, hotels were found at or nearby the town's train station for weary travelers, and later for the comfort of businessmen traveling into Bridgeport to check on the industries. In 1900, the Bovcot family owned and operated a hotel located at Second and Dekalb Streets that later became the Bridgeport Hotel. In 1914, the Bridgeport Hotel was one of five hotels operating in Bridgeport, including the Barrett Hotel, Barry's Hotel, Dewan's Hotel, and the Dillon Hotel. By the mid-1920s the hotel business in Bridgeport was diminishing and the Hotel Bridgeport was sold and became the Carneau Inn. In that same year, Bridgeport was down to three hotels, including Barrett's and the Colonial Inn. (Above, Phil and Sharon Welsh collection; below, the Historical Society of Montgomery County.)

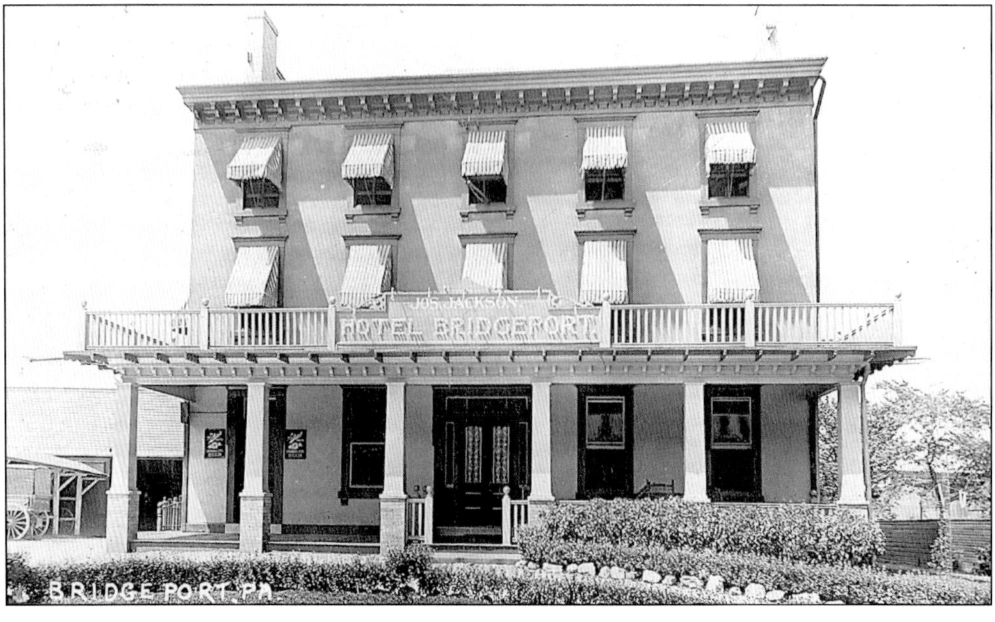

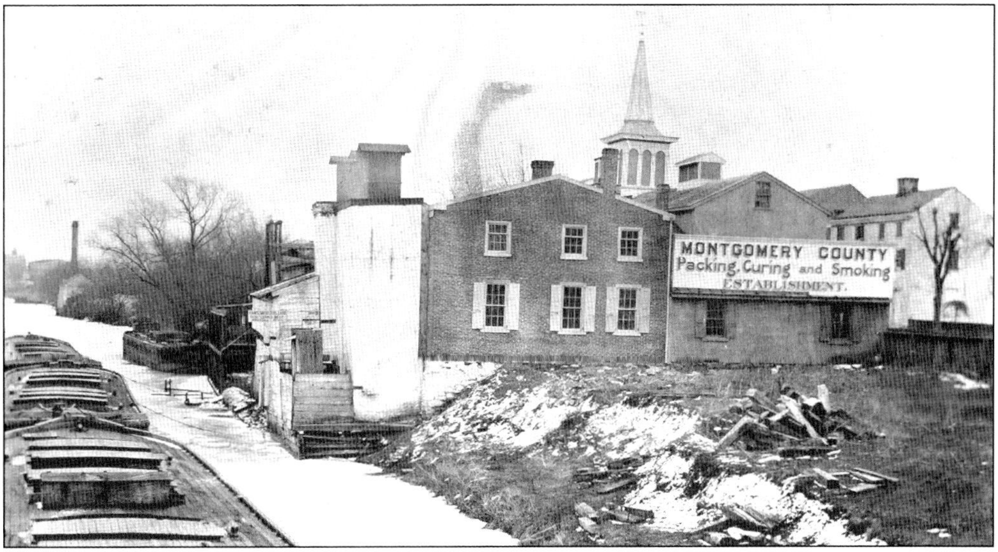

Back in the 1890s, Bridgeport was a hub for industry because of the canal along the riverfront. Goods were shipped in from all over the world, and companies like the Bridgeport Flour Mills, Andrews Brick Yard, and Hughes's Lumber thrived. The J. B. Horn Packing, Curing and Smoking Mill was one of the prominent Bridgeport mills of the day. A. H. March's meatpacking company occupied the plant for more than 40 years, from 1892 to 1934, when it moved its operations to Lederach.

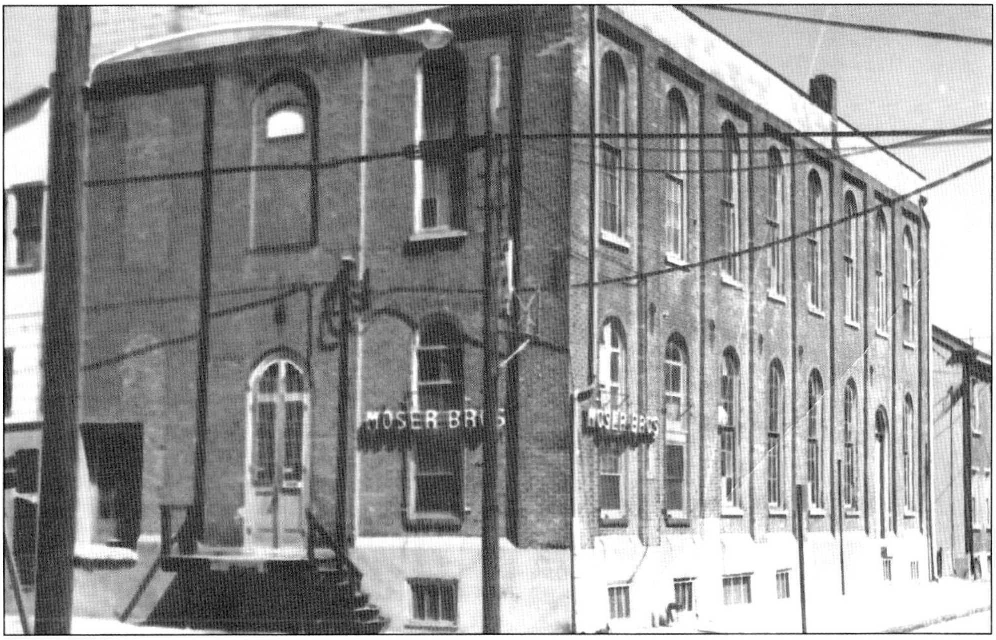

This building located at Third and Green Streets was built in 1874 as the Old Market Hall, conveniently located not far from Bridgeport's canal where incoming goods were easily accessible. In the early 1900s, the building became the town's first borough hall. The borough vacated the building when it moved into its current location at Fourth and Mill Streets in 1923. Isaac, Garrett, and Joseph Moser moved their woodworking mill from Norristown into Bridgeport in 1925, under the name of Moser Brothers. The building still stands today and is home to Country Club Editions Golf Art Gallery and RMH Image Group. (Bridgeport Hall of Fame.)

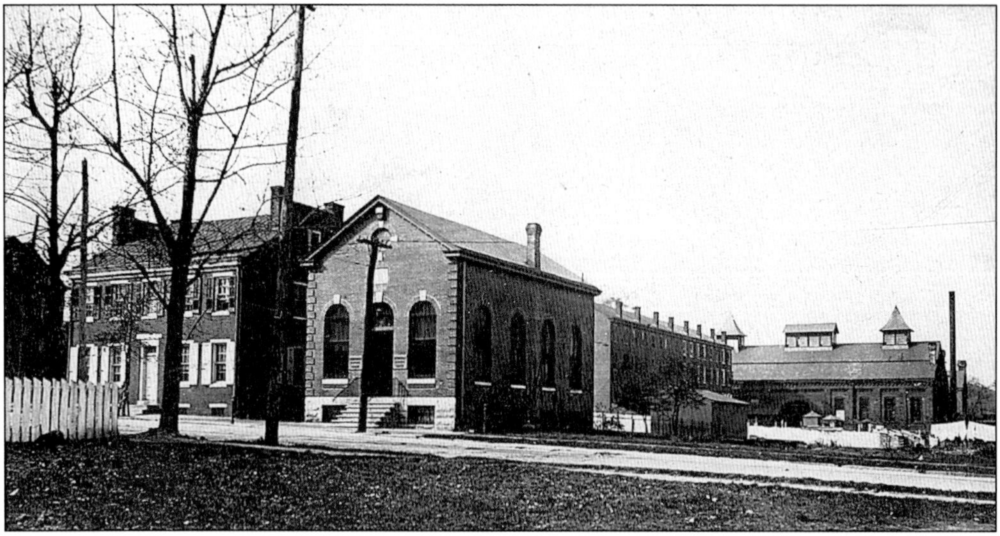

In the early 1900s, Bridgeport was in need of a bank. Montgomery County had 16 national banks and six trust companies, but none were located in Bridgeport. In 1906, a number of residents put up $50 each to start the Bridgeport National Bank. Dr. Charles Mann, who practiced his business at Third and Dekalb Streets, was appointed president of the bank by his good friend William Needler. A solid board of directors was established, including Dr. George Holstein, who was formerly a burgess, postmaster, and school director, along with John Hampton, Charles McAvoy, Iaaac Reiner, and John McCormick. This small bank building built of red brick was located on Dekalb Street between Fourth Street and the Reading Railroad. The bank moved into new quarters at Fourth and Dekalb Streets in 1928. (Phil and Sharon Welsh collection.)

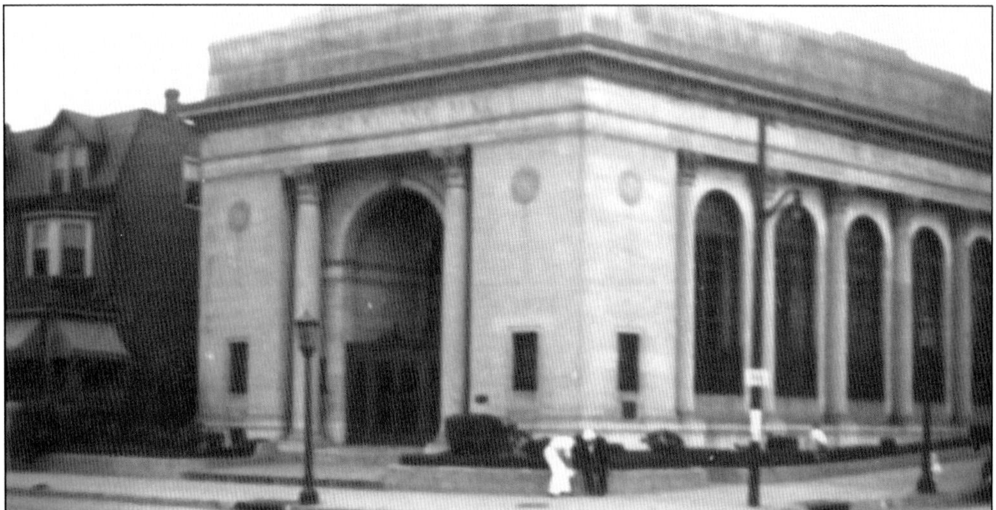

Bridgeport's first bank opened in the old Market Hall located at Third and Green Streets, the building is still standing today. The first bank was called William B. Rambo Building and Loan Association. The Bridgeport National Bank was organized in 1906 by William Needler. In 1928, the bank expanded and built a facility at Fourth and Dekalb Streets. Notice the house on the left of the bank and the pedestrian lamps out in front of the bank. Bridgeport National Bank merged several times over the years, calling itself Liberty Real Estate Bank and Trust Company and Fidelity Bank. The building is no longer used as a bank. (Bridgeport Hall of Fame.)

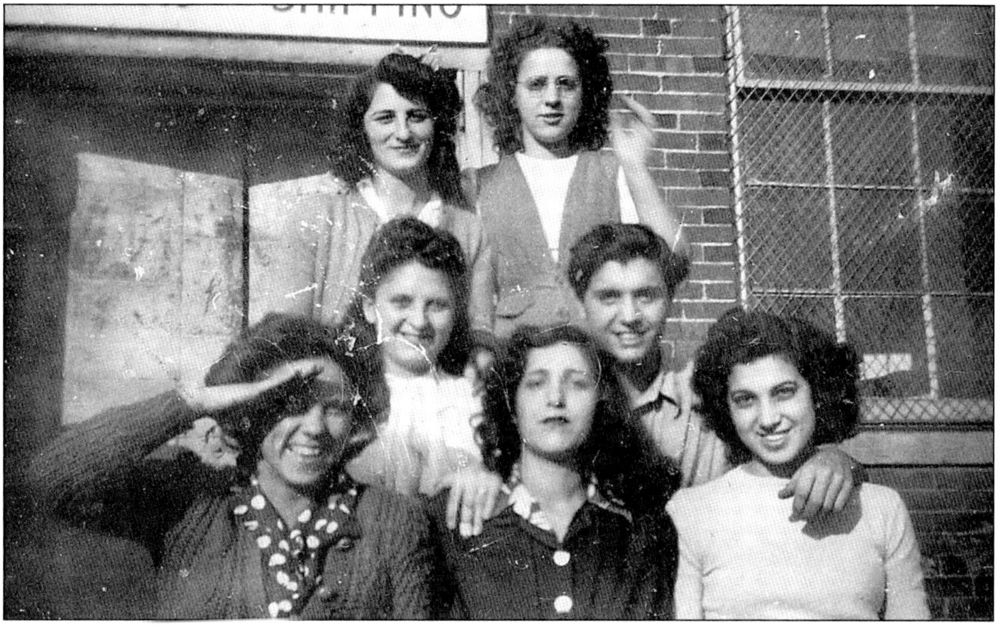

Work was not hard to find back in the mid-1940s when this picture was taken at the Bridgeport Luggage Company, especially for females. World War II was in full swing, and any and all capable males living in Bridgeport were off supporting the war effort. Margaret Pizza, top left, was enjoying a break from the job along with some coworkers outside the company's shipping and receiving doors. The Bridgeport Luggage Company was located on West Fourth Street on the lower floor of the Bridgeport Pants Factory. The company opened in 1943 and closed several years later. (Phil Johns.)

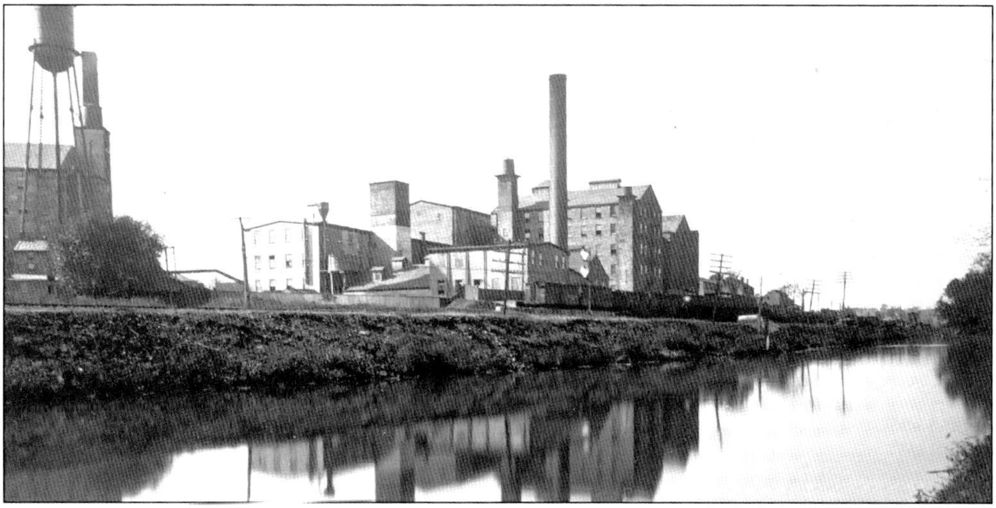

Some of Bridgeport's early industries included Hugh's Lumber Yard, Bridgeport Flour Mill, and Andrew's Brick Yard, but none of the early industries had the impact that James Lees had when he brought his company to Bridgeport. Minerva Mills later became Lees Carpet Mill, shown in this photograph, started in 1846 and operated from a multitude of buildings in several different locations for more than a century in Bridgeport. Lees's operation along the canal provided thousands of jobs for Bridgeport residents over more than a century. (Historical Society of Montgomery County.)

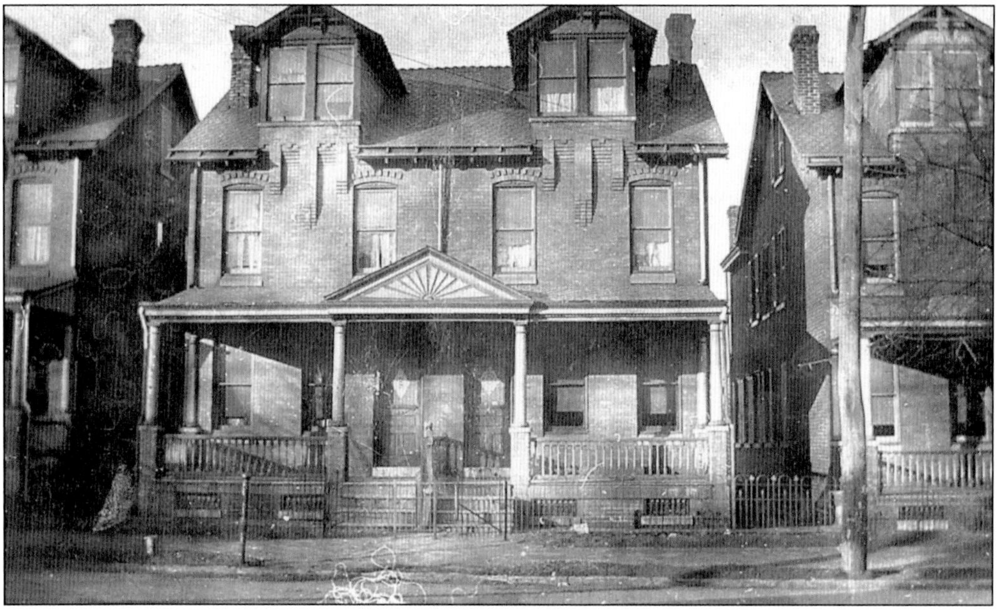

This photograph of the building located at 119 West Fourth Street in Bridgeport was taken back in 1915 and shows the typical Bridgeport residence. Most of the 4,000 residents living in the port back in the early part of the century worked at the mills and along the river, other residents were self-employed with small businesses like corner grocery stores. Both of these homes still stand today as private residences, and very little has changed, including the wooden spindles on the porch and the wrought iron railings in front. (Phil and Sharon Welsh collection.)

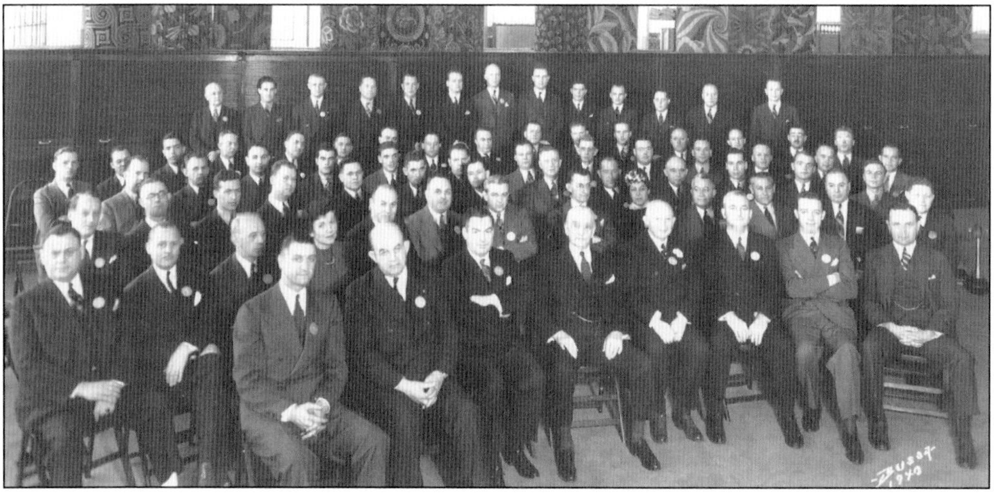

Lees Carpets was founded in 1846 by James Lees and became Bridgeport's oldest industry. The company operated multistoried mills in Bridgeport and up until the 1950s provided thousands of jobs for over more than 100 years in the borough. In 1940, salesmen and members of the sales staff from several states held a conference at James Lees and Sons, in the carpet showroom. Lees's office headquarters continued in Bridgeport until the mid-1960s. (Historical Society of Montgomery County.)

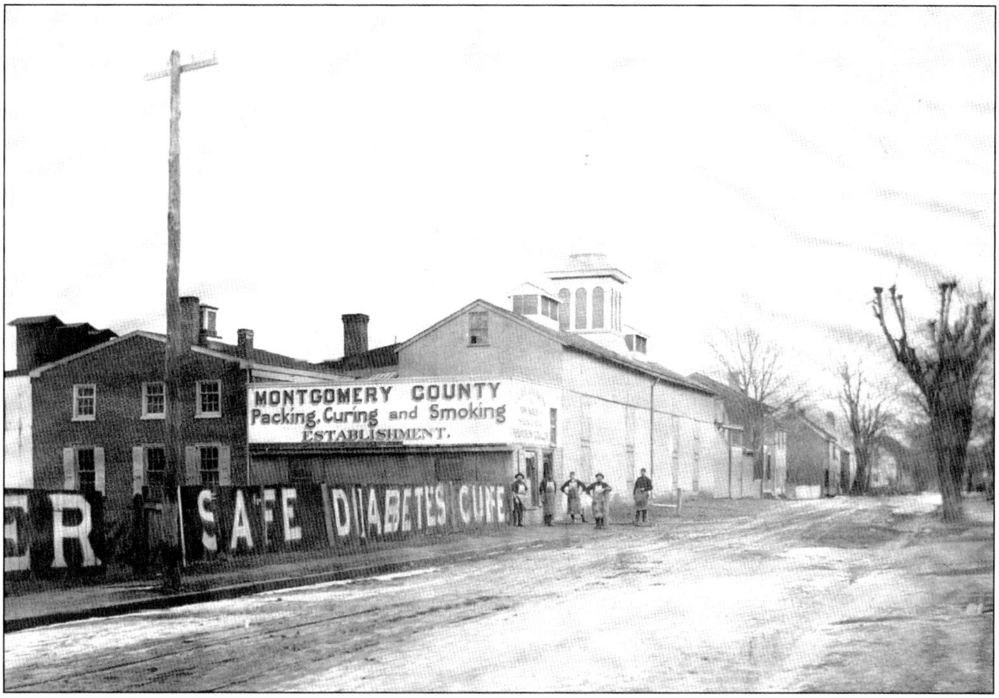

The Montgomery County Packing, Curing and Smoking Establishment was one of the early Bridgeport industries established in the 1870s along with Bridgeport Flour Mills, Hugh's Lumber Yard, and Andrew's Brick Yard. A. H. March's Packing Company was established in 1892, taking over the Montgomery County plant. March's packing company later moved out of Bridgeport in 1934. (Historical Society of Montgomery County.)

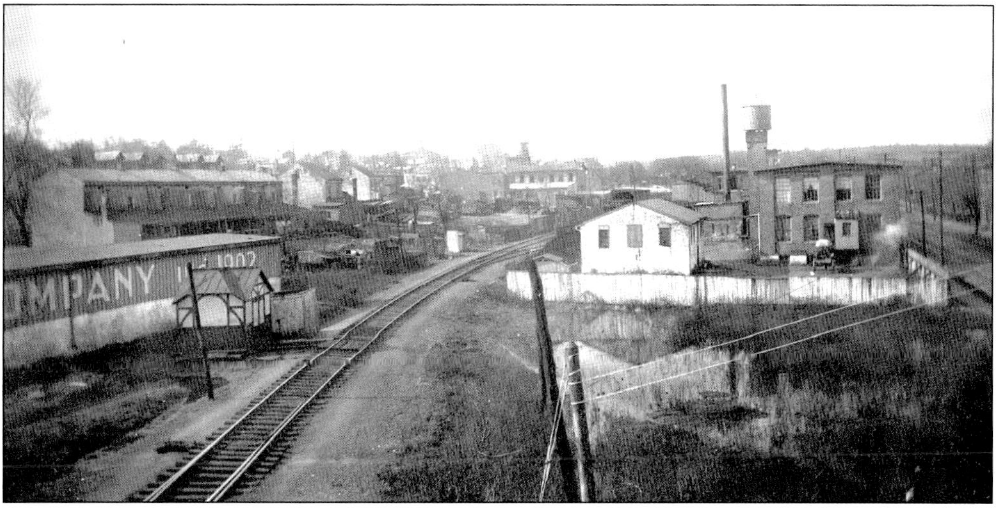

This photograph taken in the early 1900s shows the workingman's life in a small town. Back then only men were welcomed into the mills, at a rate of 20¢ per 10-hour working day. To the left is the back of the Montgomery County Packing, Curing and Smoking Establishment, a company owned by J. B. Horn, and he later sold it to March's. Work was solid and secure for Bridgeport residents, but all that would be interrupted by World War I, as many of Bridgeport's sons and daughters answered the call.

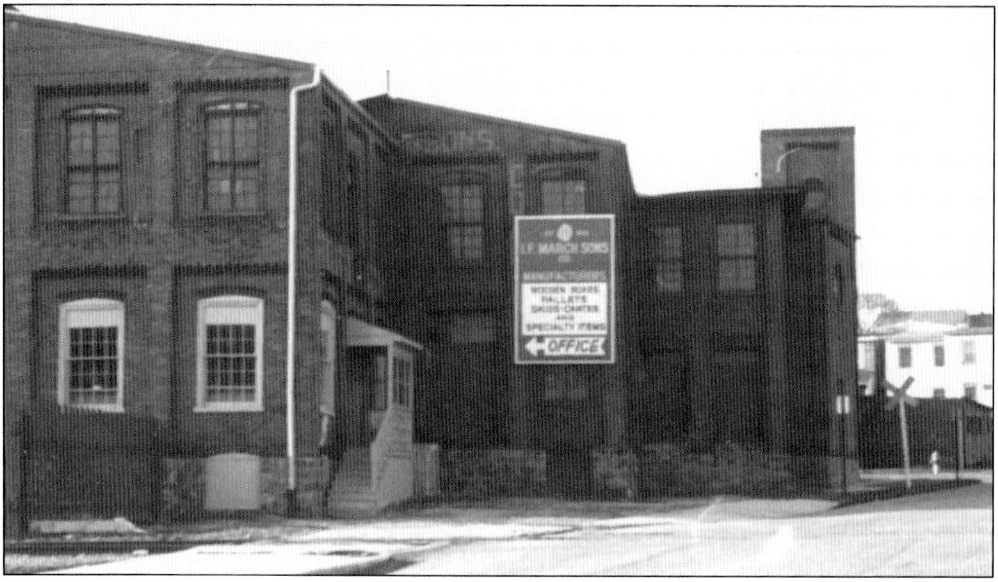

The I. F. March and Sons Company had a long, rich history with the borough. The company sold coal, lumber, and other building materials and was well established by 1886. The company moved a portion of its operations to Norristown in the mid-1970s but continued to manufacture industrial wooden boxes and crates in Bridgeport. The building was located on Mill Street and was sold in the early 1980s and reopened as the Camelot Banquet Hall. The banquet hall recently closed, and as of 2007, the building is once again for sale. (Bridgeport Hall of Fame.)

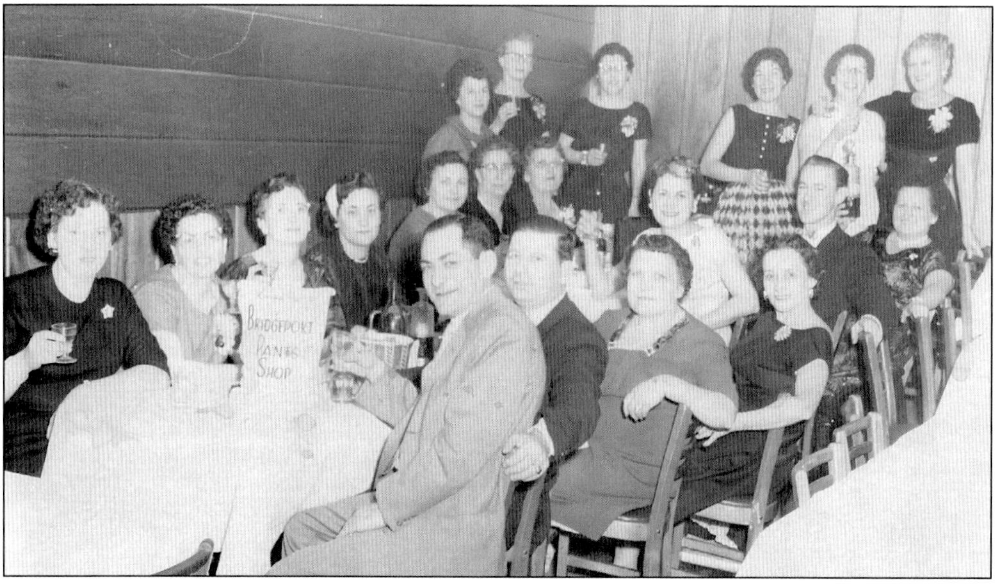

Employees of the Bridgeport Pants Factory enjoy a holiday celebration at Palumbo's Restaurant in South Philadelphia. The pants factory, once located at 54 West Fourth Street, was founded in 1929 by Hyman Freilich. The Bridgeport Pants Factory quickly became a leader in the pants industry, shipping pants and other clothing all over the world. Hyman passed the business down to his son Samuel and other family members. By the early 1990s it grew more difficult to find skilled labor, according to Freilich's grandson Mark. The business ceased operations, and the building was razed in September 1997. (Bridgeport Hall of Fame.)

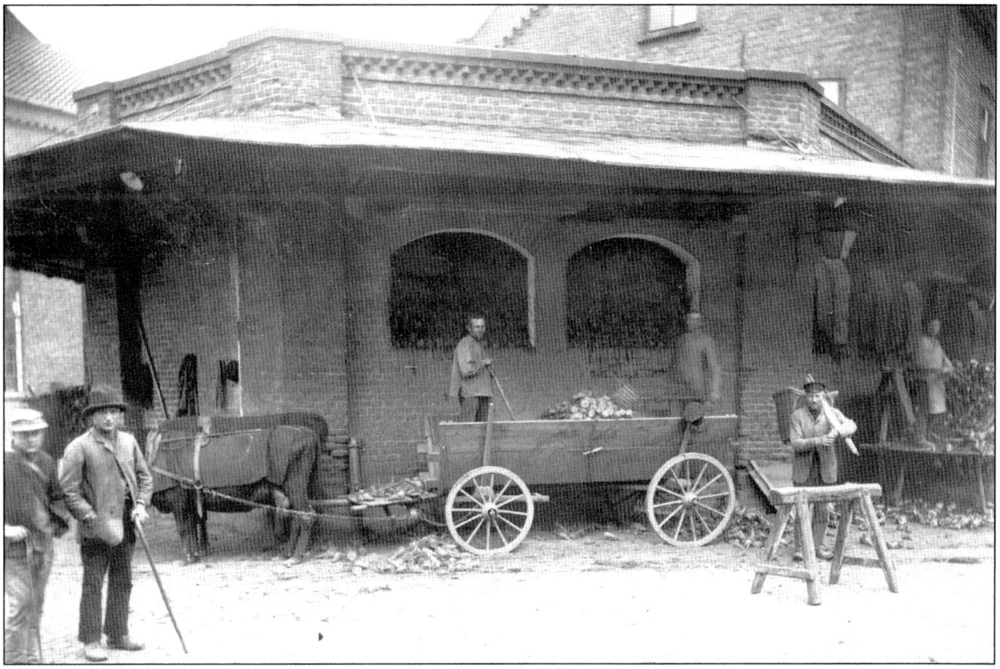

Workers at the M. R. Hughes Lumber Yard sold coal, lumber, and building materials, seen in this photograph in the late 1800s. Hughes's lumber yard closed in the early part of the 1900s, but companies like W. Davis Jr. and Company Lumber Yard and I. F. March and Sons Company continued their businesses. Moving goods like lumber and coal was a slow process in 1900 due to animal-powered wagons; the first horseless carriage appeared in Bridgeport in 1903, when Dr. Charles H. Mann drove his 1902 Stanley Steamer through Bridgeport's dirt roads to his office. (Historical Society of Montgomery County.)

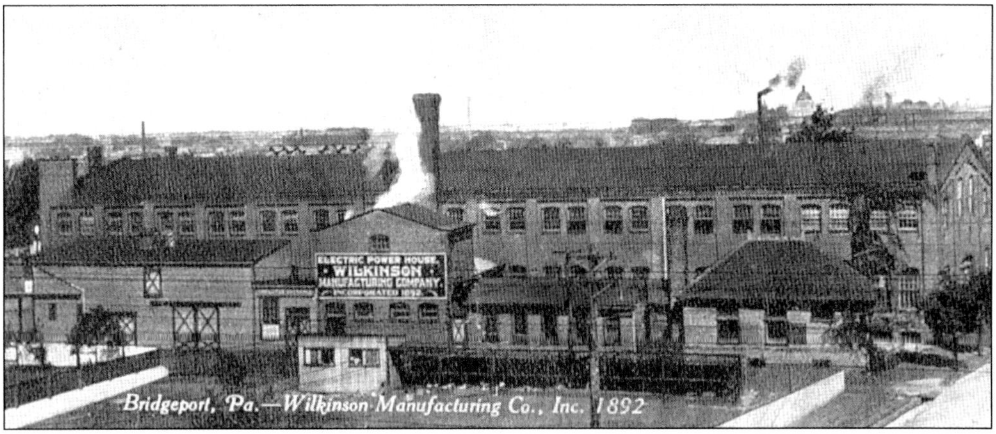

The Wilkinson Manufacturing Company was one of many industrial mills that provided thousands of jobs around the beginning of the 20th century. Established in 1892, the Wilkinson company began making mechanical stokers that fed furnaces and cleaned them of ashes. The factory was short lived, as a fire destroyed the building in 1902, but companies like A. H. March Packing Company and Bridgeport Wire and Iron Works provided needed employment. Ironically the wire and iron works building burned to the ground in 1929. It was almost a common sight back in the day to see large structures burn to the ground, all the factories were made of wood and were very flammable. (Phil and Sharon Welsh collection.)

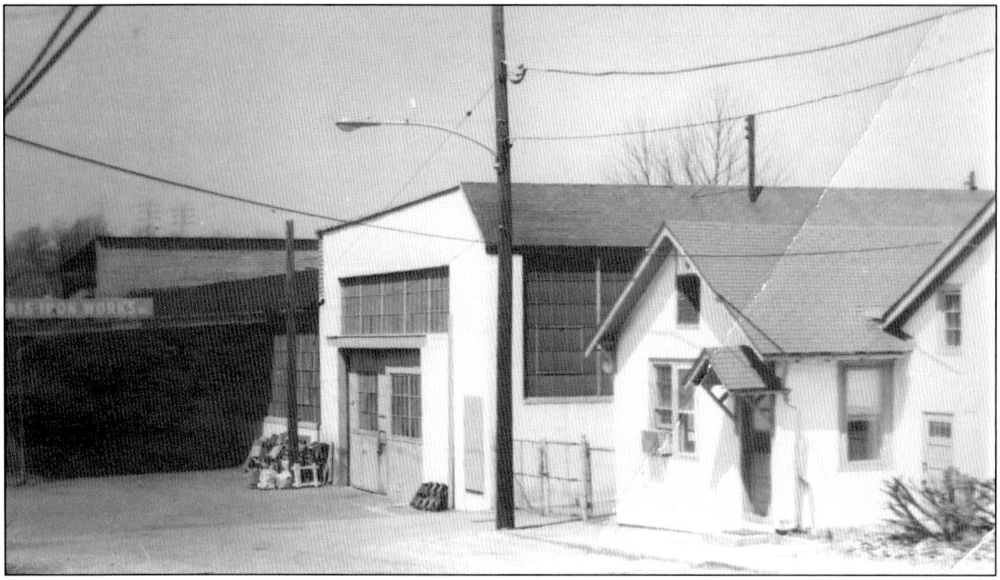

The Norris Iron Works, once located on West Sixth Avenue, was formed by John Gehret and employed hundreds of borough residents over the years. Bridgeport was a thriving borough in the 1920s before the Depression set in. The borough housed three hotels in the day to accommodate the many businesses, including Mike Tose's Trucking firm, the Energetic Worster Corporation, Rambo and Regar, and Protectus Paint Company, among dozens of others. (Bridgeport Hall of Fame.)

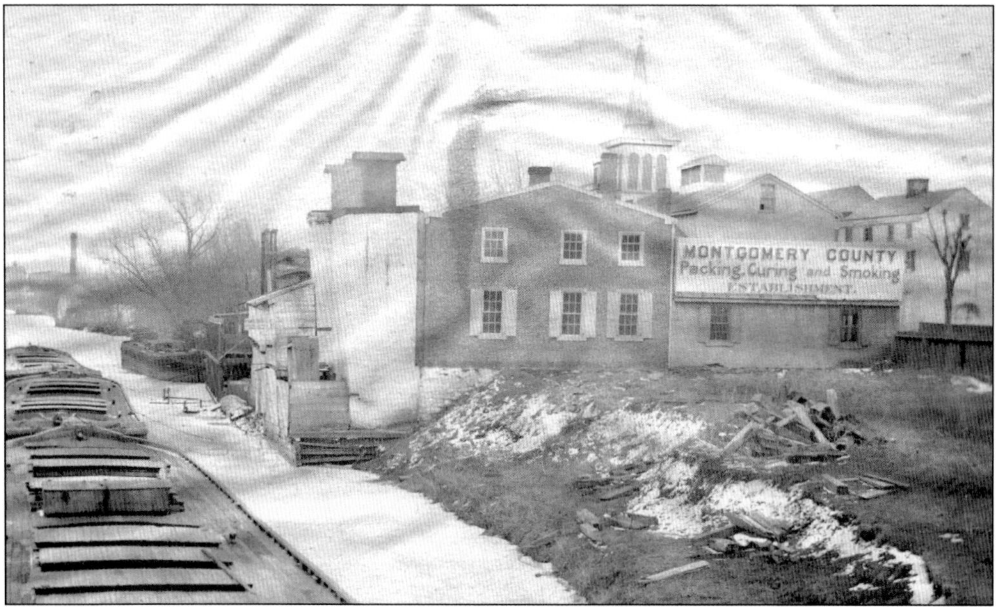

The Montgomery County Packing, Curing and Smoking Establishment, owned by J. B. Horn, was once located at Fourth and Green Streets. The meatpacking plant provided thousands of jobs to Bridgeport residents. Horn opened the business and by 1892 sold it to A. H. March, who moved the business out of Bridgeport during the Great Depression in the early 1930s. The meatpacking plant allowed many immigrants to settle in Bridgeport with the opportunity of working, raising families, and realizing the American dream. (Historical Society of Montgomery County.)

Two

CHURCHES

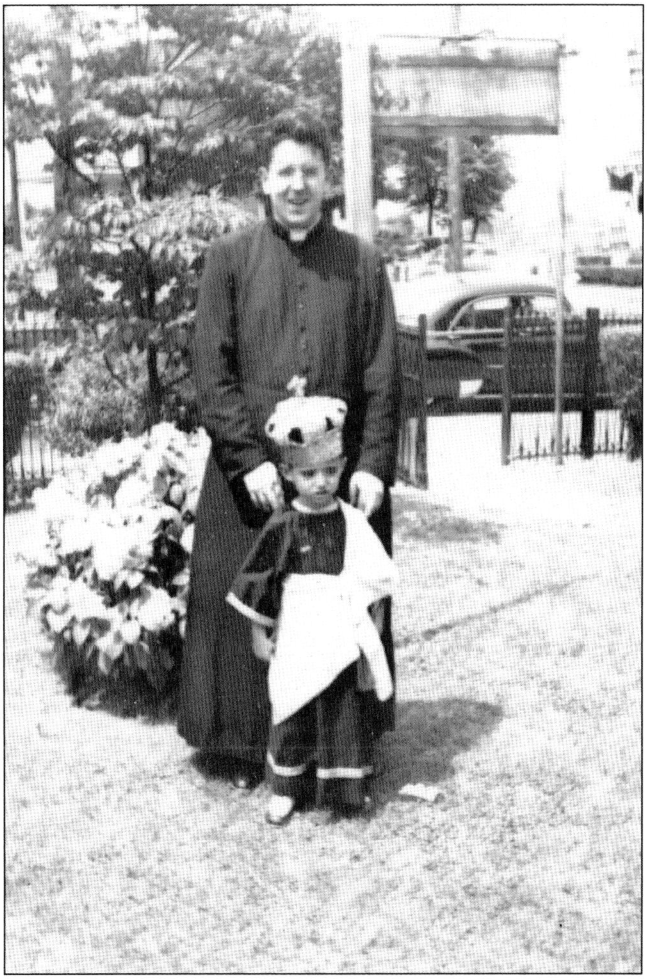

This photograph was taken in the schoolyard of Our Lady of Mount Carmel parish showing young parishioner Salvatore DiNenna with assistant pastor Rev. William Caufield. DiNenna is wearing a costume depicting St. Salvatore, patron of Montella, Italy. In a long tradition still continued in the parish, children would dress as Jesus, Mary, and various saints and walk in procession at the annual observance of the feast of Our Lady of Mount Carmel held every July. Many parishioners immigrated from Montella and settled in the area of Bridgeport and Norristown, finding work, raising families, and capturing the American dream. (Sal DiNenna.)

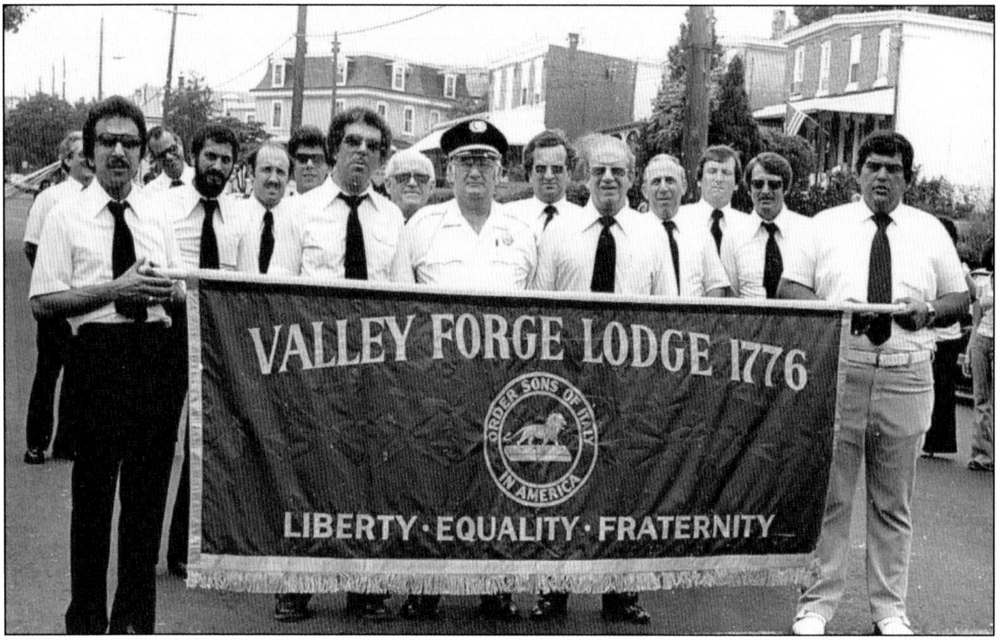

Members of the Valley Forge Lodge 1776 Order Sons of Italy prepare to march in the annual Our Lady of Mount Carmel Feast held each year in July. The three men standing behind the banner in this 1973 photograph are, from left to right, Rudy DiGiacomo, Chief Joseph Colilluri of the Bridgeport Police Force, and Reds Barbone. The feast is sponsored each year by the Congrega Society, but hundreds of volunteers are needed to help with the event. (Our Lady of Mount Carmel Church.)

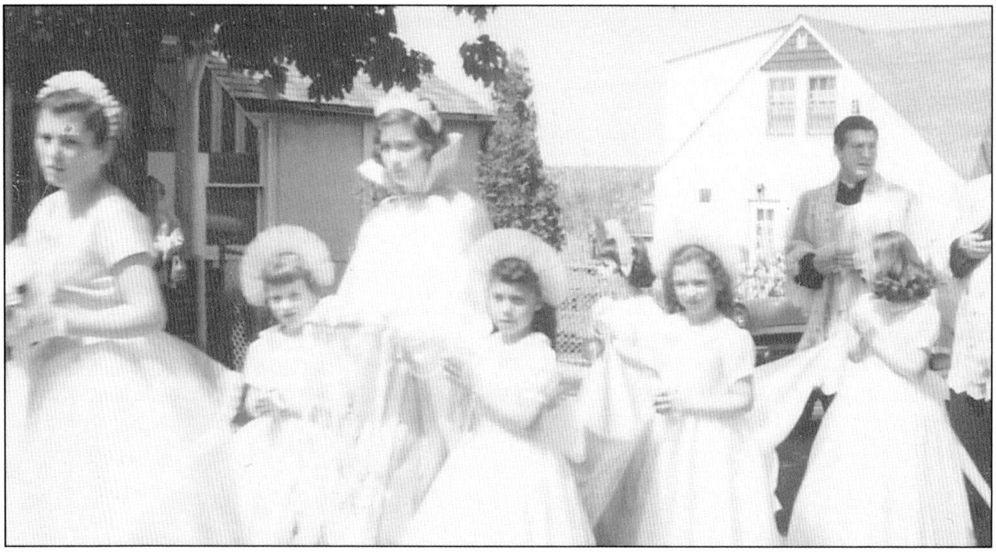

The May procession has been an annual event since Our Lady of Mount Carmel School opened back in 1952. One of the early processions was photographed in 1957 along Bush Street showing eighth graders Mary Ann Pachella (left) and May Queen Rosemarie Tredice. Members of her court included first graders Rosemary Iacovino, Rosemary Diana, Antonia Santucci (not visible), Philomena Roberto, Claire Marie Ritrovato, and Nancy Palumbo, and assistant pastor Rev. Edward Iannucci. (Philomena Roberto Johns.)

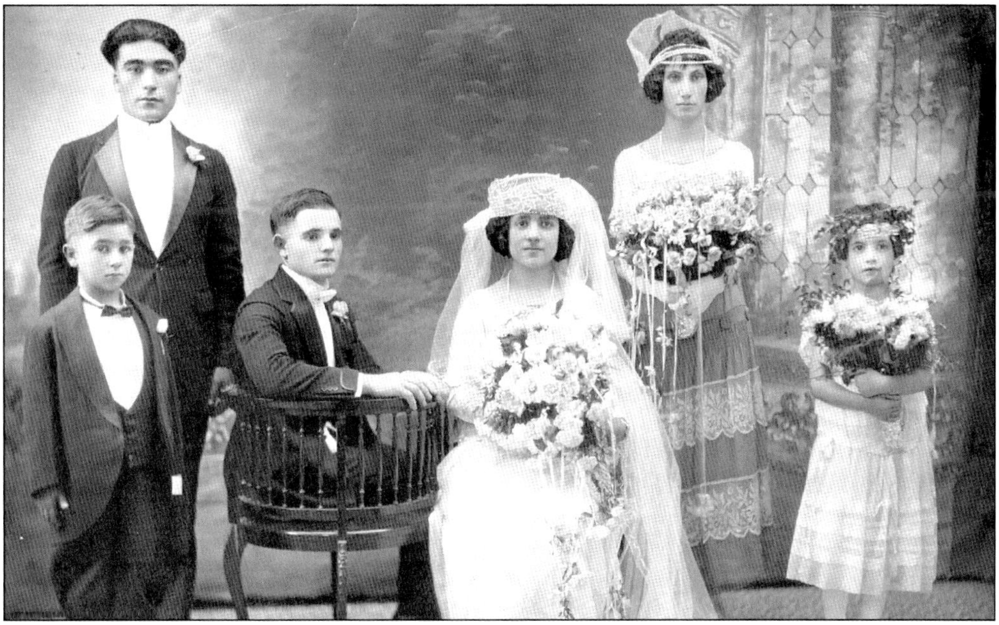

Our Lady of Mount Carmel Church began in a rented building, a stable, and a storage place, and on August 9, 1924, the official establishment of the new Italian parish marked a new era in the small industrial borough known as Bridgeport. Just three weeks after opening ceremonies at the church, the very first wedding was performed. Salvatore and Michelina DiNenna were the first couple to be officially married at Our Lady of Mount Carmel Church. The best man and matron of honor were Carmen and Angie Subranni. The flower girl and ring bearer are unidentified. (Sal DiNenna.)

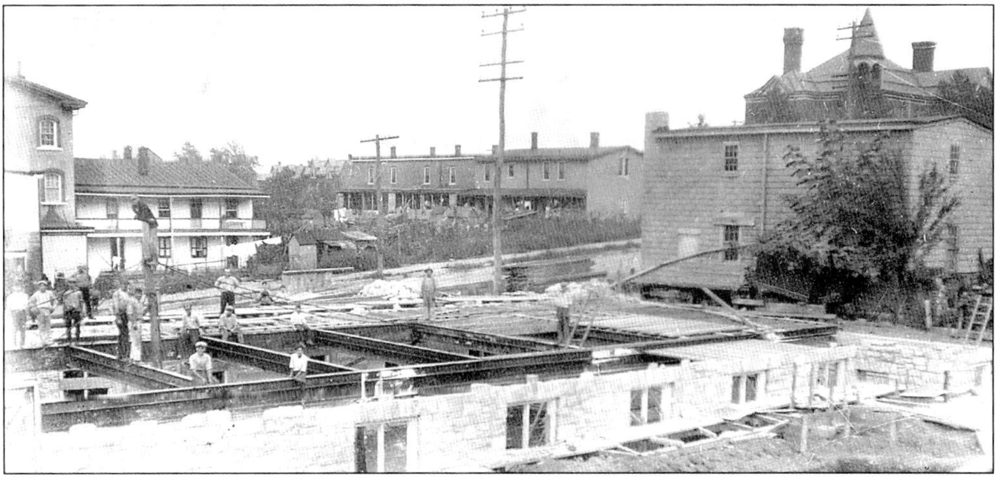

In the early 1920s, Bridgeport had trolley cars clanging along the tracks and hucksters set up on the busy street corners selling everything from food to footwear. James Bell was running his store on the corner of Holstein and Ford Streets from Monday through Saturday. On Sunday, Bell would rent his storage place and animal stable, located at 112 Holstein Street, to a group of Italian worshipers led by Rev. John Colantonio. Colantonio believed that the Italian group of worshipers could build a church, and on ground donated by Joseph and Philomena Phillips at the corner of Ford street and Beech Alley construction began on a basement church in 1924. It was called Our Lady of Mount Carmel Church, and the rest is church history.

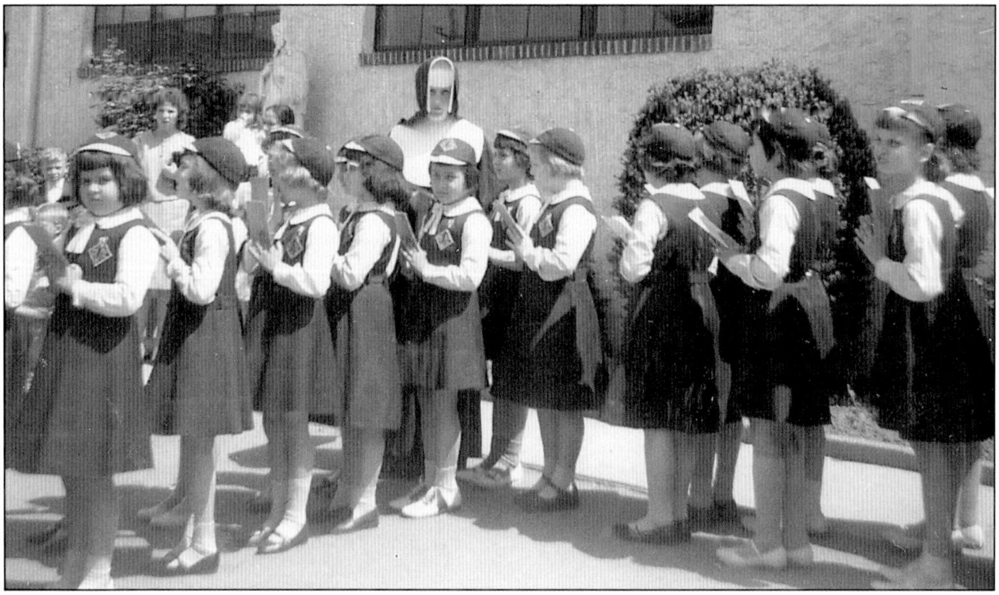

Students of Our Lady of Mount Carmel Parish line up in front of the school for the annual May procession back in 1963. When the school opened in 1952 it had an enrollment of 266 students; Our Lady of Mount Carmel enjoyed a heavy enrollment throughout the 1950s and 1960s. Bridgeport had three Catholic schools within a few blocks of each other, and declining enrollment forced the merger of these schools in later years. Notice the knee-length school dresses and matching caps, needed for females to enter the church back then. (Philomena Roberto Johns.)

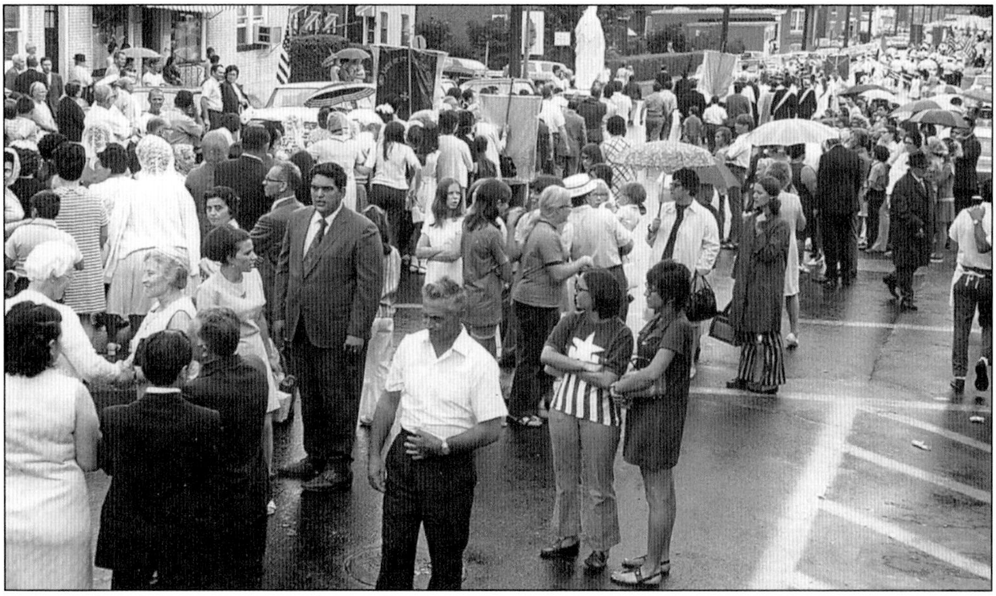

Our Lady of Mount Carmel parishioners and visitors were waiting in the rain for the 42nd annual feast procession to get underway. The procession held every year since 1924 began with a small ceremony, but by 1971, when this photograph was taken, thousands of locals and visitors were participating in the weekend events. Our Lady of Mount Carmel Church was founded in 1924.

On October 26, 1947, Margaret Pizza and Albert Roberto were married and are seen outside Our Lady of Mount Carmel Church when it was still called a basement church. The basement church was completed in 1926 on ground donated by Joseph and Philomena Phillips at 502 Ford Street. Nearly two years after their wedding on August 24, 1949, the completed church was dedicated. When the Robertos were married in 1947, they quickly learned that the average cost of a new house in Bridgeport was $6,650, a new car at Kinnane Chevrolet located at 421 Dekalb Street cost $1,290, and the price of a movie ticket at the Broadway Theatre had jumped to 55¢ per ticket. (Phil Johns.)

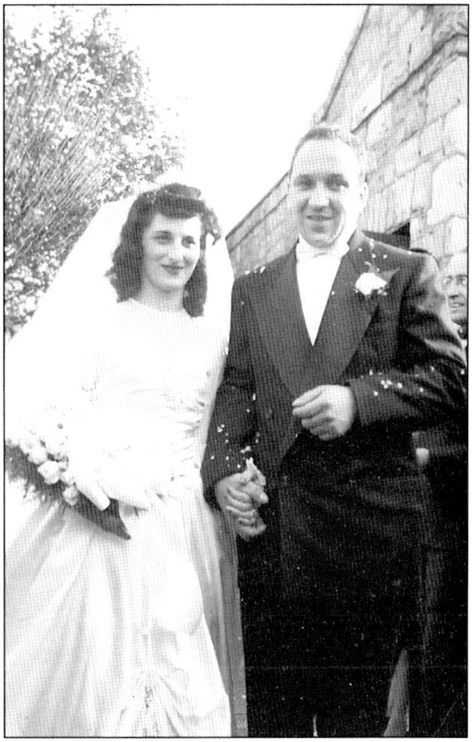

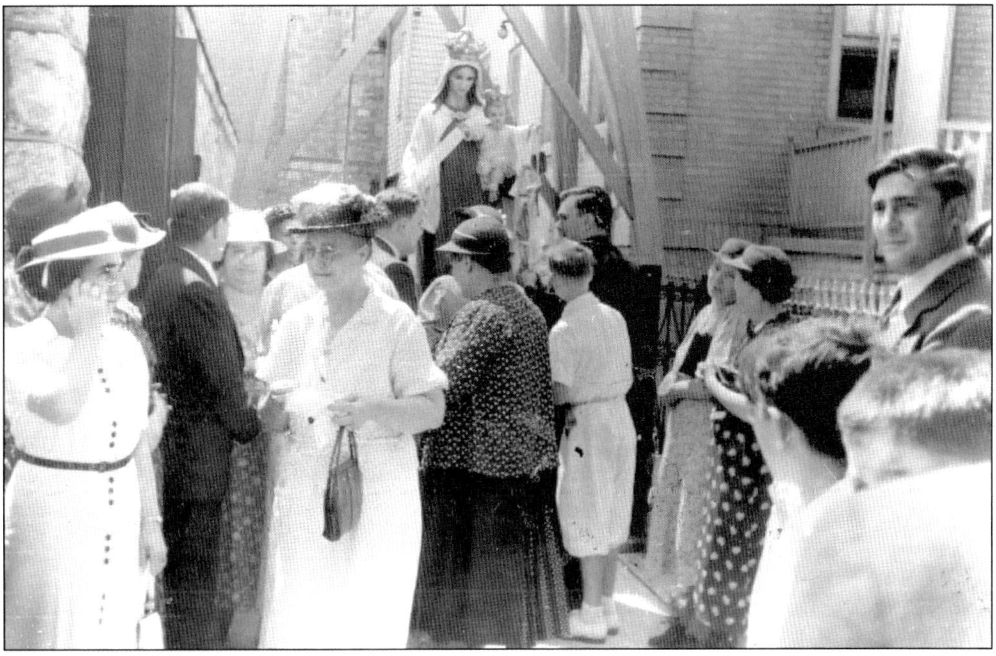

Members of Our Lady of Mount Carmel Church gather outside the church following a summer Sunday service. Noticeable in the photograph are Mrs. Paciello, Nick Ivone, Mrs. Pizza, Emilio Rociole, George Rociola, and Tony Santillo. Notice the men dressed in suits and the females with dresses and of course beautiful hats, the Catholic Church required females to cover their heads when entering the church, a rule that was in effect until the 1970s. (Rose Valerio.)

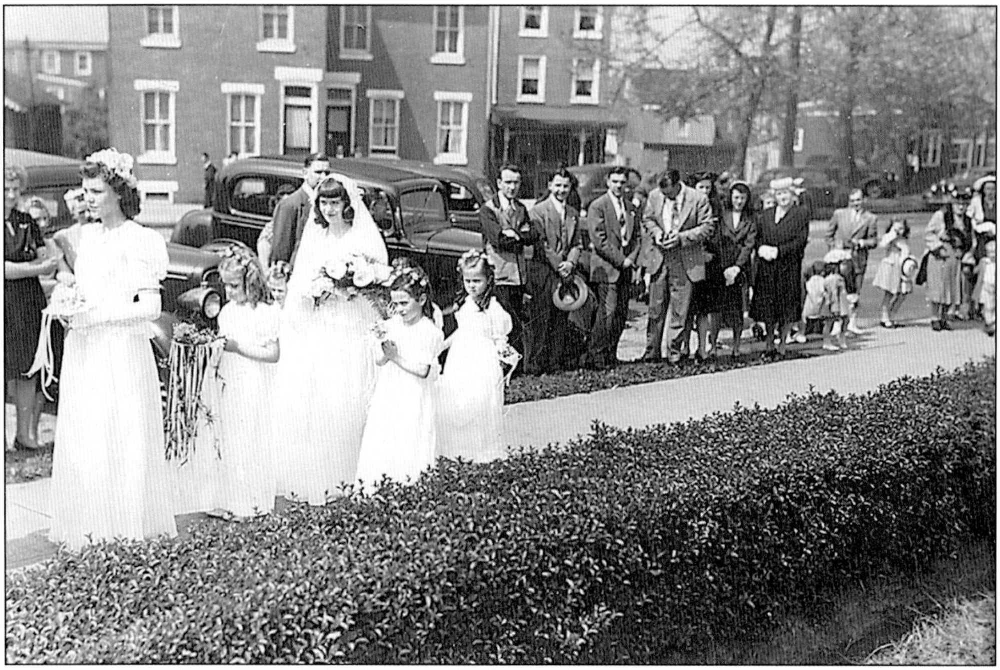

St. Augustine Church established a parochial school in 1896, and not long after that, May processions became a yearly passage for the schoolchildren. Proud parents look on in these 1947 photographs as May Queen Margie Lockern, on the far left, marches with her court in the photograph above. In 1947, America was enjoying the postwar economic surge that allowed many of the returning soldiers to purchase homes in Bridgeport at an average cost of $6,650. While this sounds cheap, keep in mind that the average yearly income was still under $3,000 per year.

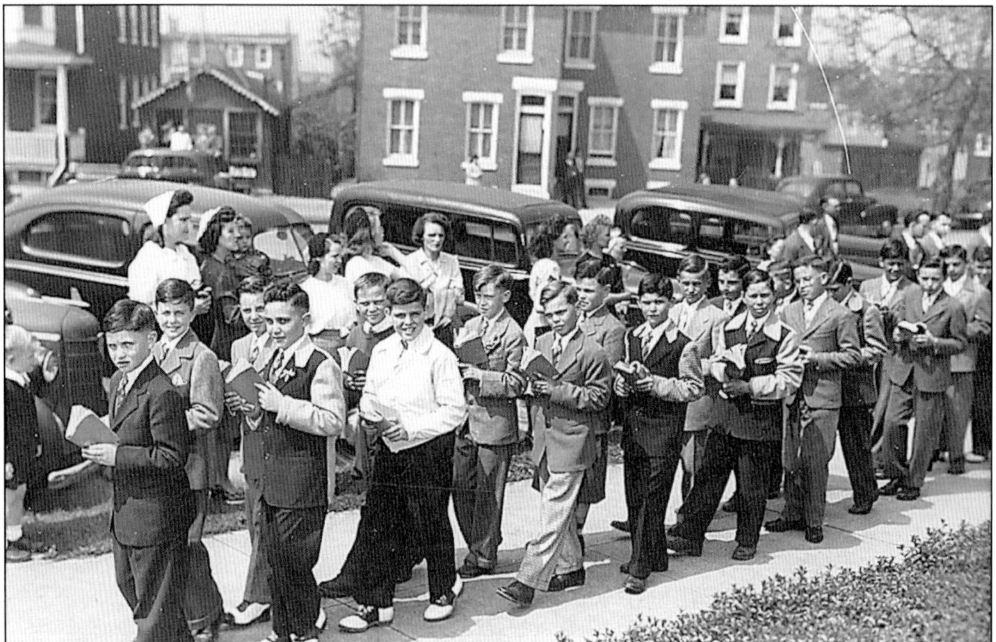

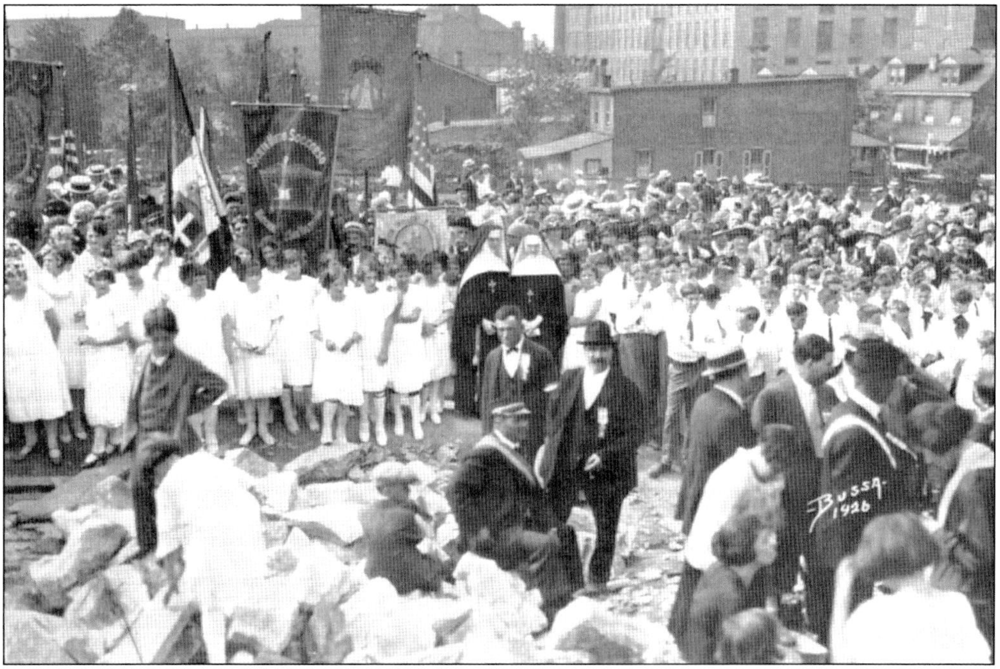

Sacred Heart Church in Swedesburg was established in 1907, at a time when the ethnic character of the Catholic immigration from Europe became so popular that the Catholic Church was forced to build national parishes. Within 15 years of its formation, it was clear that Sacred Heart needed bigger quarters and a bigger church to house its members. In 1926, the cornerstone was dedicated for the new church as hundreds of residents and members of the church gathered for the ceremony. Notice the Bridgeport mills in the background. (Ed Dybicz.)

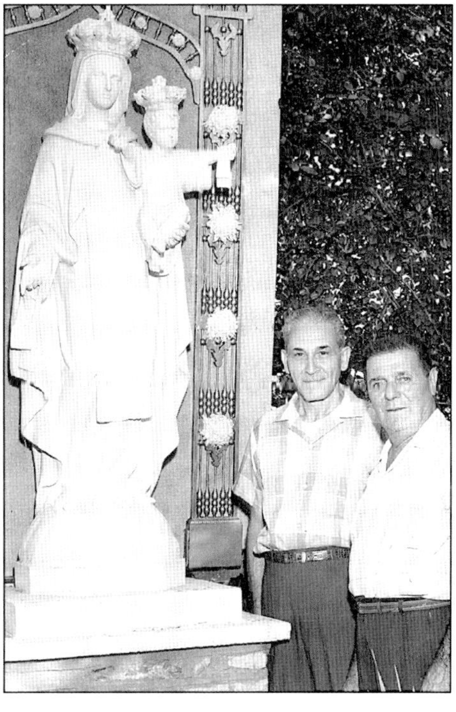

Henry Churchill and Frank Petrucci were cochairmen of Our Lady of Mount Carmel Feast back in the summer of 1960. In 1960, times were different in Bridgeport with 76 retail establishments still located in the borough, and Bridgeport still had a high school. Over the years not much had changed about the feast, which started back in 1924, the year the church formed. Two years later, in 1926, the church population had swelled to more than 1,200 parishioners.

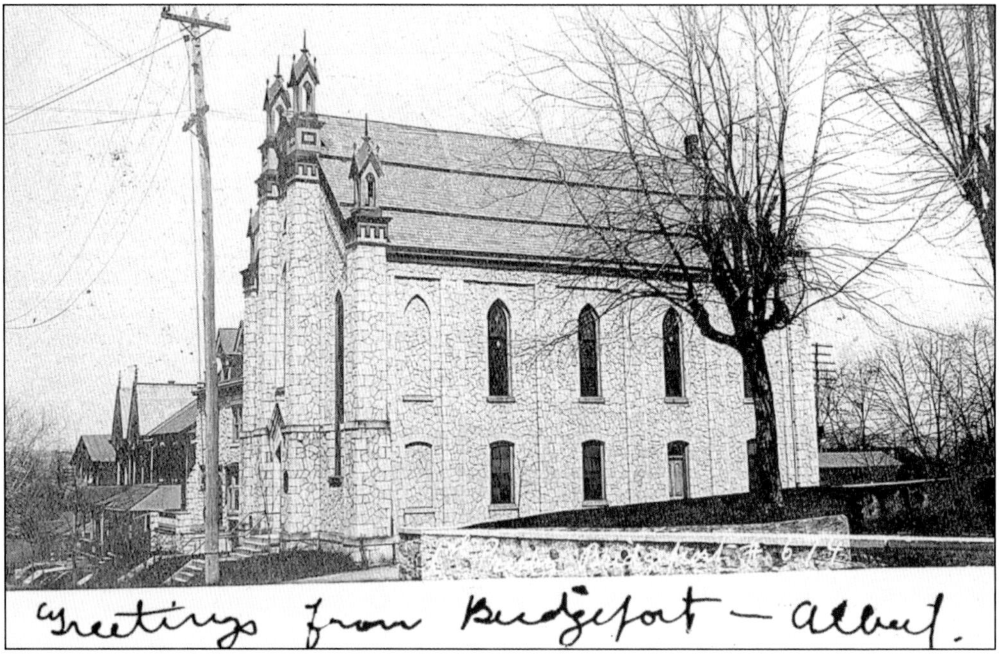

The Bridgeport Presbyterian Church was established in 1875 at Sixth and Dekalb Streets. Bridgeport Presbyterians first attended services in Norristown and later in Mogeetown before building a church of their own. This 1908 image of the church shows the exterior stonework, but the church also had a beautiful interior with stonework from Brown and Roberts quarry from Sixth and Ford Streets. (Phil and Sharon Welsh collection.)

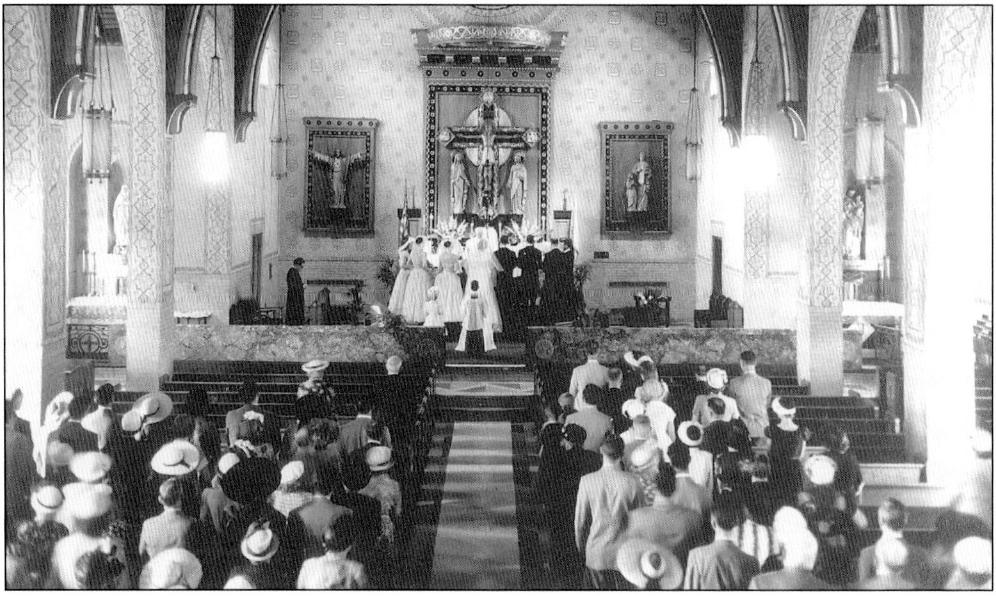

In 1950, the borough of Bridgeport was preparing to celebrate 100 years of incorporation, and Albert Wagner and Helen O'Hara were entering into marriage at St. Augustine's Church. This photograph taken from the church balcony shows the interior of the church that was established in December 1892. The very first wedding was held at St. Augustine's Church on January 4, 1893, when Hugh Dale married Mary McDermott. (St. Augustine Church.)

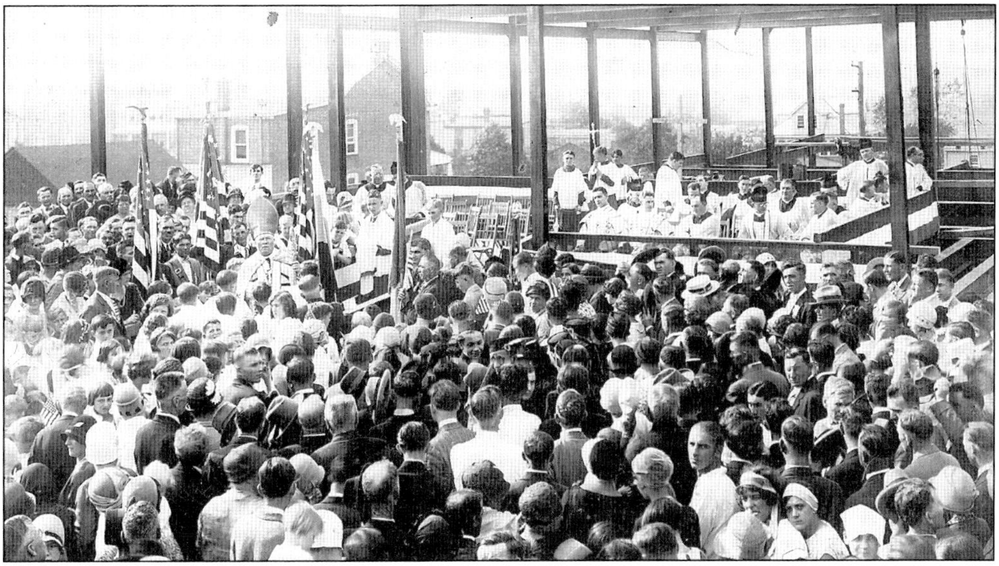

The steel structure in the background is in the early stages of construction for Our Mother of Sorrows Church back in 1928. The event seen was the ceremonial laying of the cornerstone on September 16, 1928. Dennis Cardinal Dougherty can be seen just to the left in the center of the picture preaching to the more than 2,000 residents taking part in the fall ceremony. The church was officially blessed and opened on Easter Sunday, March 31, 1929. On that joyous day in March no one knew that the Great Depression was breathing down on the mortgage of the church. This was a real tribute to the parishioners who worked to pay that mortgage off. (St. Augustine Church.)

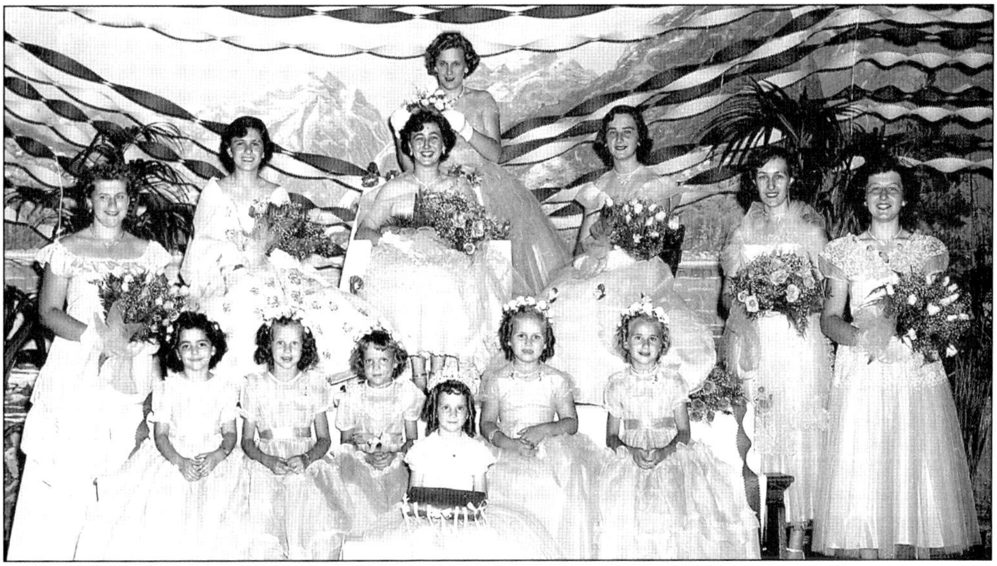

Our Mother of Sorrows School was exploding with activity back in 1951 when this May procession court photograph was taken. Not only was the school a beehive of activity in 1951, but so was the borough of Bridgeport. Mayor Anthony Borzillo and the town council were celebrating 100 years of incorporation of the borough with Bridgeport's population at an all-time high with nearly 6,000 residents. Forty years after this picture was taken the school closed in the 1990s, and exactly 50 years after this picture was taken the church of Our Mother of Sorrows closed in June 2001. (St. Augustine Church.)

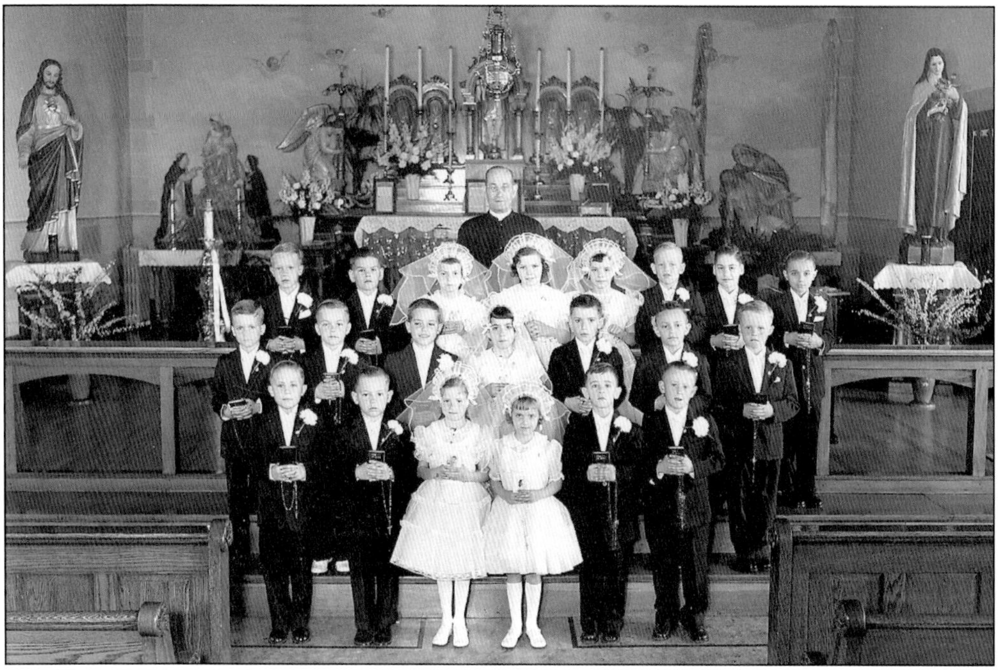

First Holy Communion classes at Our Mother of Sorrows School show a severe reduction in student population in a 20-year span. The photograph above, taken in 1956, shows 21 students receiving the sacrament of First Holy Communion holding onto their Bible and rosary beads. The photograph below, taken 20 years later in 1976, had eight students. Our Mother of Sorrows School later merged with St. Augustine's and Mount Carmel Schools in Bridgeport. As of the early 21st century, Bridgeport has no parochial schools within the borough limits. (St. Augustine Church.)

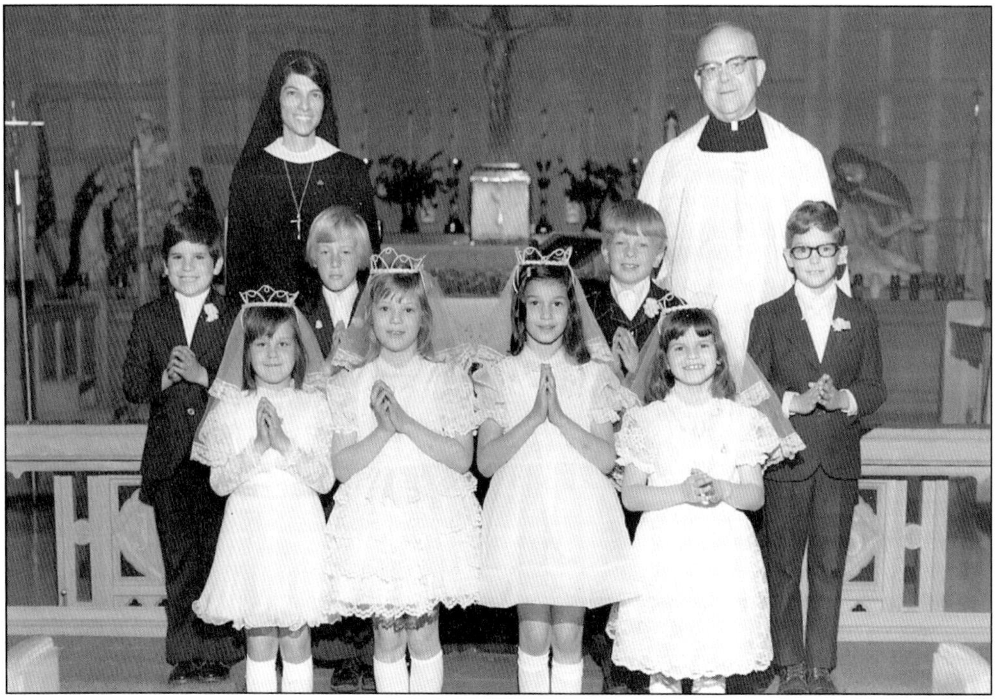

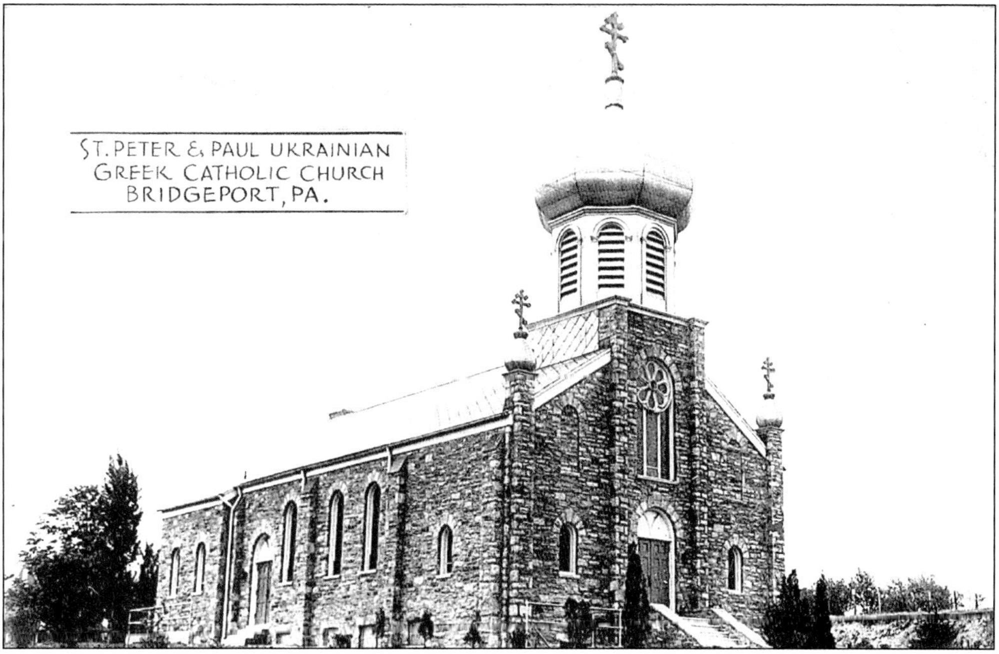

St. Peter and Paul Ukrainian Greek Catholic Church had very humble beginnings in Bridgeport. In the spring of 1924, a group of immigrants from western Ukraine gathered at Temperance Hall (St. Monica's Hall) to worship and lay the groundwork for a church. Rev. Eugene Bartosh led the congregation for 10 years, and on May 30, 1936, a new church was dedicated at Union and Hurst Streets. In 1944, a school building was added at a time when Bridgeport hit a population peak with more than 6,000 residents. (Phil and Sharon Welsh collection.)

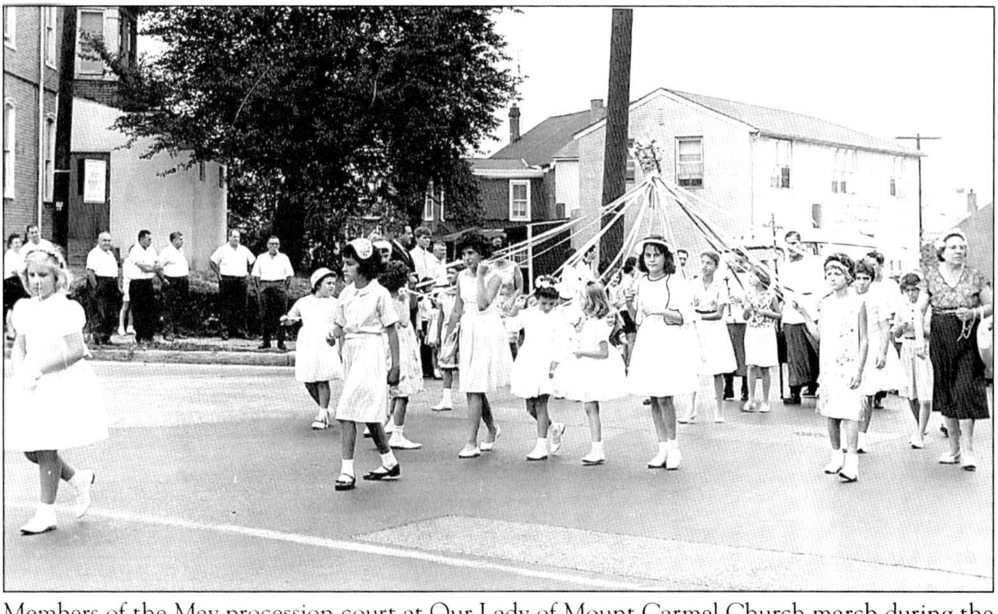

Members of the May procession court at Our Lady of Mount Carmel Church march during the annual church procession back in the 1960s. Our Lady of Mount Carmel Church was established in August 1924, and by 1952 the church dedicated its elementary school with an enrollment of 266 students. The annual May procession was a spring tradition for more than 20 years.

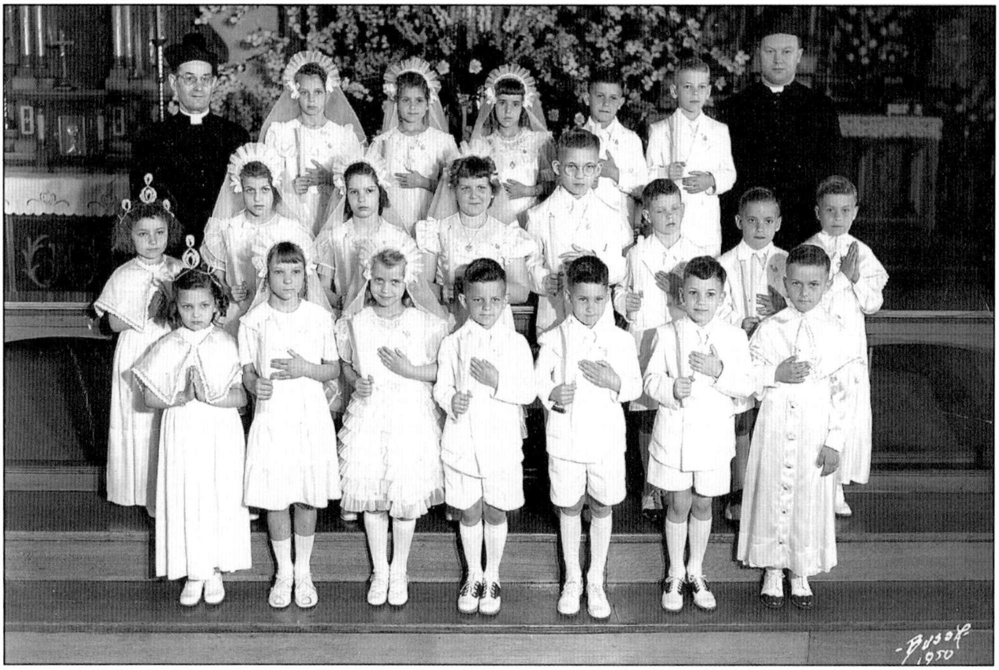

These two interesting photographs were taken at Our Mother of Sorrows Church at the annual May procession. The photograph above was taken in 1950 with the boys and girls dressed all in white. Notice the boys in white shorts, knee-high white socks, and saddle shoes. The girls had different dresses and two types of headgear, while the photograph below, taken in 1968, shows the girls all dressed the same with identical headgear, and the boys dressed in black suits. In 1950, Bridgeport had six schools in the borough, including three public elementary schools, one high school, and two parochial schools. Mount Carmel Parochial School was not opened until 1952, when it enrolled more than 300 students. (St. Augustine Church.)

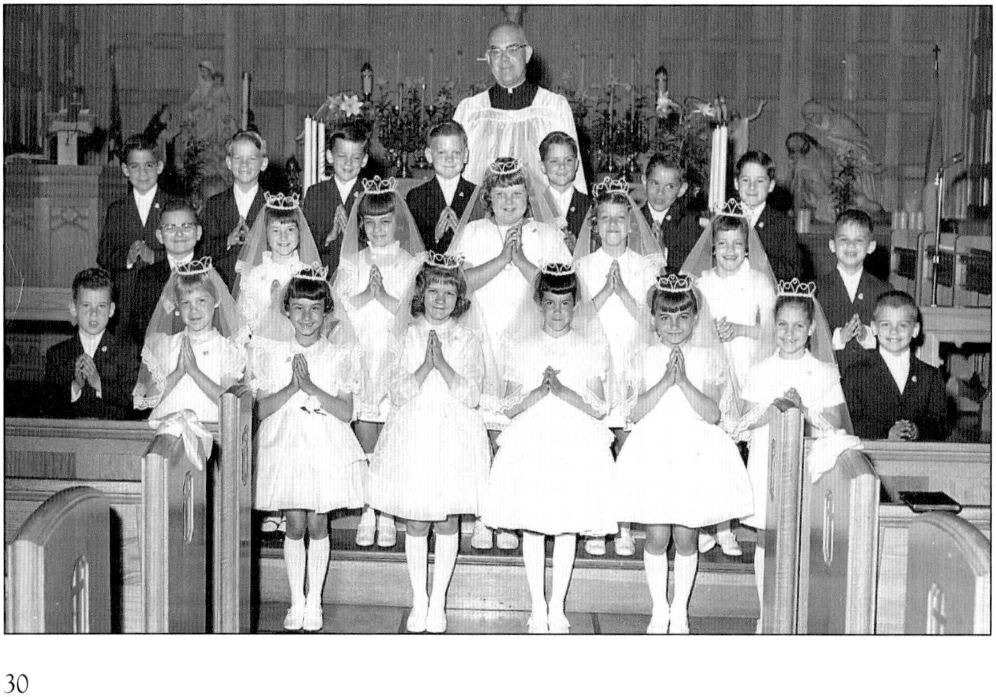

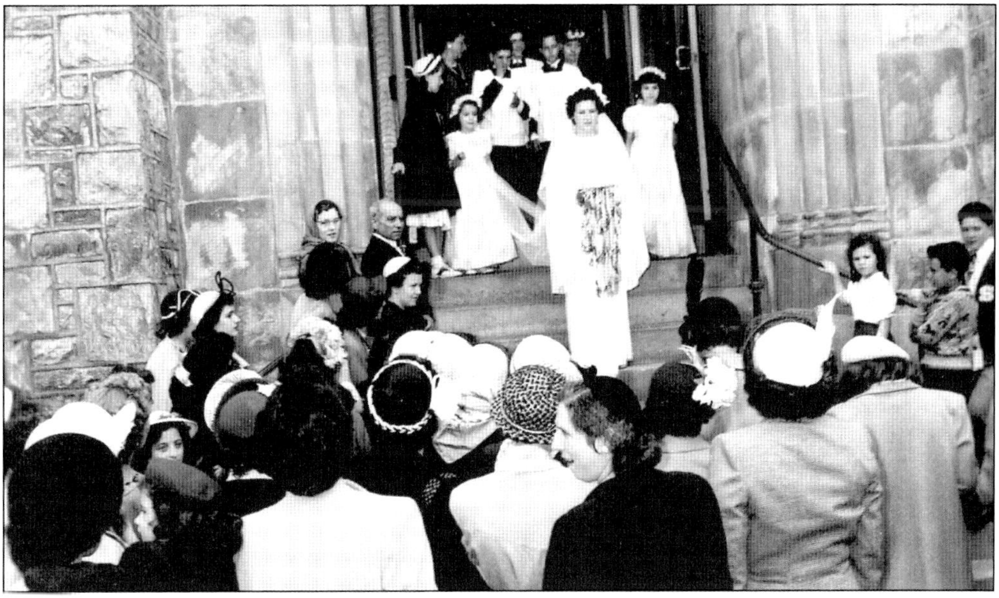

Eleanor Pignoli, the 1950 May queen, leads her court out of Mount Carmel Church as the annual May queen procession took place on Ford Street. Both St. Augustine's and Our Lady of Mount Carmel grade schools were enjoying an all-time attendance high in 1950, but that would soon change. In 1954, the boundaries of the church were changed when Mother of Divine Providence Church was founded to serve the residents of Upper Merion Township and King of Prussia. In the late 1950s and early 1960s, both Bridgeport schools realized a declining enrollment. Both schools are closed today. (Rocky Pignoli.)

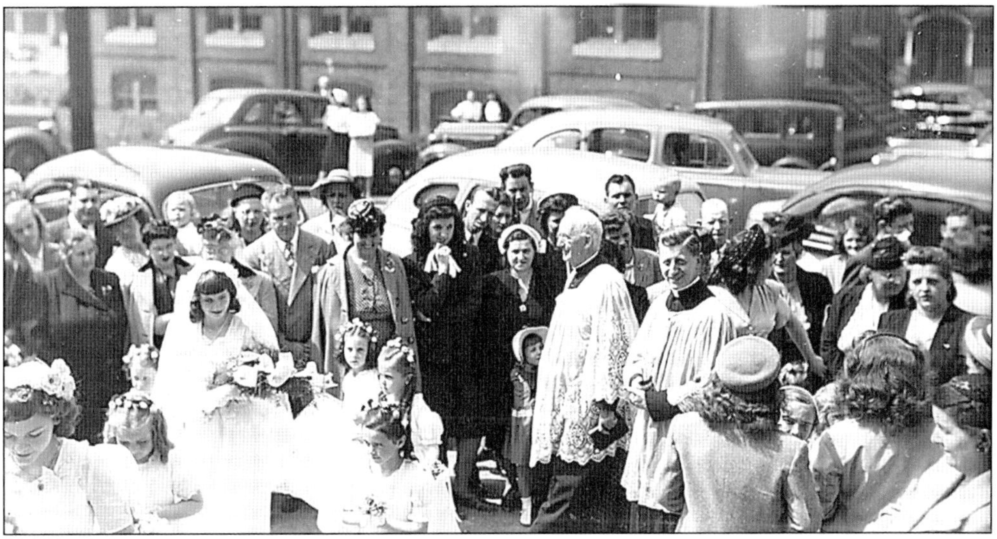

Fr. James V. McEnery, of St. Augustine's Church, seen in the center of the photograph, was one of two assistant priests who encouraged renewed vigor in the church's organizations following World War II. While the Sodality and Holy Name Society had very active memberships, McEnery boosted the membership of the youth involvement with the parish Boy Scout troop and the Catholic Youth Organization (CYO). The 1947 May queen Margie Lockern can be seen in the left of the photograph outside St. Augustine's Church. In the background is Temperance Hall, later called St Augustine's Parish Hall. (Rocky Pignoli.)

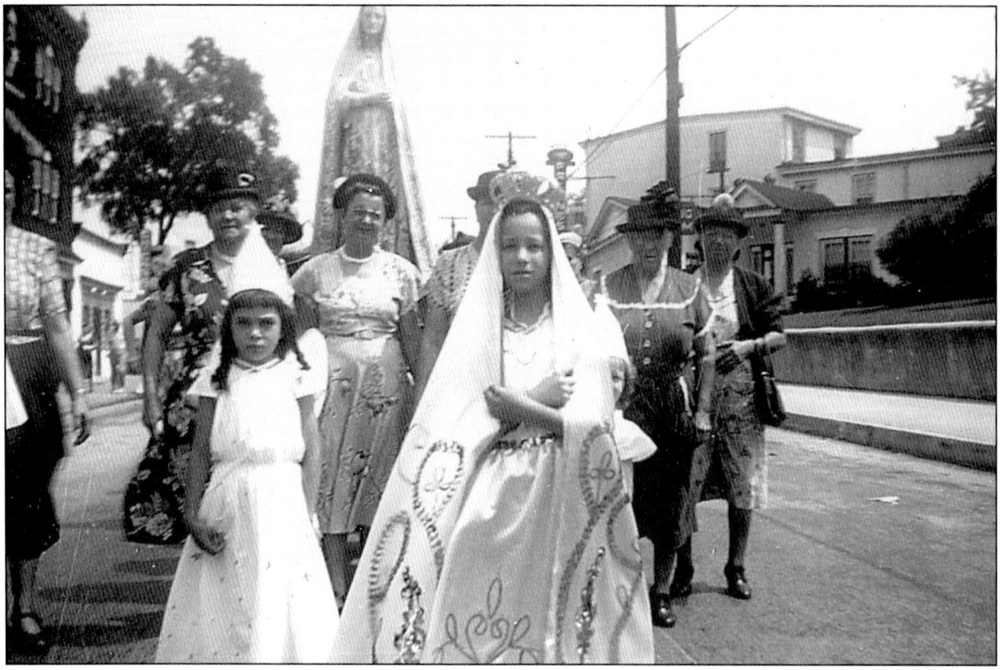

For more than 80 years, thousands of people have flocked to Bridgeport to take part in the Grande Festa Italiana, better known as "the Feast." Our Lady of Mount Carmel Church, founded in 1924, hosts the three-day event that concludes with a procession, as seen back in the early 1940s along Fourth Street. The Friendship Grill can be seen in both photographs, and Chick's Bar can be seen above on the left. Pastor Joseph Megna can be seen below leading the procession along Fourth Street. (Rocky Pignoli.)

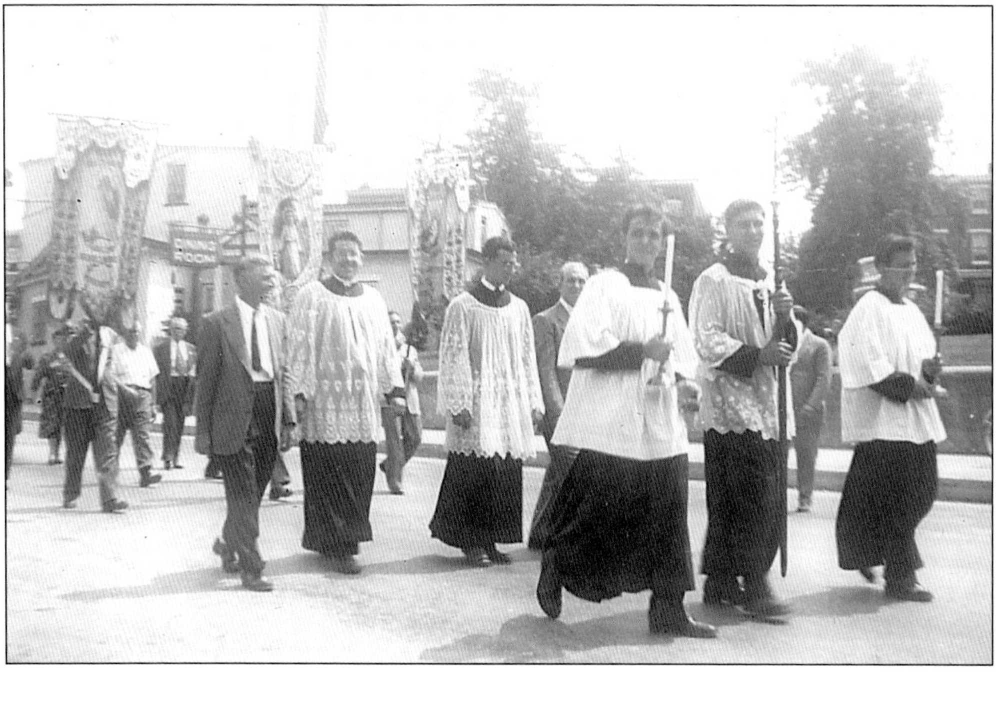

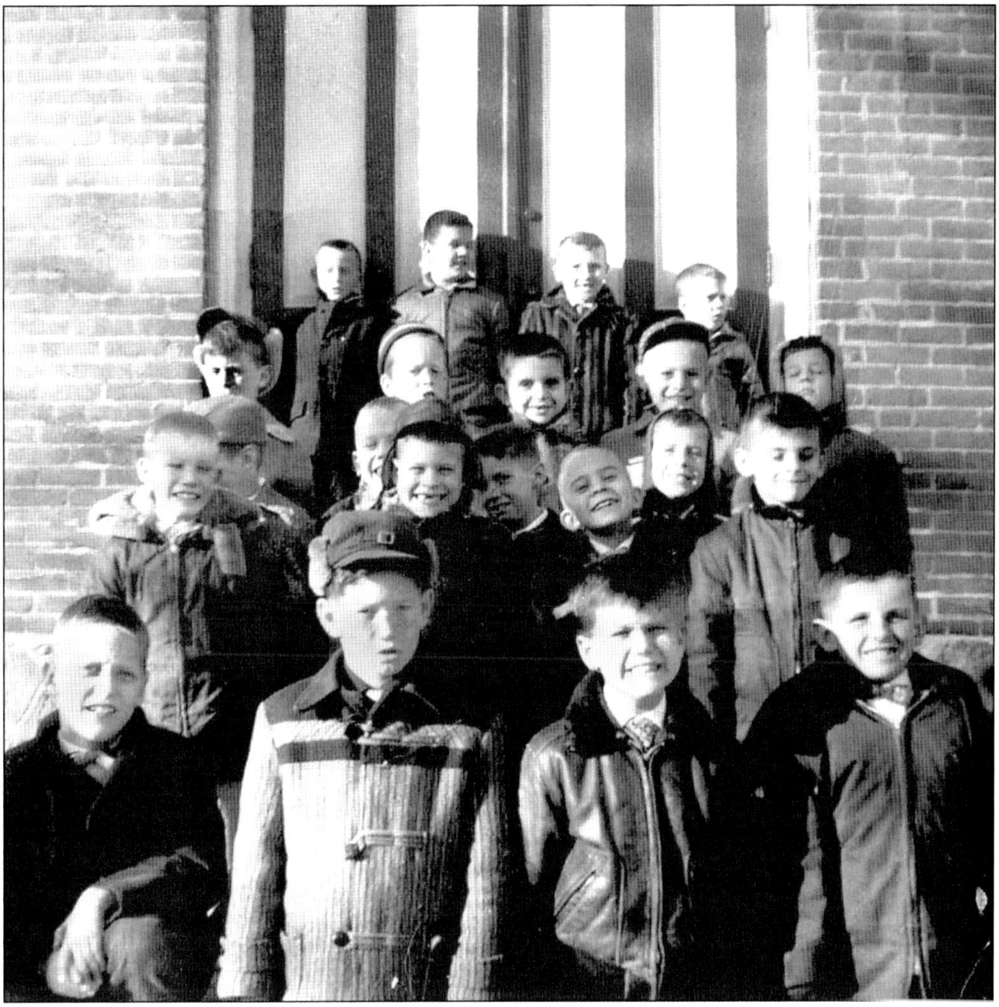

Students pose outside St. Augustine School back in 1960. St. Augustine Church was established in December 1892 and just four years later in 1896, St. Augustine School was founded, educating young parishioners in grades 1 through 8. A number of students seen in this photograph include Jim Richey, Ron Fonock, Tom Brady, Jim Garvey, Bill Whitmore, Ralph Zecca, Chuck Flynn, Joe Kelly, Bill Sally, Tom Kane, and Don Pearson.

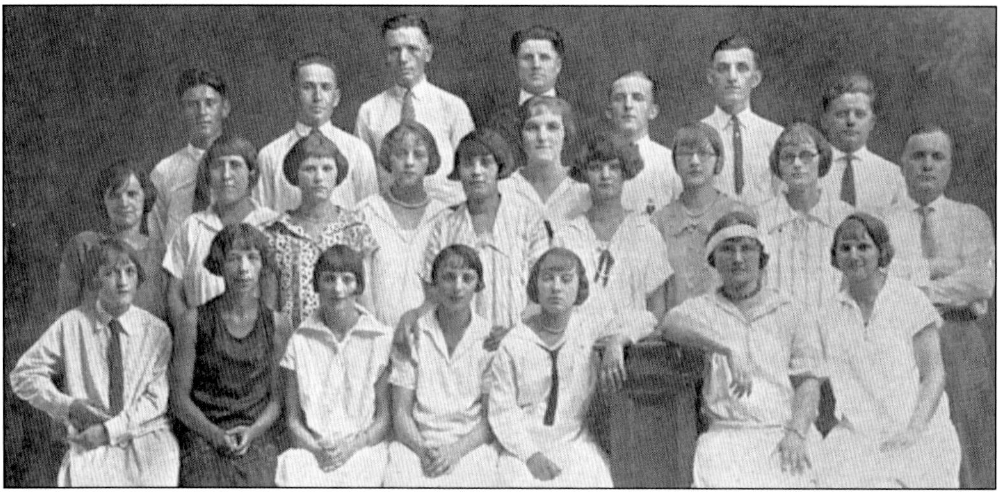

Sacred Heart Church was established in 1907, and as with all churches many activities became affiliated with the church, such as this group of the St. Cecill's Choir shown in 1927. Shown from left to right are (first row) Agnes Kopacz Golas, unidentified, Mary Zaremba Kozlowski, Bertha Zaremba Valerio, Stella Rotay Bernsteil, Stella Wysocki Wanik, and Myrtle Zaremba Dob; (second row) Helen Pisiak Palaszewski, Edna Yarosh Molnar, Sophie Dybicz Jakielaszek, Julie Kurish Rozccki, Charlotte Sujkowski, Sr. M. Hubertine, Josephine Wolfrom Jordan, Dora Kowalski Tyson, Anastasia Jastrzemski Maciejewski, and Walter Rojewski; (third row) Alex Kurish, Anthony Polchlopek, Frank Walania, organist Mr. Albert, Michael Dybicz, Paul Flack, and John Gadzinski. (Ed Dybicz.)

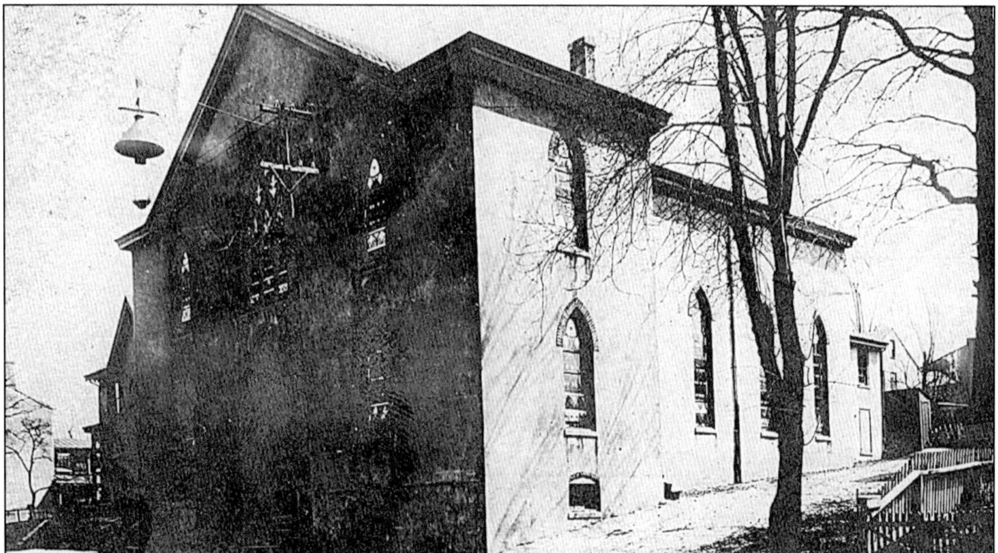

Bridgeport's first church was the Baptist church established in July 1846. The Reverend William Smith of Norristown began services in an old schoolhouse and collected no compensation. Sunday school began a year later, and in 1849, money was collected to purchase a site located at Fourth Street above Dekalb Street. The church was completed in late 1850 and held services in Bridgeport until 1961, when the congregation moved to Valley Forge and Steuben Roads in Upper Merion Township. The photograph above depicts the church in its heyday back in 1907. (Phil and Sharon Welsh collection.)

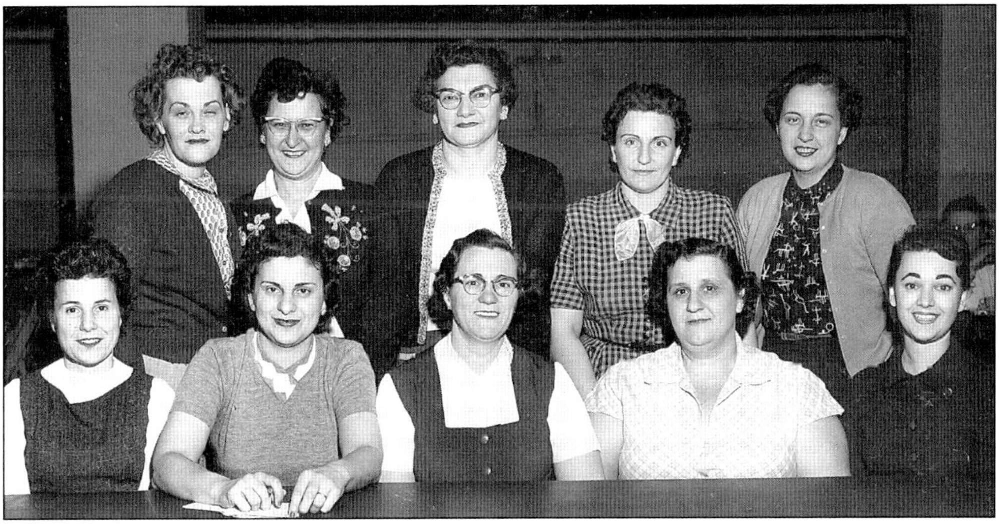

A group of the mothers club from Our Lady of Mount Carmel Parochial School in Bridgeport gathered for this 1958 photograph while discussing a benefit covered-dish social. From left to right are (first row) Mrs. William Morello, Mrs. Joseph Interrante, Mrs. Dominic Mastrangelo, Mrs. Joseph Rosiello, and Mrs. Leonard Berry; (second row) Mrs. Carmen Desimone, Mrs. Pat Valerio, Mrs. Pat Prestia, Mrs. Joseph Valerio, and Mrs. Rocco Longo. (Our Lady of Mount Carmel Church.)

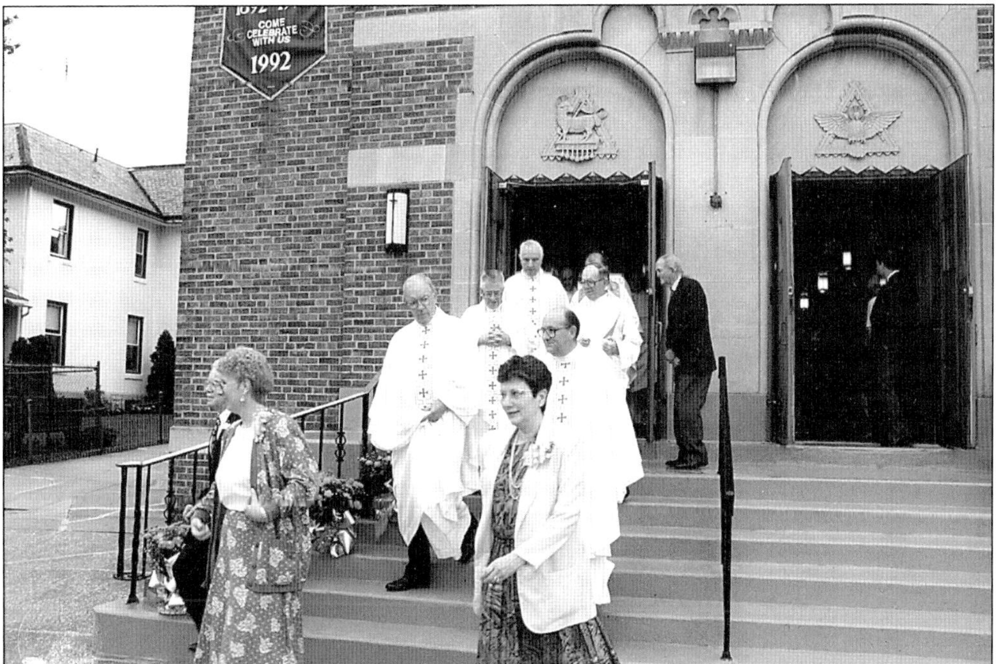

St. Augustine's Church celebrated 100 years of service to the community back in 1992 with a yearlong calendar of events to mark the event. Fr. Michael John Gately celebrated the church's first mass on July 18, 1892, at the former bonnet factory located on Ford Street. St. Augustine started with more than 300 families and at one time had 350 students attending St. Augustine's school. (St. Augustine's Church.)

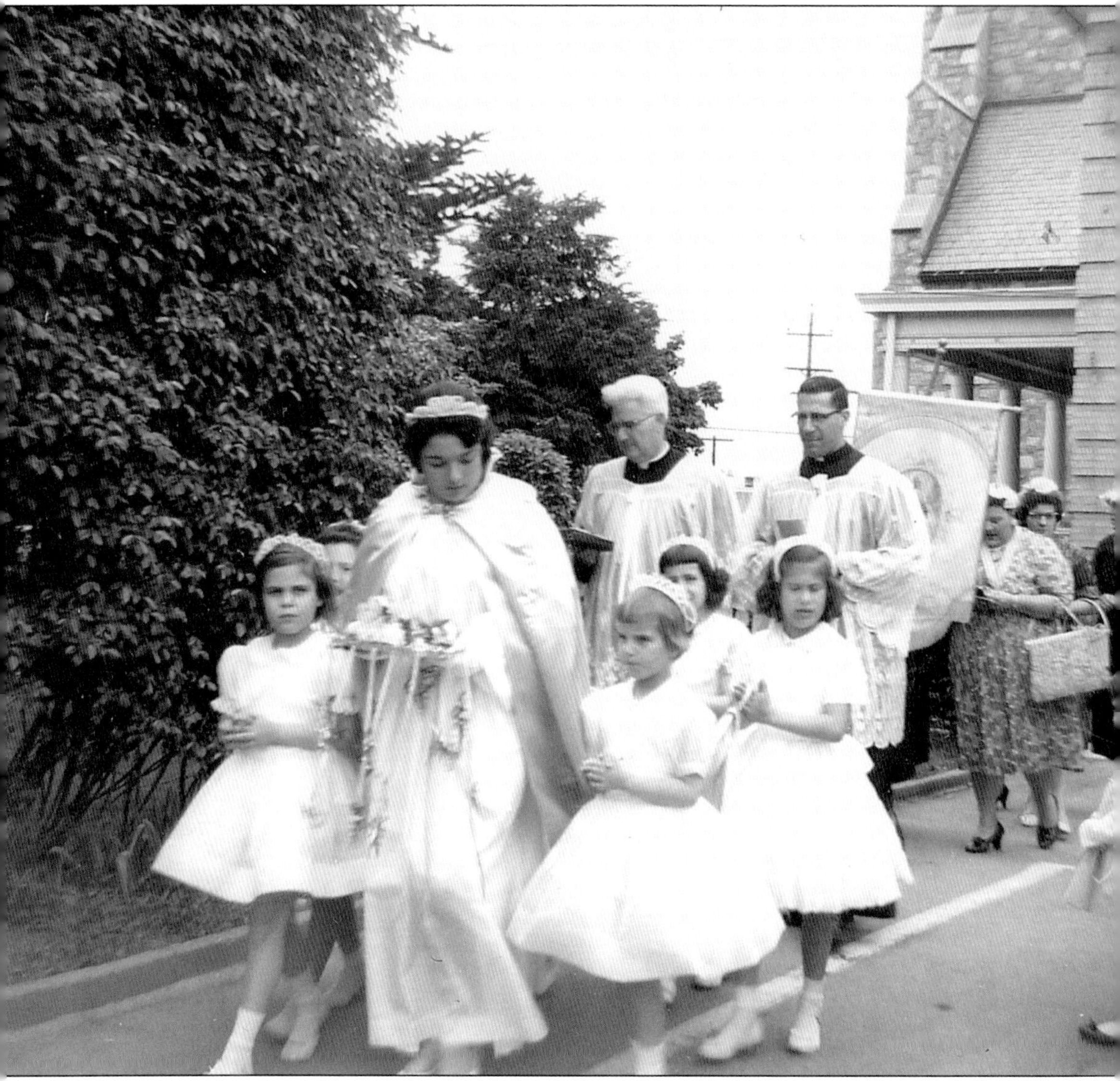

In 1962, Our Lady of Mount Carmel School was celebrating its 10th anniversary and the annual May procession was underway. The May queen in the center of the photograph is Mary Rose Amato with her court. The priest on the left is longtime pastor Ed Craney, and next to him is Pastor Arthur Centrella. Due to changing geographic conditions, the parish school was consolidated with St. Augustine Church in 1977 and further consolidated in 1998 with Sacred Heart Parish in Swedesburg. Due to declining enrollment, the school closed its doors for good in 2005. (Philomena Roberto Johns.)

Three

FIRE AND POLICE

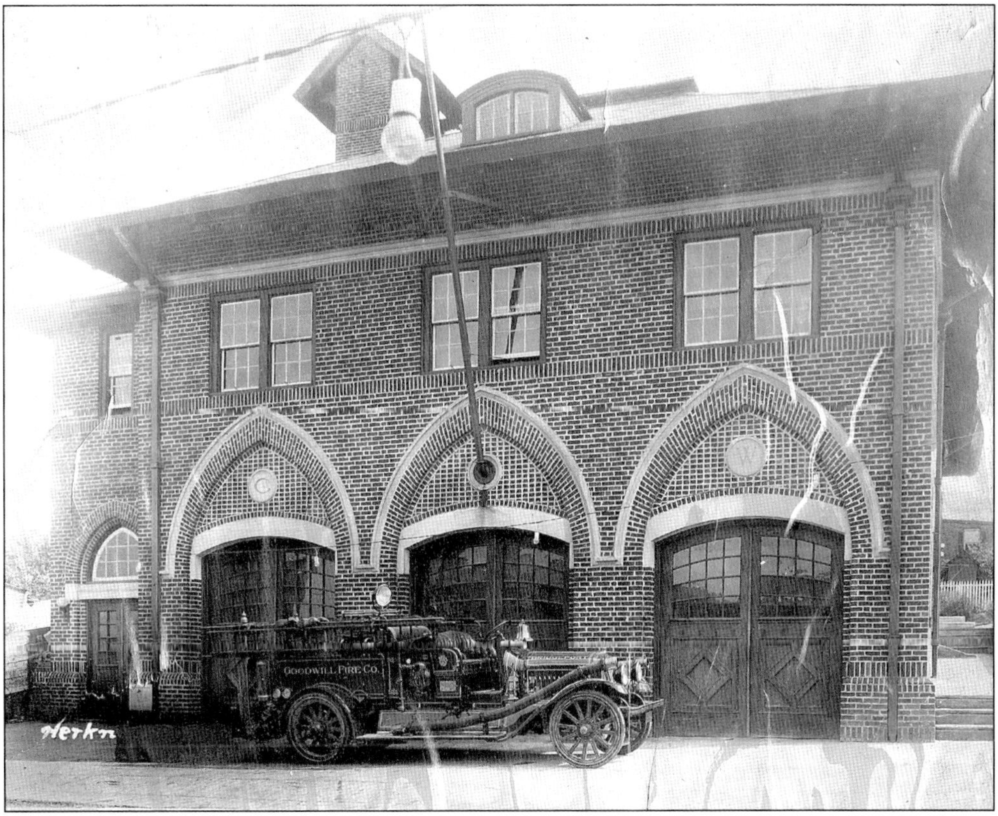

The Goodwill Fire Company plays a vital roll in the safety of Bridgeport's residents. Founded on February 1, 1915, Bridgeport was growing at a rapid pace, and the need for a second fire company was evident. The Goodwill Fire Company has been involved in every major fire and flood in the borough for nearly 100 years. This 1920s photograph was taken shortly after the Goodwill company built its firehouse and was showing off its first fire truck.

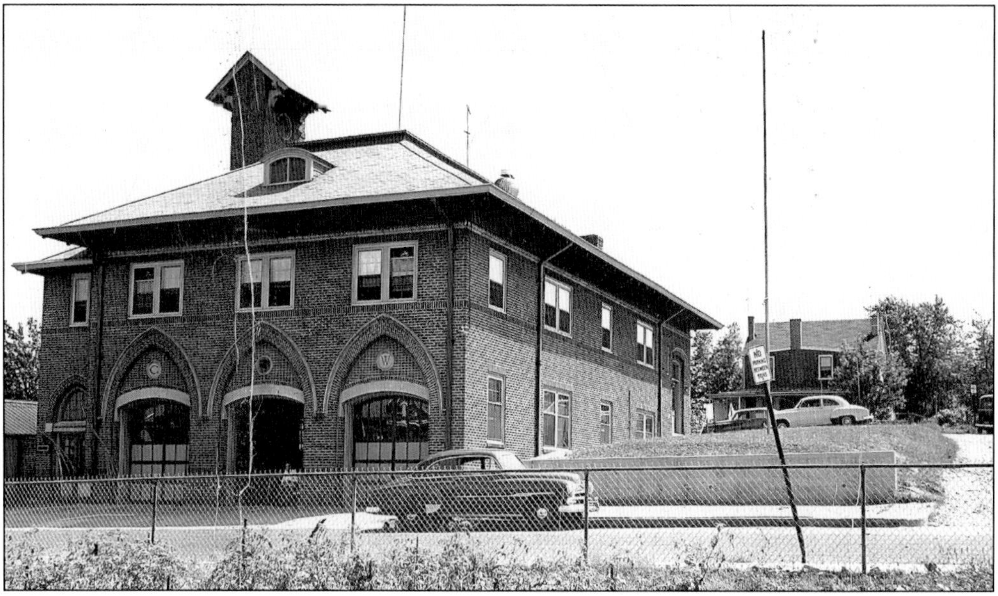

This photograph shows the Goodwill Fire Company in 1953, just before a major addition was constructed less than a year later on a plot of ground shown on the right of the photograph. Goodwill Fire Company was established in 1915, and the building was constructed in 1922. The company continues to serve Bridgeport and surrounding communities. (Goodwill Fire Company.)

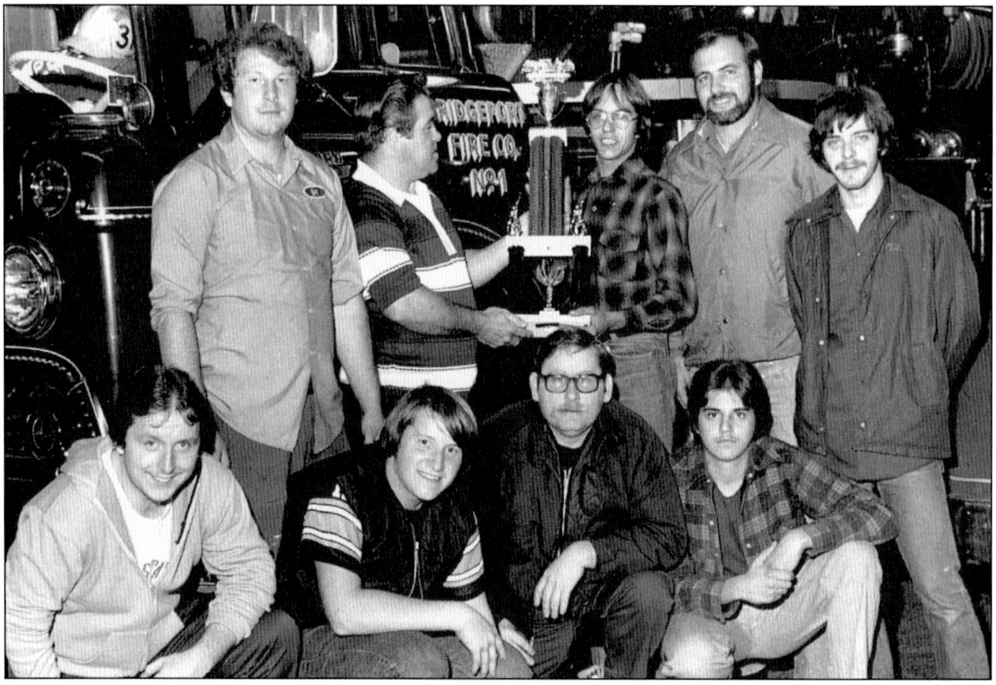

Members of the Bridgeport Fire Company No. 1 were all smiles back in 1979 after winning a first-place trophy in the annual Conshohocken Halloween parade. Showing off the trophy are, from left to right, (first row) Jerry Griffith, Terry Frymoyer, Vern Ward, and Scott Hemmerle; (second row) Joe Jeffers, Joe Lanigan, Dale Hemmerle, Gus Puleo, and Mickey Horning. (Bridgeport Fire Company No. 1.)

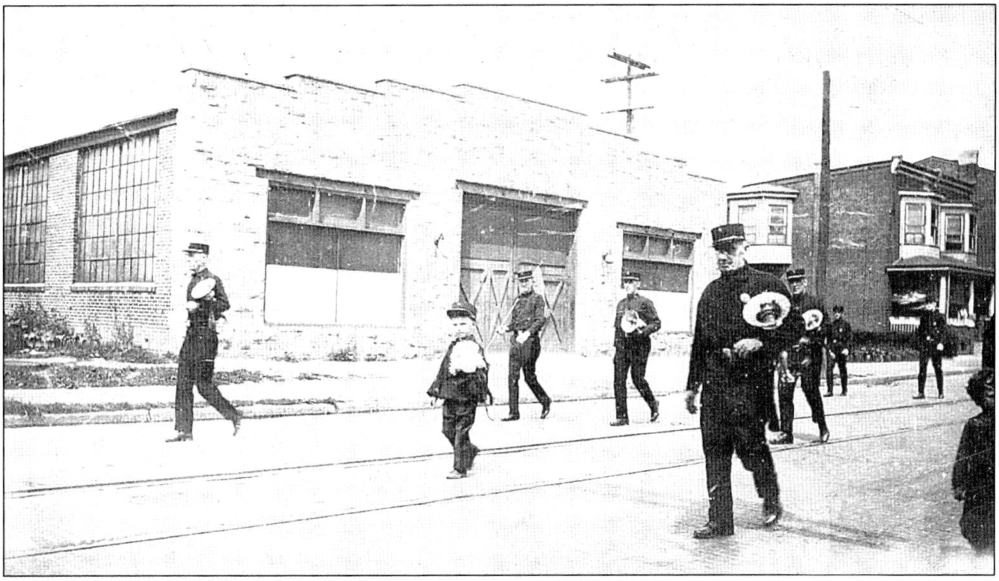

Members of the Bridgeport Fire Company No. 1, led by John Nash, march along West Fourth Street back in 1924. The members march past the Mike Tose Garage once located at 25 West Fourth Street. Bridgeport Fire Company No. 1 was formed in the fall of 1891, following a meeting at the Coats Hardware Store. In 1924, when this picture was taken, Bridgeport was enjoying part of what became known as the Roaring Twenties. (Bridgeport Fire Company No. 1.)

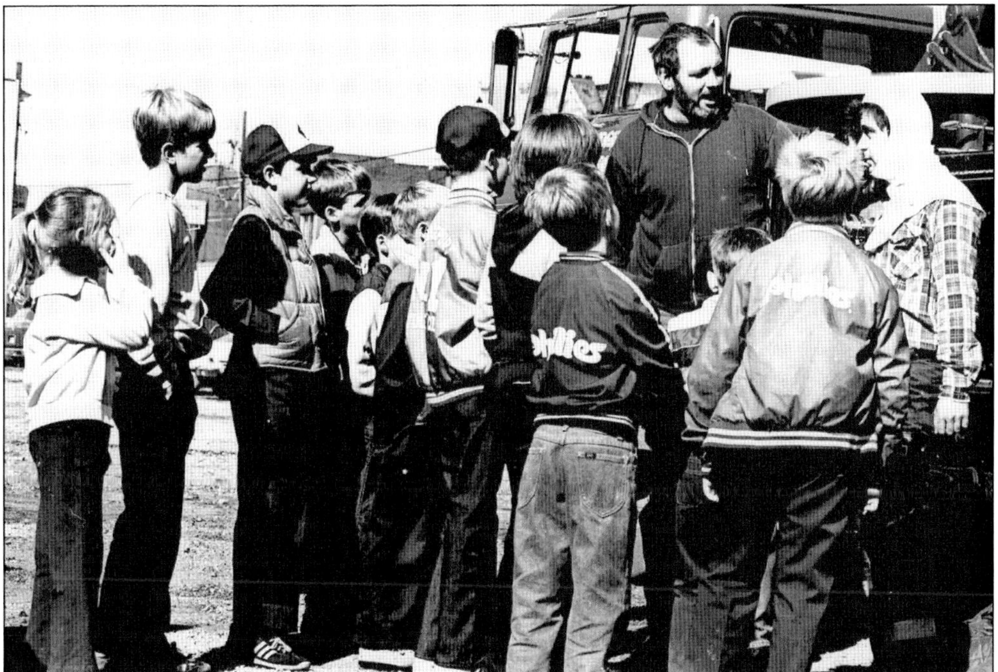

Members of the Bridgeport Cub Scout Troop gather around officials of the Bridgeport Fire Company No. 1 back in October 1983 during Fire Prevention Week to listen to firemen give fire-prevention tips. This is a yearly tradition for firemen to help educate residents in the community, especially young residents. (Bridgeport Fire Company.)

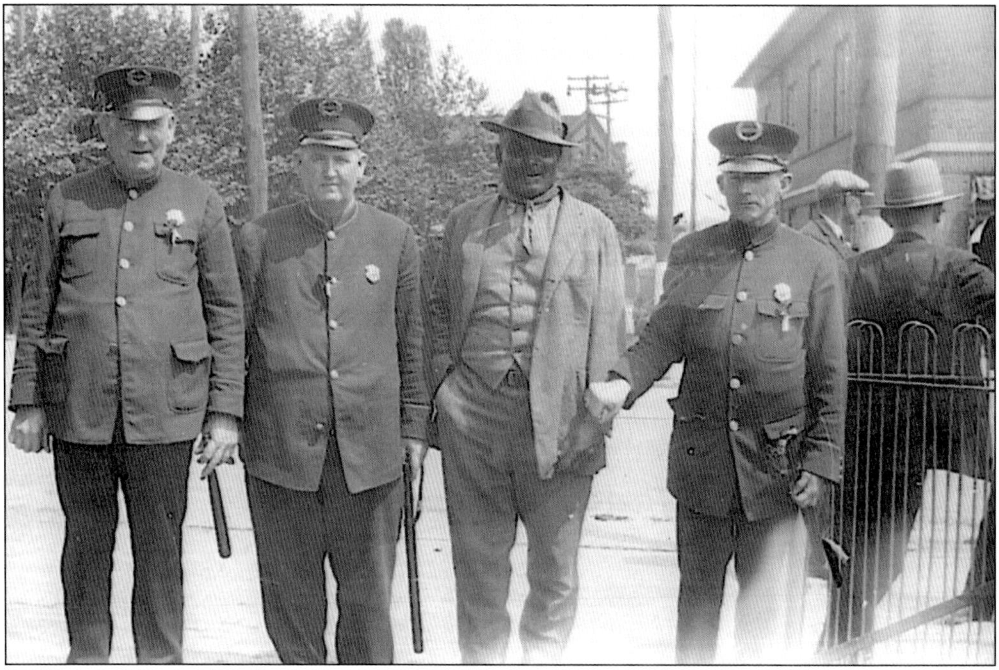

Bridgeport's borough police department was out in force in 1930, when this photograph was taken. Shortly after this photograph was taken, the department was increased to four officers to help protect Bridgeport's 5,500 residents. Shown in the photograph from left to right are Tom Butler, Joe McGrory, Ike Atley (who worked for March's lumberyard delivering coal for many years by horse and wagon), and Henry Finneran. Notice the police were all armed with billy clubs.

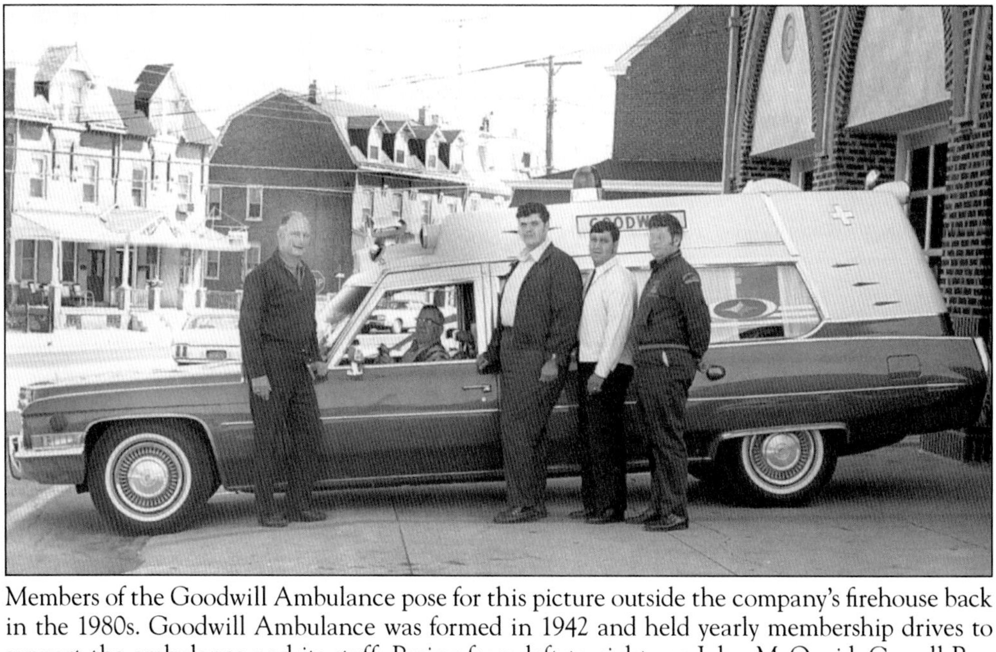

Members of the Goodwill Ambulance pose for this picture outside the company's firehouse back in the 1980s. Goodwill Ambulance was formed in 1942 and held yearly membership drives to support the ambulance and its staff. Posing from left to right are John McQuaid, Carroll Rex (sitting in the car), unidentified, Bill Campbell, and Robert Raft. (Goodwill Fire Company.)

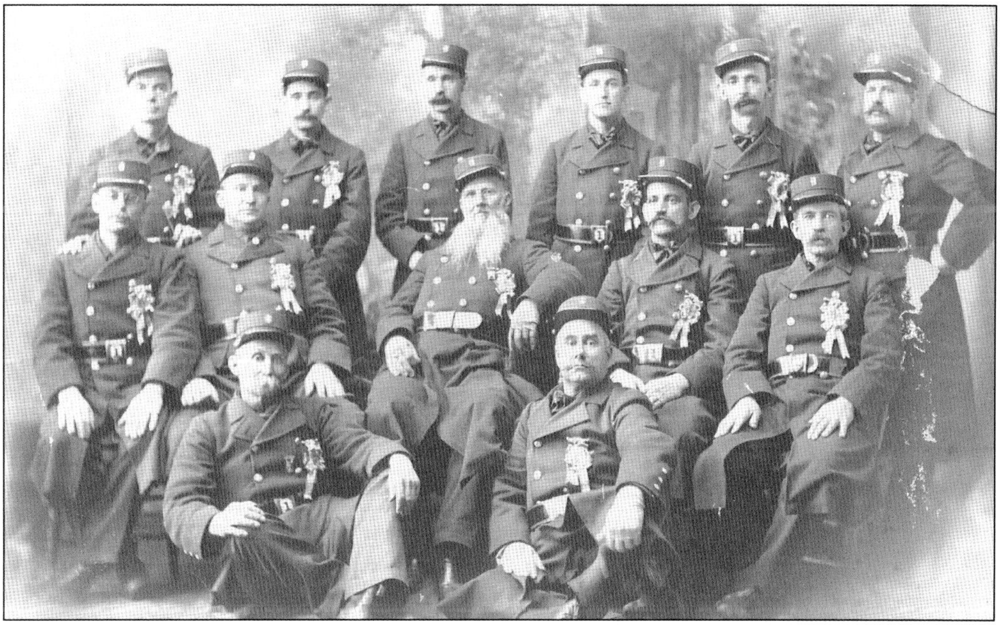

Bridgeport Fire Company was organized on October 22, 1891. Bridgeport Fire Company No. 1 quickly made a name for itself in Montgomery County, and within two years Bridgeport was making its company known across the state of Pennsylvania. Company members would travel to conventions, such as when this photograph was taken at the Johnstown Convention in 1893, just two years after it organized. Sitting in the middle of the photograph with the long white beard is Sam Coats, the company's first fire chief, who remained in that position for 22 years. (Bridgeport Hall of Fame.)

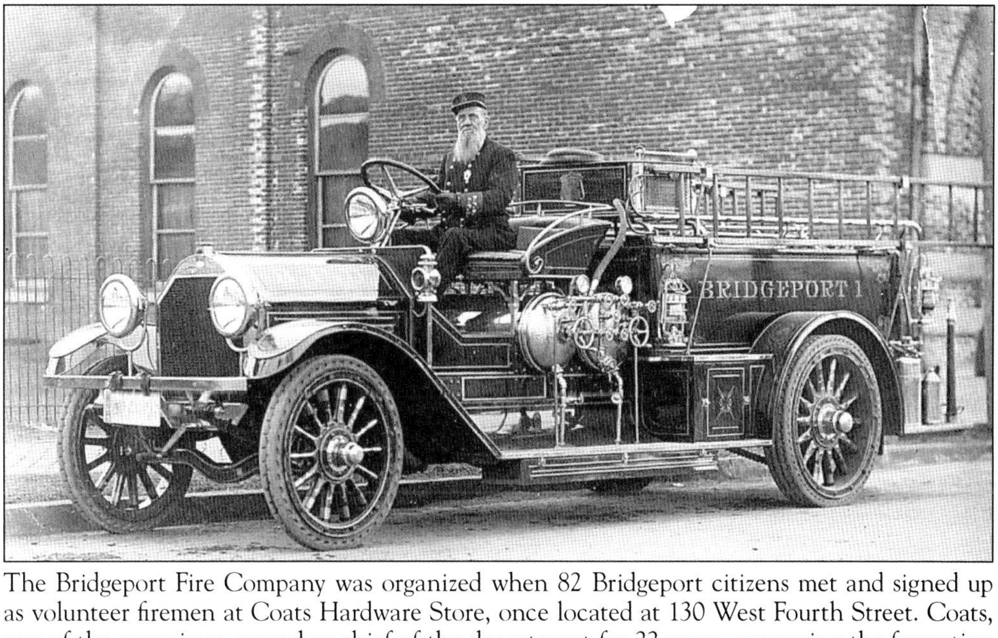

The Bridgeport Fire Company was organized when 82 Bridgeport citizens met and signed up as volunteer firemen at Coats Hardware Store, once located at 130 West Fourth Street. Coats, one of the organizers, served as chief of the department for 22 years, overseeing the formation and growth of the company. Coats is seen here sitting on the Bridgeport Fire Company 1924 Brockway fire truck outside the company's firehouse on West Fourth Street.

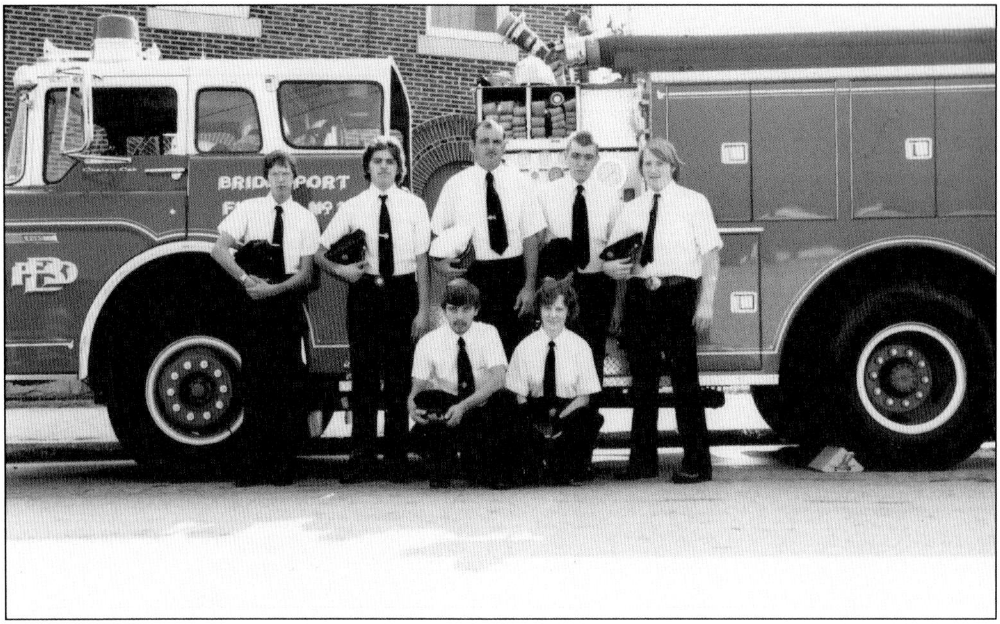

Members of the Bridgeport Fire Company line up in front of the firehouse before departing for a parade in 1980. Bridgeport Fire Company No. 1 was established in October 1891 and has served Bridgeport and surrounding communities for more than a century. From left to right are (first row) Mickey Horning and Doris Hritz; (second row) Dale Hemmerle, Scott Hemmerle, Gus Puleo, unidentified, and Terry Frymoyer. (Bridgeport Fire Company No. 1.)

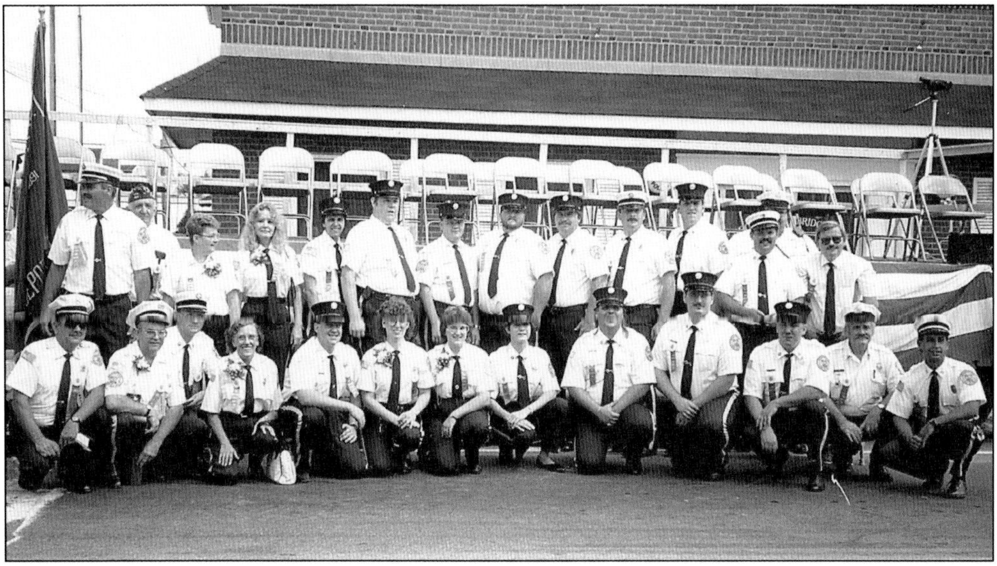

Members of the Bridgeport Fire Company No. 1 gather to celebrate the company's centennial in 1991. The Bridgeport Fire Company was organized in 1891, following a series of devastating fires from 1886 through 1890. Bridgeport was thriving with a number of large mills, including Lee's Carpets, Eureka, I. F. March Sons, and A. H. March's meatpacking plant, among others. All of the mills were built of wood, and following a number fires burning these structures to the ground while waiting for hand-pulled water wagons from Norristown to arrive, Bridgeport formed its own company in 1891. (Bridgeport Fire Company No. 1.)

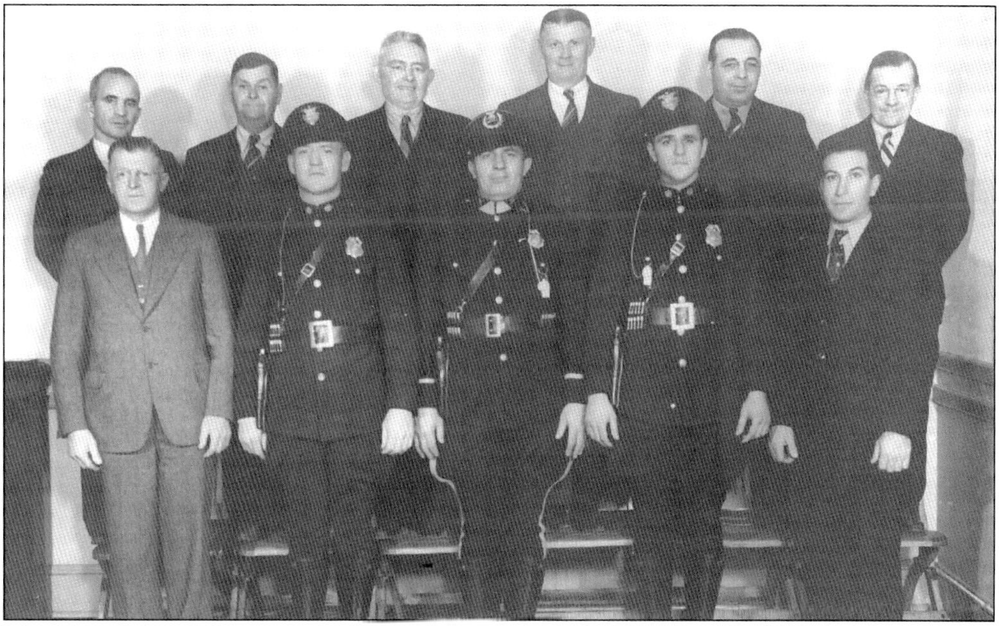

Members of the Bridgeport Police Department pose with borough officials back in 1939. Police chief Orfio Collilouri is standing in the center. In 1939, the police department had one police car that would patrol the borough's two car dealerships, four gas stations, and 25 grocery stores.

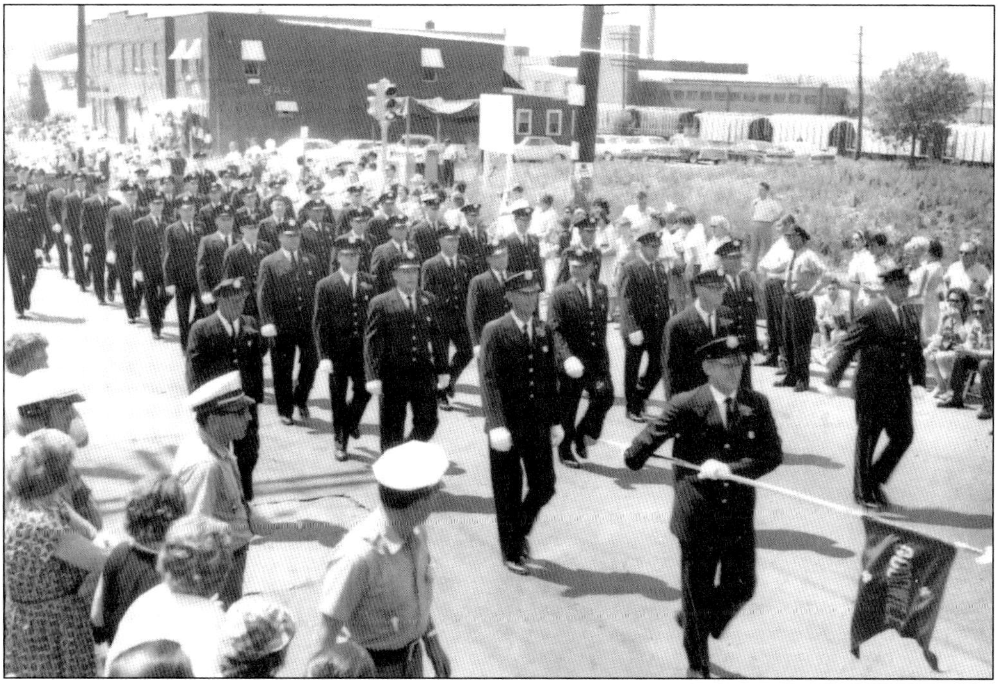

Bridgeport has a long, rich history in firefighting, generations of families have dedicated a good portion of their lives to serve and protect the borough. Good Will Fire Company, founded in 1915, celebrated 50 years of service with a huge parade back on June 5, 1965. Thousands of Bridgeport residents turned out on a mild sunny day to watch Good Will's 50 members march up Fourth Street.

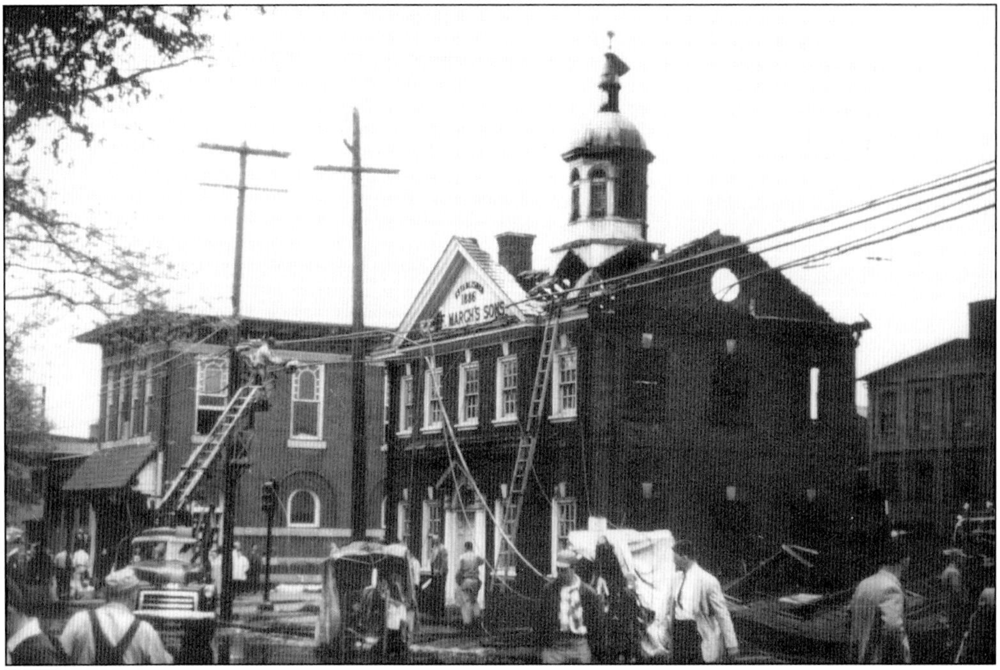

In May 1956, 10 fire companies from throughout Montgomery County fought an overnight blaze at Fourth and Mill Streets in Bridgeport that caused more than $1 million in damage to the I. F. March Lumber Yard. In 1956, the fire ran from one end of the block to the other. At Fourth and Mill Street was March's office building (seen in the photograph above). The building was an exact replica of Carpenters Hall in Philadelphia. The brickwork, molding, doors, cornice, and cupola were exact imitations of the famous Philadelphia building.

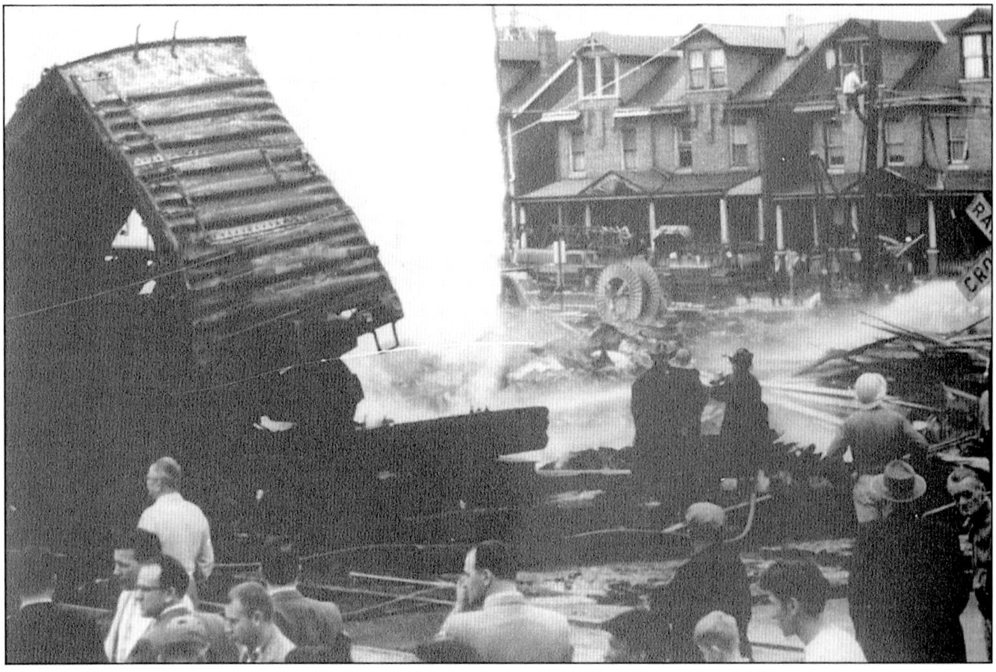

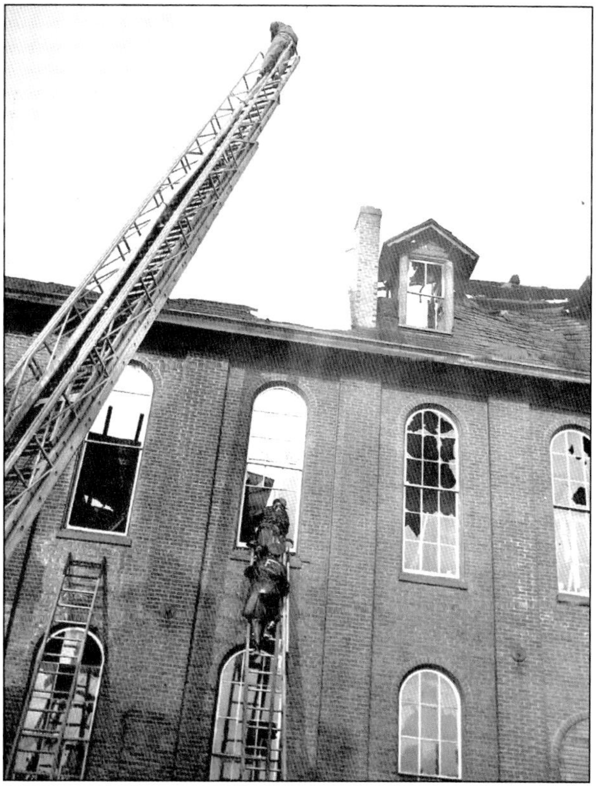

Both Bridgeport fire companies responded to a fire at Moser Brothers Building located at Third and Green Streets back on November 23, 1946. The fire did significant damage to the building that was an old borough market and former borough hall. Most of the second floor and the entire roof was damaged beyond repair and was later completely rebuilt. The building stands today and is an office building, among other things, including the Country Club Editions Golf Art Gallery. (Richard Schildt and Bridgeport Fire Company No. 1.)

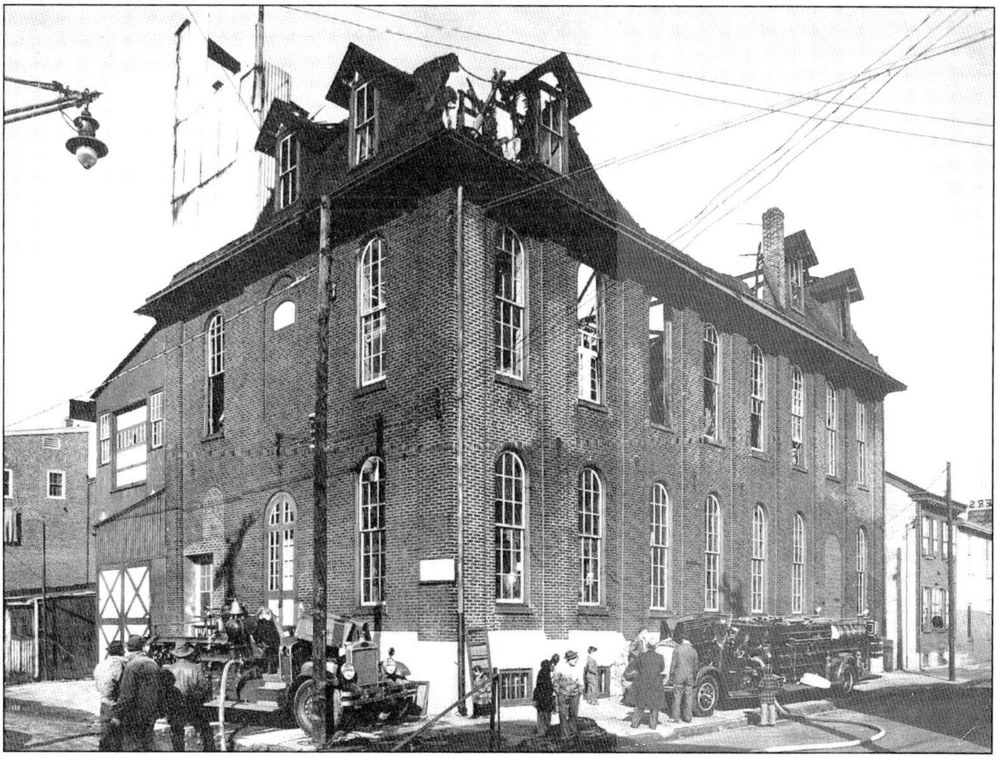

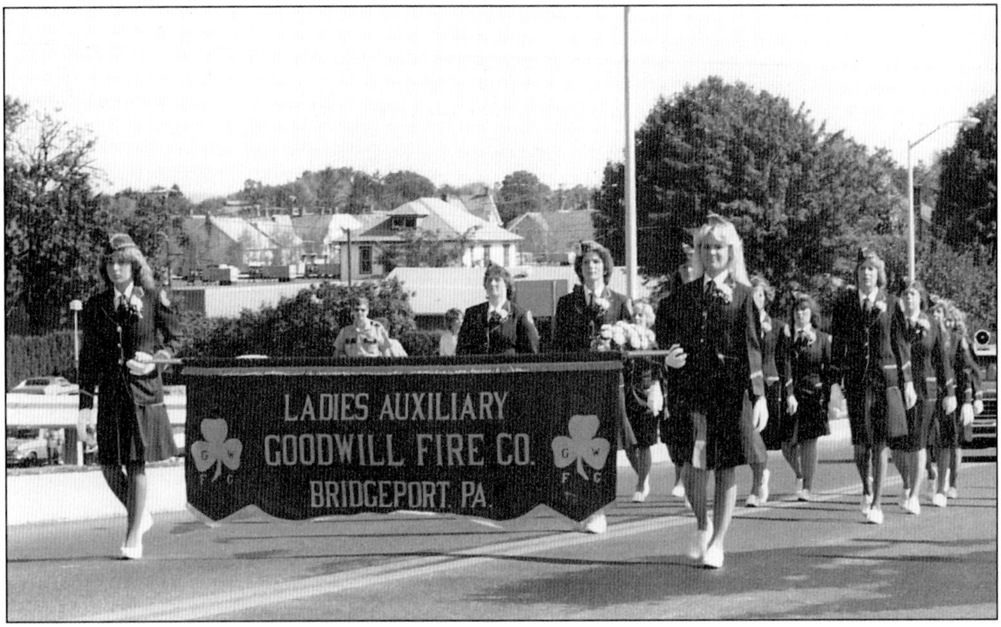

Members of the Goodwill Fire Company Ladies Auxiliary march in a parade back in the 1980s. For decades fire companies were supported by ladies auxiliaries that would provide refreshments at the scene of fires and help raise money for needed equipment. The president of the ladies auxiliary back in the 1980s was Ilene Nicoli, seen in the center of this photograph marching behind the banner. Goodwill Fire Company no longer has a ladies auxiliary unit. (Goodwill Fire Company.)

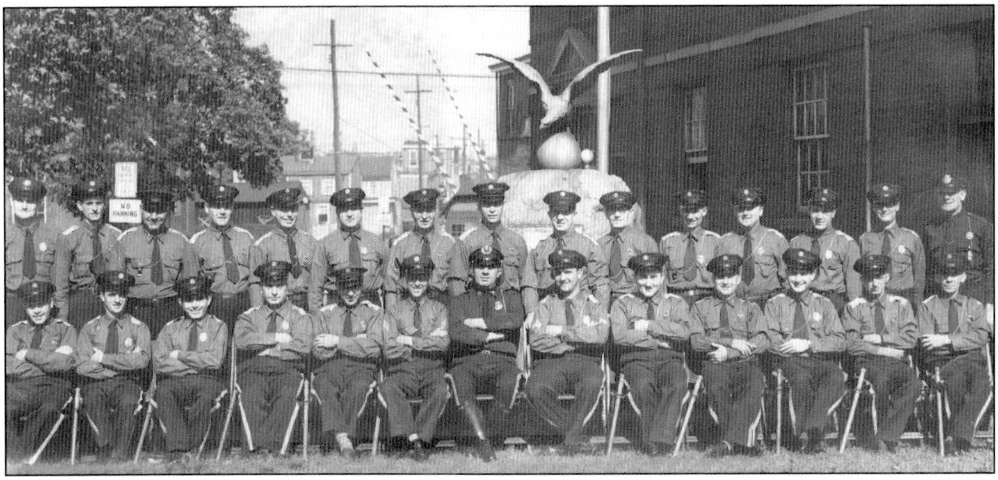

Although Bridgeport incorporated as a borough in 1851, it was not until 1870 that a one-man police force was formed in the person of Samuel Aikins. By 1940 Bridgeport had a five-man police department, but when the war broke out the force was reduced to four. Like many small towns throughout the country Bridgeport formed an auxiliary police department to assist the police with security and other functions. Posing with the 26 auxiliary police back in 1942 in a photograph taken outside borough hall are police chief Orfio Collilouri, sitting in the center of the first row, and officer Ben Waters, on the far right in the second row. Collilouri served the police department for 42 years, from 1926 to 1968; his son Chief Joseph "Murph" Collilouri served the department for 31 years, from 1948 to 1979. (Bridgeport Hall of Fame.)

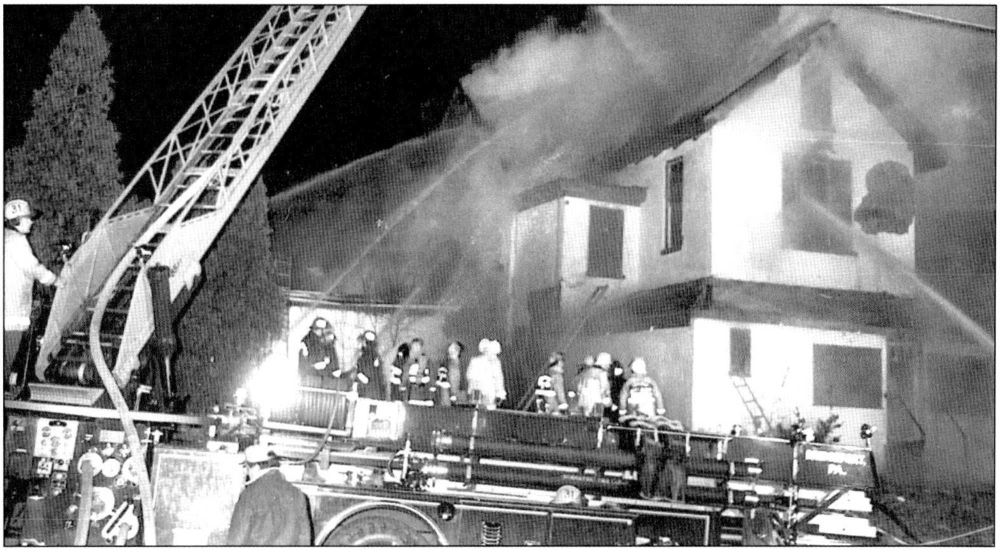

Firemen from Bridgeport Fire Company No. 1 and the Goodwill Fire Company are seen battling a 1975 New Year's Eve fire at the former Burgundy Inn in near-zero-degree temperatures. At the time of the fire the former inn was one of the oldest structures in the borough. The building had two previous fires in recent years, including fires in 1972 and again in 1973. The building located at Fifth and Ford Streets was razed in 1976, making way for apartments and Studio 8 Color Specialist. (Bridgeport Fire Company No. 1.)

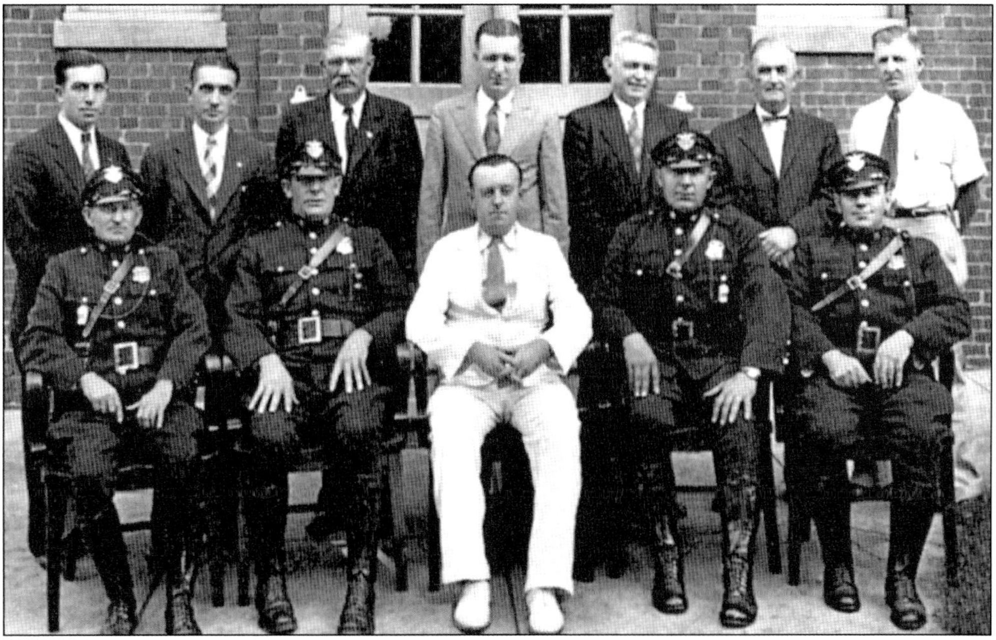

While a town watchman was appointed as early as 1870, the Bridgeport Police Department was not officially established until the early 1900s. By 1935 when this photograph was taken, Bridgeport had increased its police department to five, James Hughes was superintendent, and Orfio Collilouri was a sergeant. When Hughes resigned in 1935, Collilouri was named chief of police and held that position until his death in 1968. Bridgeport police purchased their first police car in 1934 and a second one in 1940.

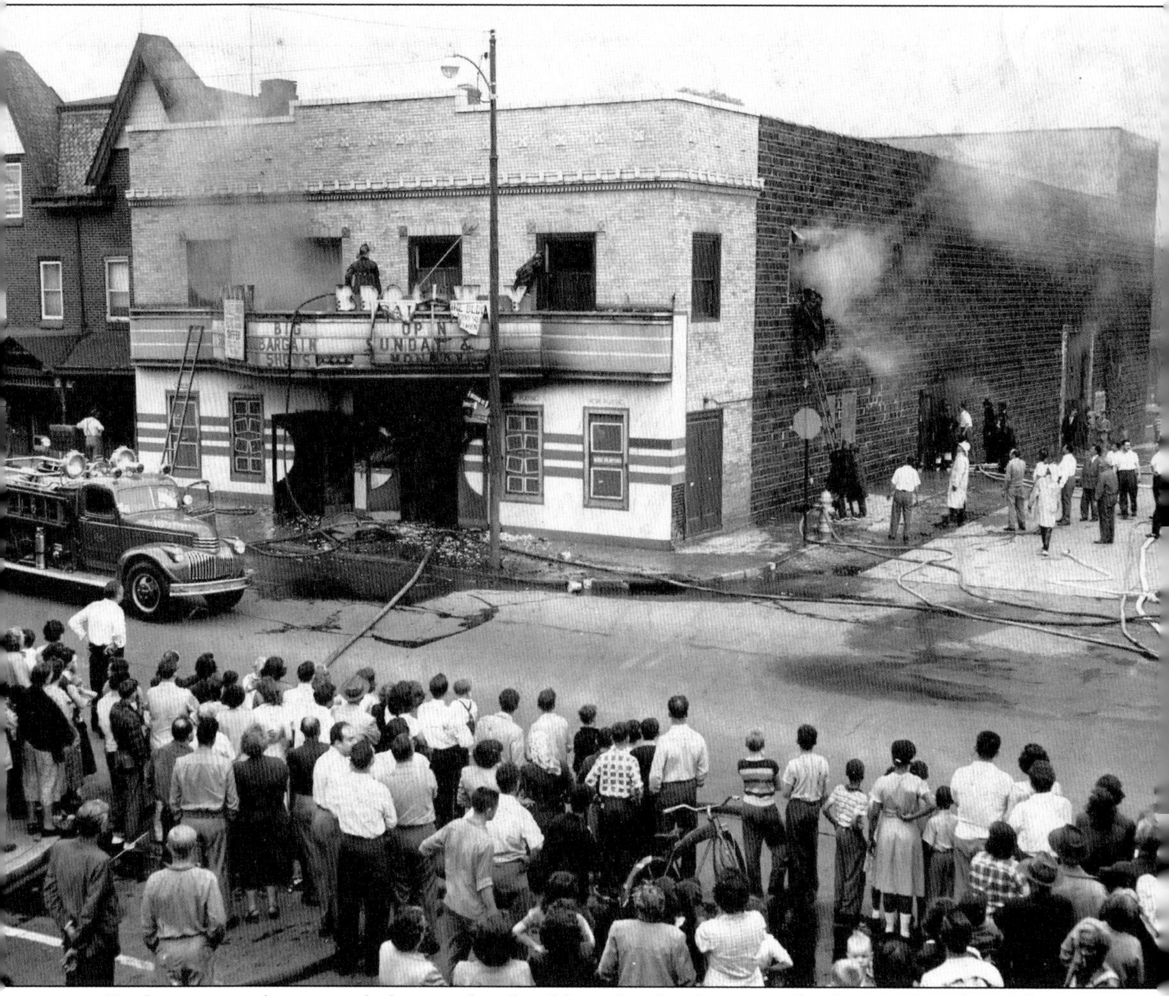

Bridgeport residents watch firemen battle a blaze that broke out at the former Broadway Theatre on Sunday, May 25, 1952. The theater closed about six months earlier and was purchased by Charles Differ, who rented the building to Philadelphia Textile Finishers, Inc., of Norristown. Twenty years earlier the theater suffered another fire that caused more than $3,000 in damage. The 1931 fire broke out following a live performance by the York Juvenile Minstrels, a show that benefited the Good Will Fire Company. A spark ignited curtains on the stage, and ironically residents ran into the theater, grabbing seats in the theater's main floor. According to the *Norristown Times Herald*, residents were hanging over the balcony railing watching and applauding the firemen as they battled the blaze on the stage. Nine firemen were affected by smoke or injured at the 1952 blaze and were treated at the scene by members of the Good Will Ambulance team. (Bridgeport Fire Company No. 1.)

Four

SCHOOLS

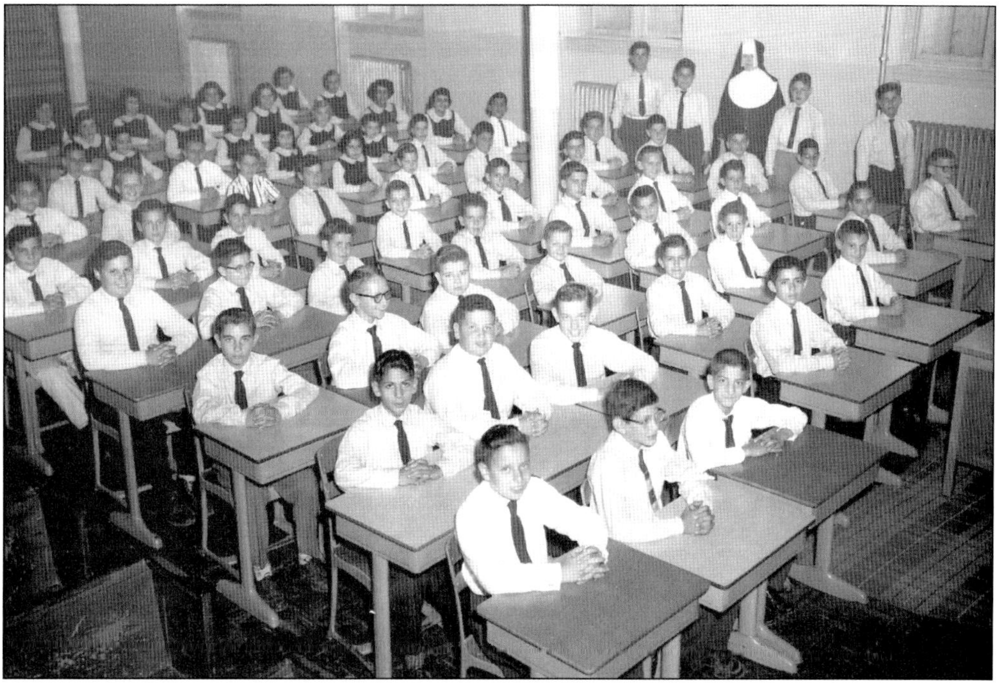

Our Lady of Mount Carmel School opened in September 1952 with an enrollment of 266 students in grades 1 through 8. This photograph was taken in 1957 of the fifth- and sixth-grade combined class. Within five years the amount of students outgrew the school and classes were being held in the church basement; notice the remaining pews in the lower left-hand corner of the photograph. The teacher against the wall was Sr. Mary Bridget, IHM (Immaculate Heart of Mary community). The young girl in the second seat, second isle from the windows is Maria Filiponi, now an IHM sister. Another future IHM was in that same class, Sr. Angela Mastrangela. The student in the front row, extreme right corner (only part of desk is visible), is Nicholas Pagano Jr. Pagano was ordained a priest on May 20, 2006, for the Diocese of Lexington, Kentucky. (Sal DiNenna.)

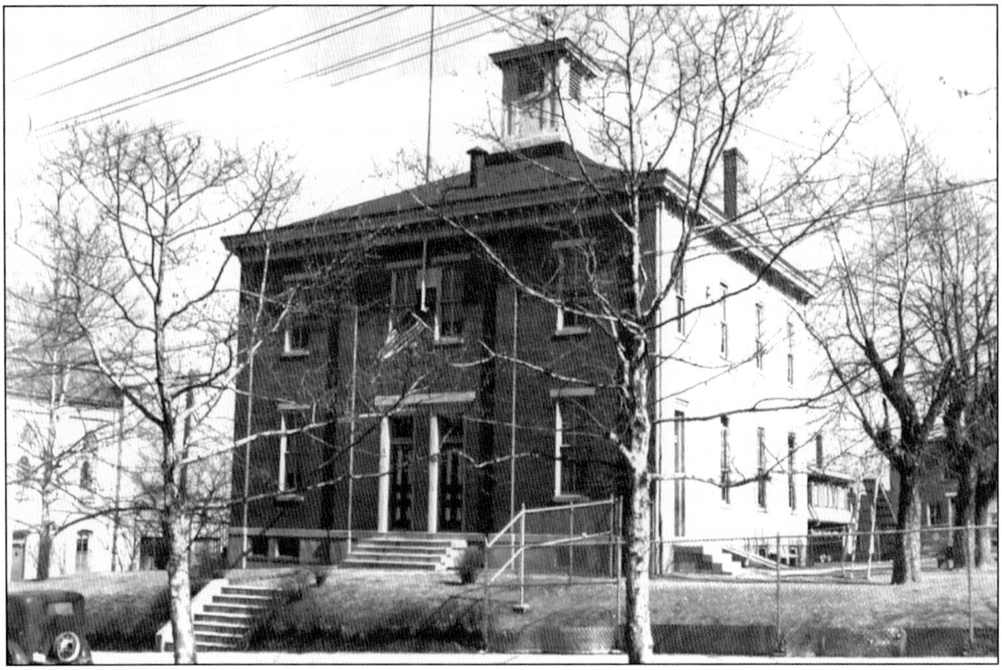

Bridgeport was incorporated as a borough in 1851, and five years later, in 1856, the town's first schoolhouse was erected at 601 Dekalb Street. While the borough was in its infancy nearly 1,000 people took up residence near the river where jobs were plenty in the mills. The Dekalb Street schoolhouse also served the community as an early meeting place for a number of religious groups until they could secure their own churches. The borough sold the building in 1953, and a group of townhouses now occupy the site at Sixth and Dekalb Streets. (Bridgeport Hall of Fame.)

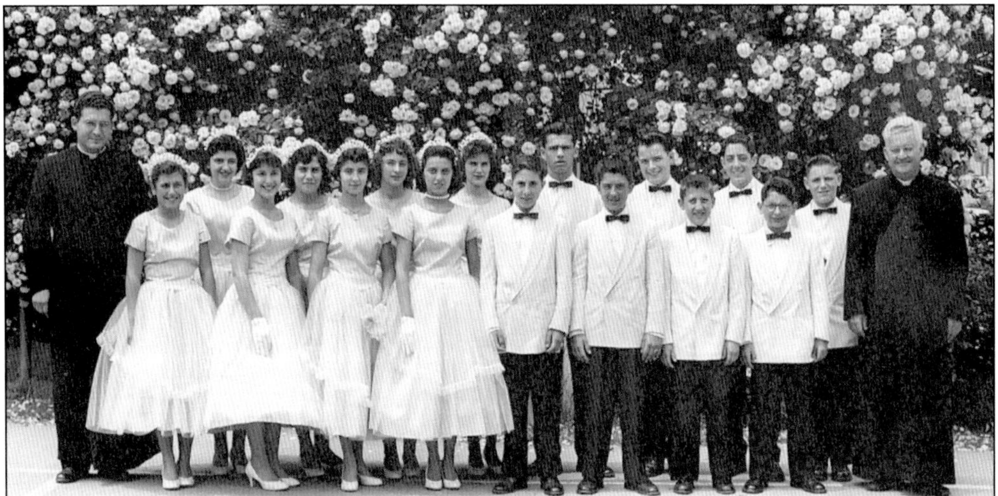

Eighth-grade graduates of Our Lady of Mount Carmel Parochial School back in the spring of 1956 included the students and two parish priests. From left to right are Rev. Edward Iannucci, Mary Ann Pachella, Jean Trolio, Antoinette Romanelli, Carmelina Churchill, Joanne Reed, Rachel DeMarco, Joanne Pretzello, Marie Mastercola, Gerald DeJoseph, William Yacovelli, Albert Pastino, John Melle, Carmen DeSterano, Carl Januzelli, Theodore Battaglio, Joseph Pignoli, and Rev. Edward Craney. (Joanne Hector.)

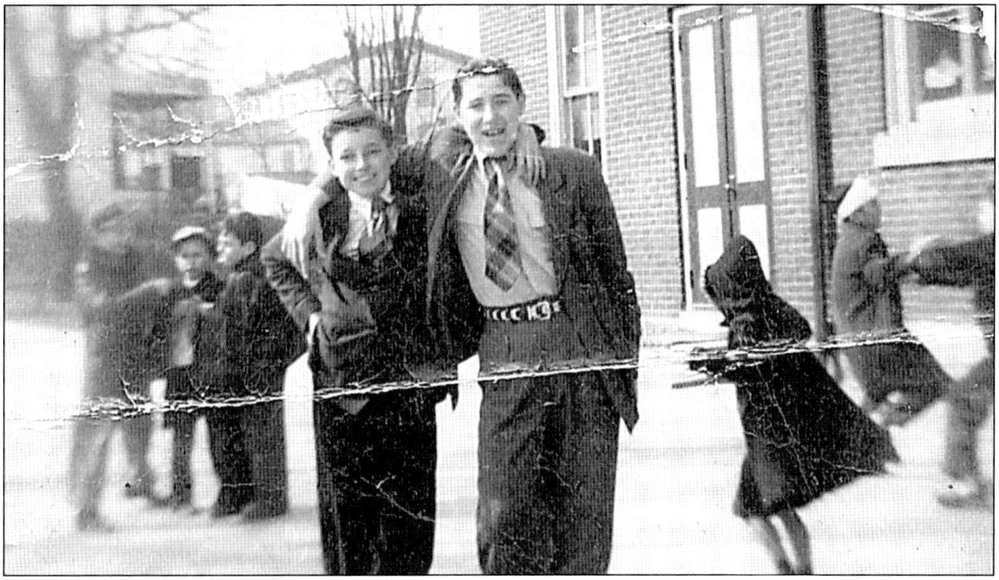

In 1940, John McGuire (left) and Rocky Pignoli were two of the 311 children attending St. Augustine's grade school as the two were photographed during a recess break in the schoolyard. Sr. M. Anselm was mother superior back then as 145 boys and 166 girls attended grades 1 through 8. The school's enrollment would grow to more than 350 children in the 1950s before the decline started in the 1960s. St. Augustine's School closed in 2000. (Rocky Pignoli.)

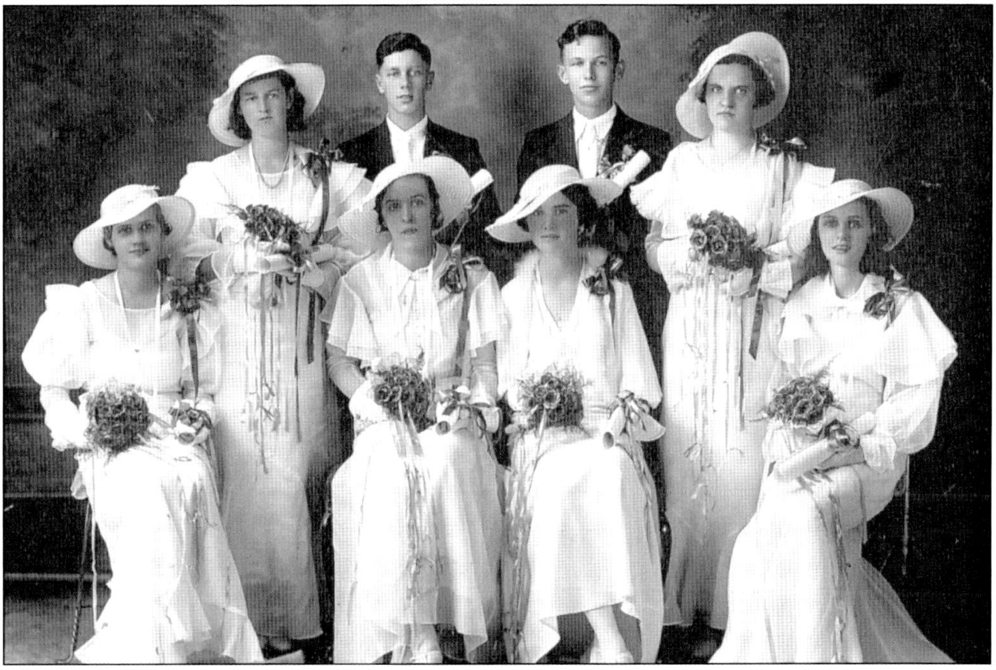

This was the last commercial class to graduate from St. Augustine's School, back in 1934. Graduating commercial classes were students in 9th and 10th grade who studied secretarial and standard job positions of the day. In 1935, all classes above eighth grade were discontinued. In 1934, St. Augustine School had 315 students registered, a number that would decline starting in the 1950s. (St. Augustine Church.)

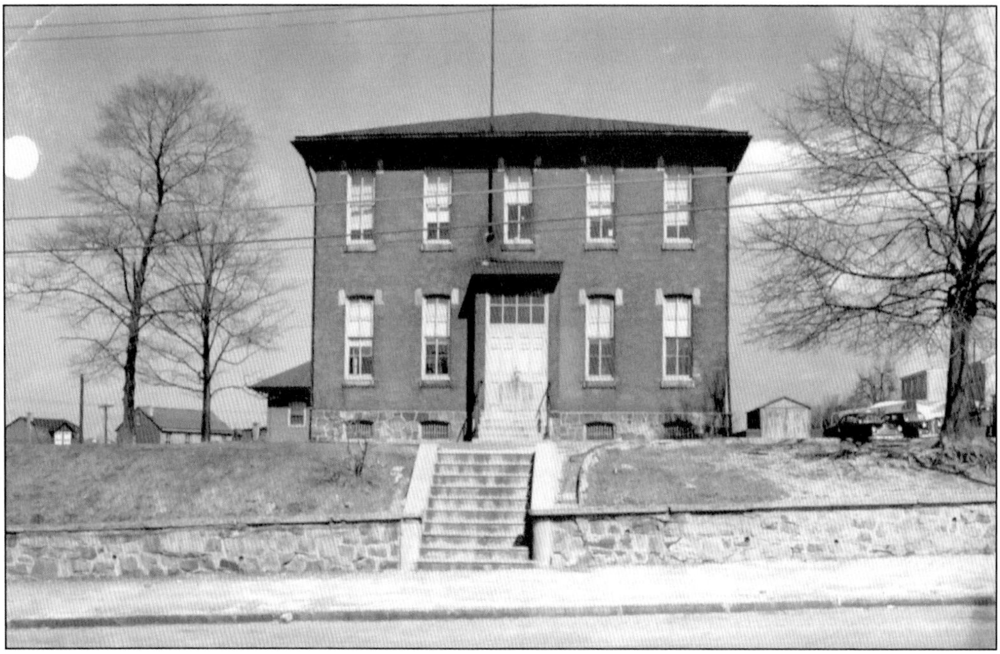

Bridgeport was experiencing a population growth in the late 1870s, and a second schoolhouse was needed to accommodate residents living on the other side of town. The first schoolhouse was built in 1856 on Dekalb Street. The Holstein Street School shown above was erected in 1882 at 209 Holstein Street. In a 20-year period, from 1870 to 1890, the town's population surged from 1,600 residents to 2,600 residents due to the growing industry. The school was sold in 1953, and a gas station was added onto the property and the schoolhouse was later used for apartments. The schoolhouse still stands, and the Raimo and Mill Automobile Repair Shop now occupies the site. (Bridgeport Hall of Fame.)

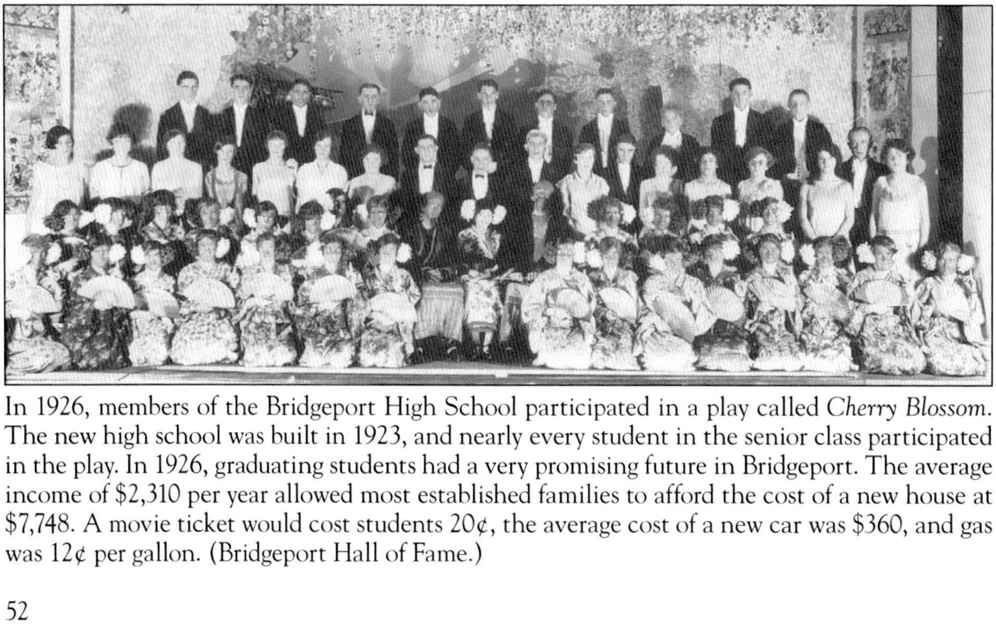

In 1926, members of the Bridgeport High School participated in a play called *Cherry Blossom*. The new high school was built in 1923, and nearly every student in the senior class participated in the play. In 1926, graduating students had a very promising future in Bridgeport. The average income of $2,310 per year allowed most established families to afford the cost of a new house at $7,748. A movie ticket would cost students 20¢, the average cost of a new car was $360, and gas was 12¢ per gallon. (Bridgeport Hall of Fame.)

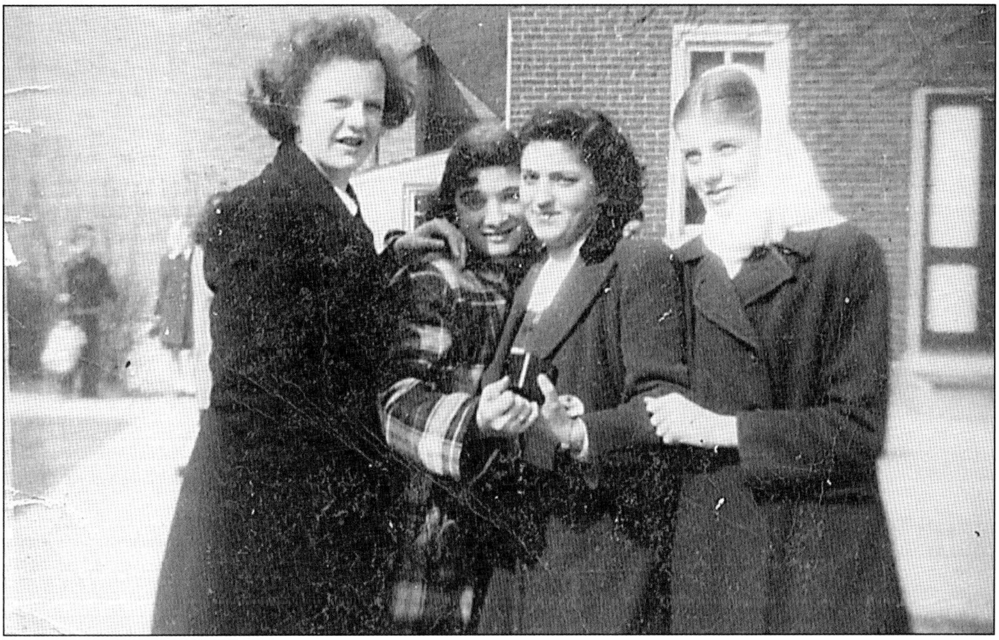

A group of childhood friends gathered in the St. Augustine's schoolyard for this photograph in the winter of 1949. Eighth-grade students, from left to right, included Patricia Grant, Connie Petroleti, Rosemary Raniri, and Doris Thomas. While more than 150 sisters taught at St. Augustine's over the years, Sr. M. Avila, Sr. Mary Madeleine, Sr. Marie Barat, and Sr. Maria Josepha were just a few who taught back in 1949. (Rocky Pignoli.)

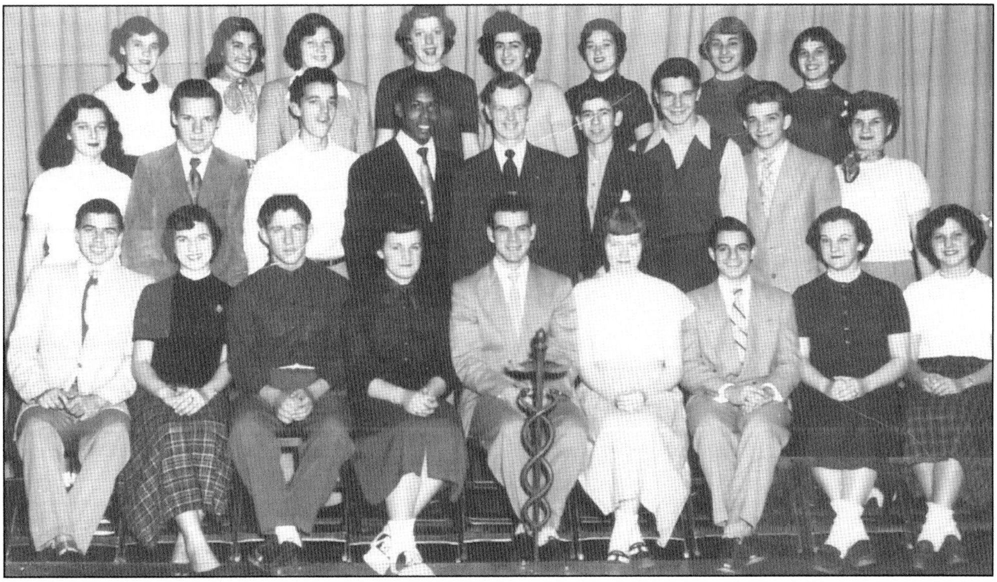

Members of the 1952 Bridgeport High School junior and senior council pose for a picture before graduation. The class of 52 had an exciting year as the girls' basketball team posted the first undefeated season in the school's 30-year history. Students could shop the local department stores, including Charles DeJohn Department Store located on Fourth Street and Spillane's 5 and 10 Cent Store located at 118 Holstein Street A couple of the 43 graduating students included Lou Carfagno, Marie DeStefano, James Lawless, and Doris Smith. (Bridgeport Hall of Fame.)

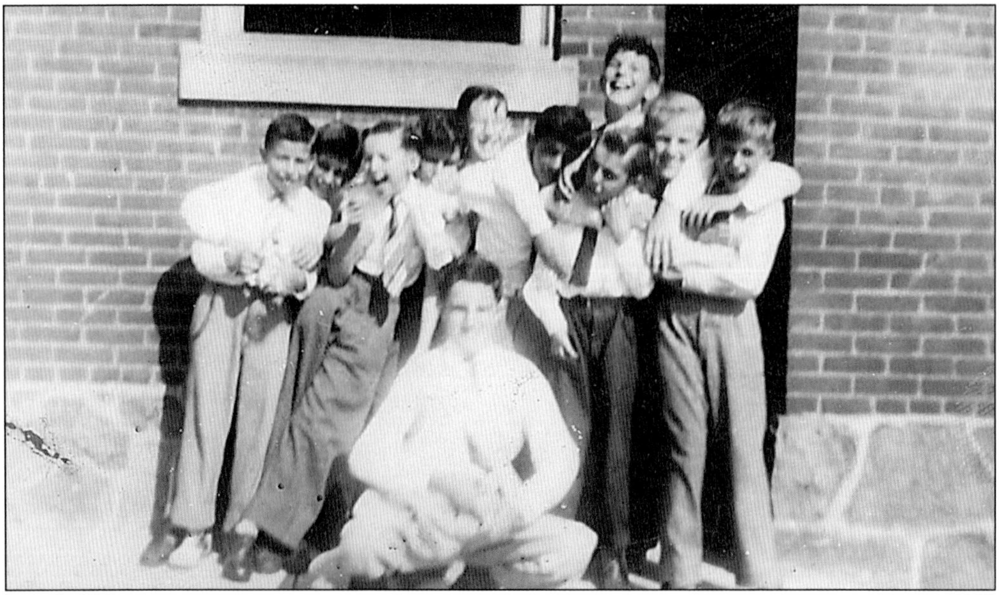

A bunch of school friends from St. Augustine's School on Bush Street were seen playing in the schoolyard back in the early 1940s when St. Augustine's School had more than 300 students. Included in the photograph are Robert McTague, John McGuire, Charles Epright, Cap Masintonio, Dave Maloney, Franny Poore, Joseph Rotay, Eddie Tomchiek, and Charles Denofi. The first schoolhouse was built in Bridgeport before the town was incorporated in 1842; St. Augustine's School was established in 1896. (Rocky Pignoli.)

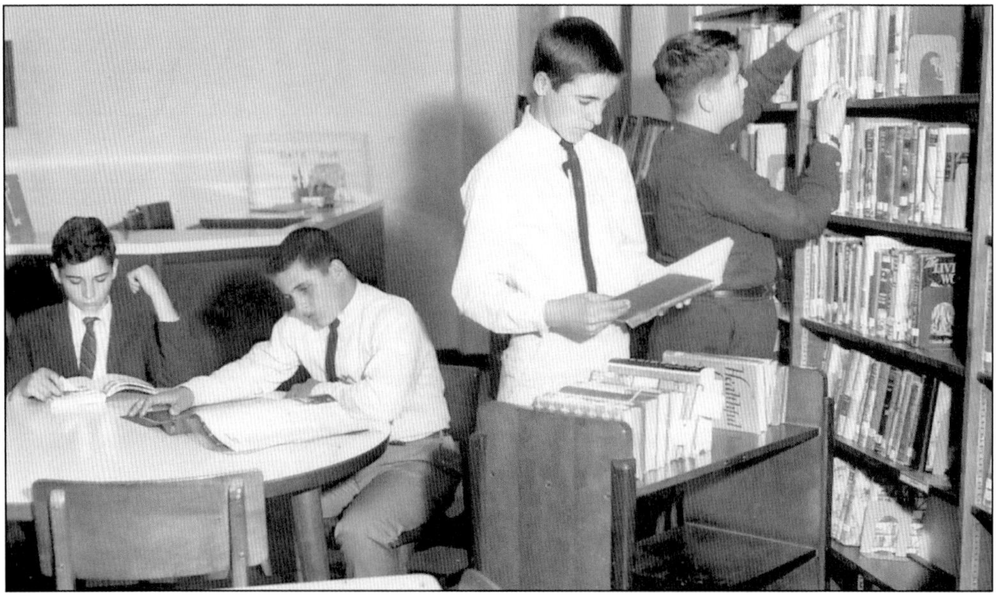

Bridgeport High School, once located at Seventh and Ford Streets, was the absolute pride of the borough from 1924 until the school merged with Upper Merion Township in 1966. Just one year before the school closed, students were photographed taking part in Library Week at the school in April 1965. Students taking part included, from left to right, David Wroua, Raymond Perone, and Daniel Puscar, all ninth graders, and James Wilkinson, who was in eighth grade. (Bridgeport Hall of Fame.)

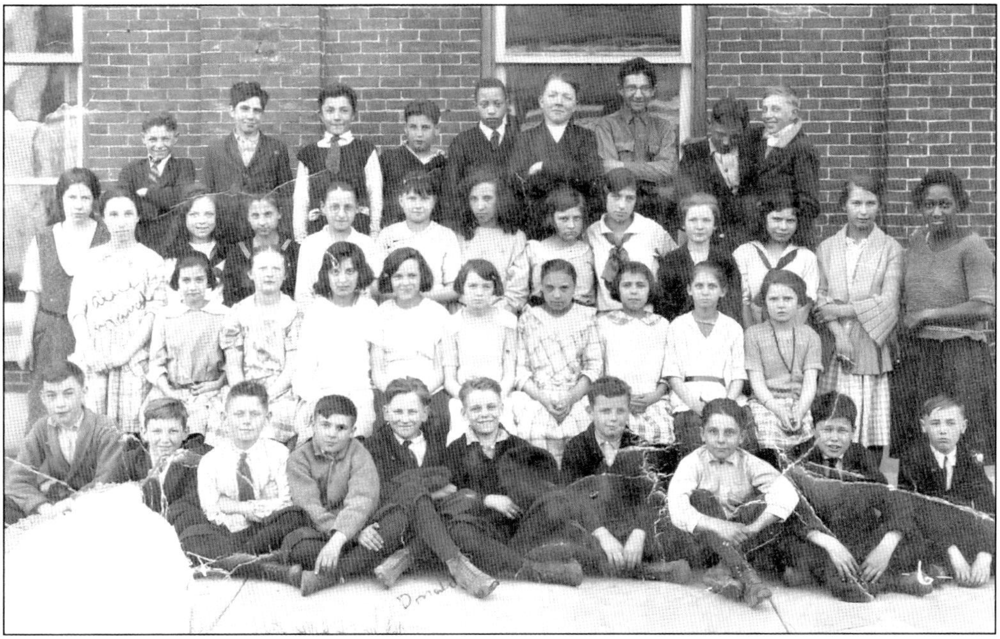

This 1920s Bridgeport Elementary School class photograph shows well-dressed students, and notice the high-topped laced shoes on the boys sitting in the first row. Sam Volpe is among the boys in the first row, while Christine Chiccarine, Florence Hughes, Elsie Beech, Rose Marnelli, and Emma Shields are in the second row. Ellen Maiale, Helen Richards, and Mary Young are in the third row, and Leroy Smith and Donald Coats are among the students in the fourth row. (Bridgeport Hall of Fame.)

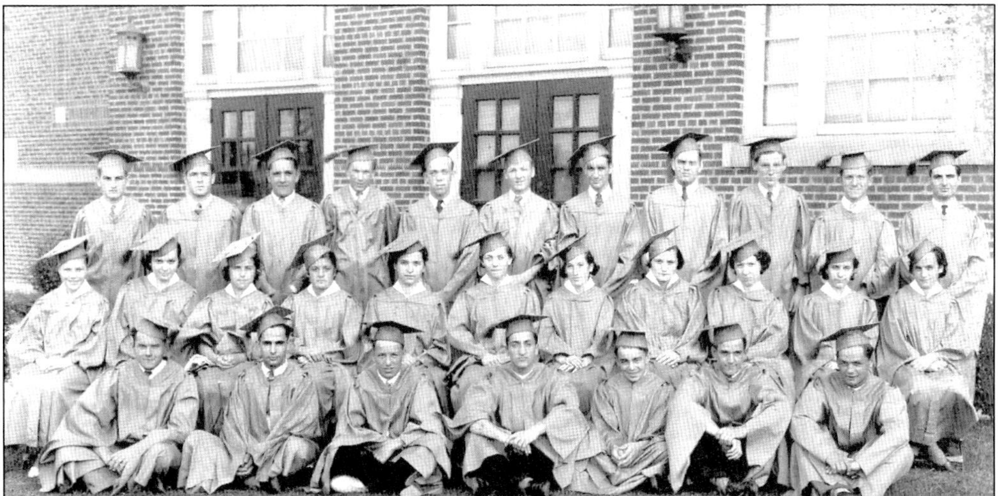

In 1934, when these Bridgeport High School students graduated, the first state liquor store opened in Pennsylvania, and in February 1934, the first high school automobile driving course was offered in State College Pennsylvania. When these students graduated the average income was up to $1,601 per year, and if they wanted to further their education at Harvard University they would have been required to pay a tuition cost of $410 per year. On the cheaper side a 25¢ movie ticket to the Broadway Theatre would have allowed them to witness Shirley Temple appearing in her first movie.

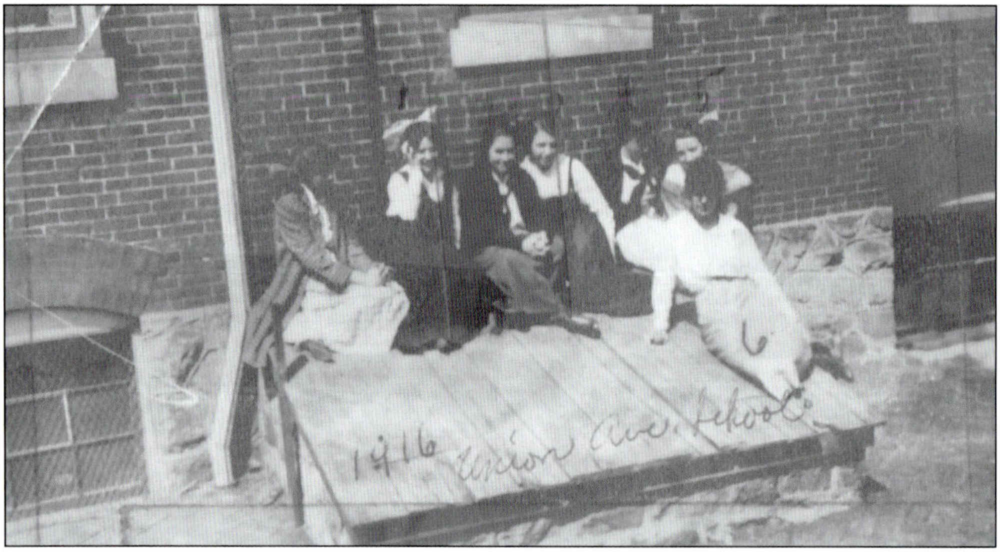

Seven Bridgeport High School girls were photographed sitting behind the Union Avenue School in the fall of 1916. From left to right are Mary Supplee, Elsie Smith, Bertha Milligan, Sophia Leewton, Helen Hoffman, Helen Star, and Bee Hall. In the spring of 1917, eight students graduated from the high school. (Bridgeport Hall of Fame.)

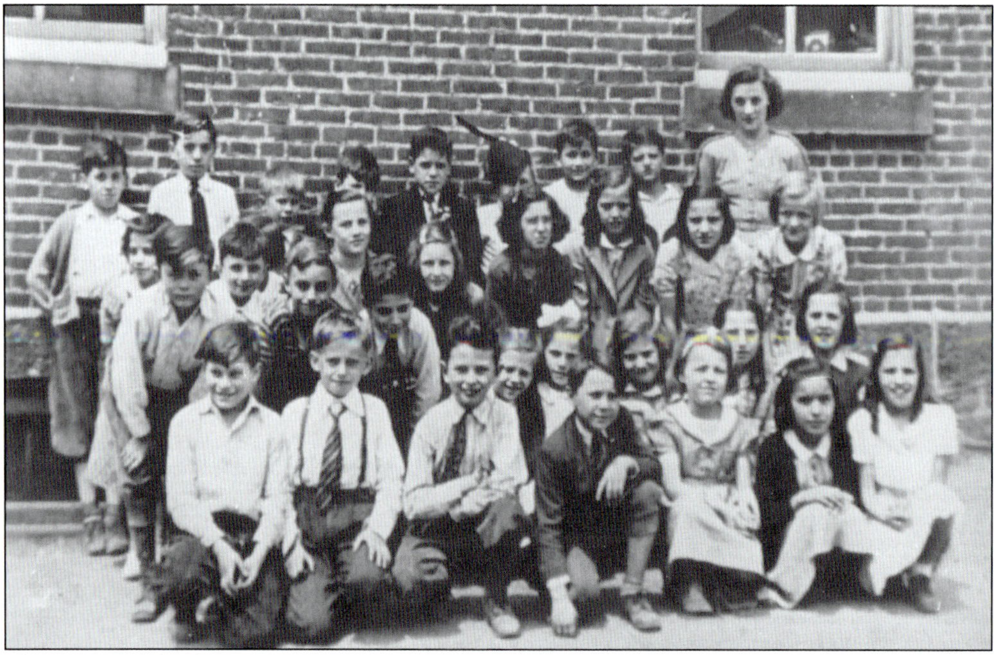

This group of third-grade students from the Holstein Street School poses for a class photograph back in the mid-1930s outside the school building. In the mid-1930s, Bridgeport was nearing a population peak with nearly 6,000 residents living in the borough. The school was located at 209 Holstein Street and was built in 1882. Joe Palumbo can be seen in the fourth row, fifth student from the left. (Bridgeport Hall of Fame.)

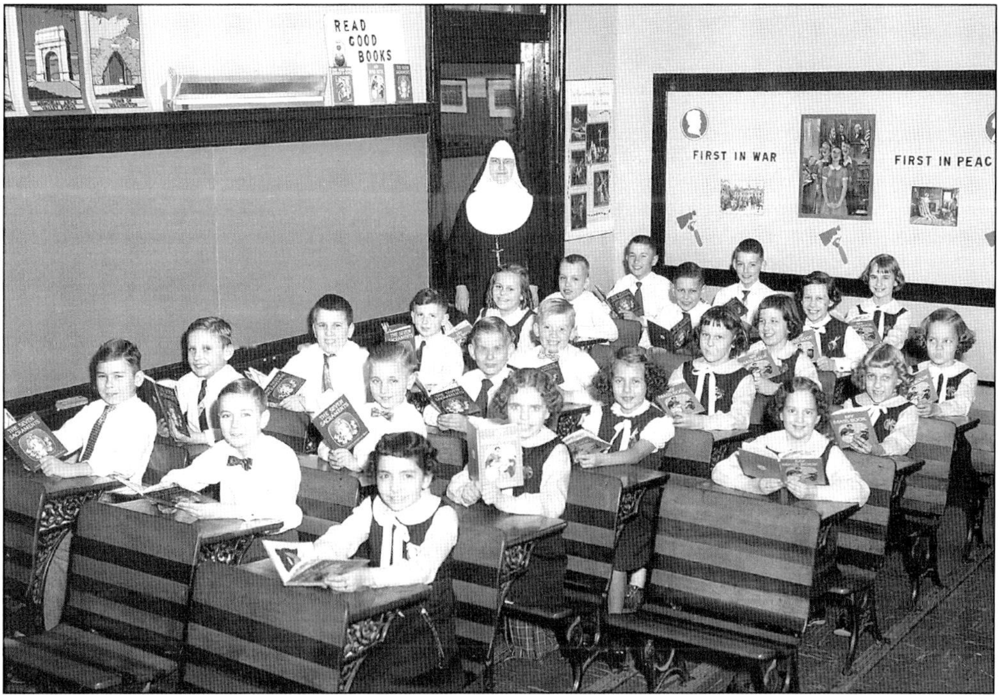

In September 1929, Our Mother of Sorrows School welcomed its first students into the newly constructed school. In the early years, students participated in grades 1 through 4, other grades were added in later years. The photograph above shows students at their desks in the early 1940s, the boys are holding books titled *The Seven Sacraments*, while the girls hold *My Mass Book*. The photograph below shows the graduating class from Our Mother of Sorrows School in 1942. (St. Augustine Church.)

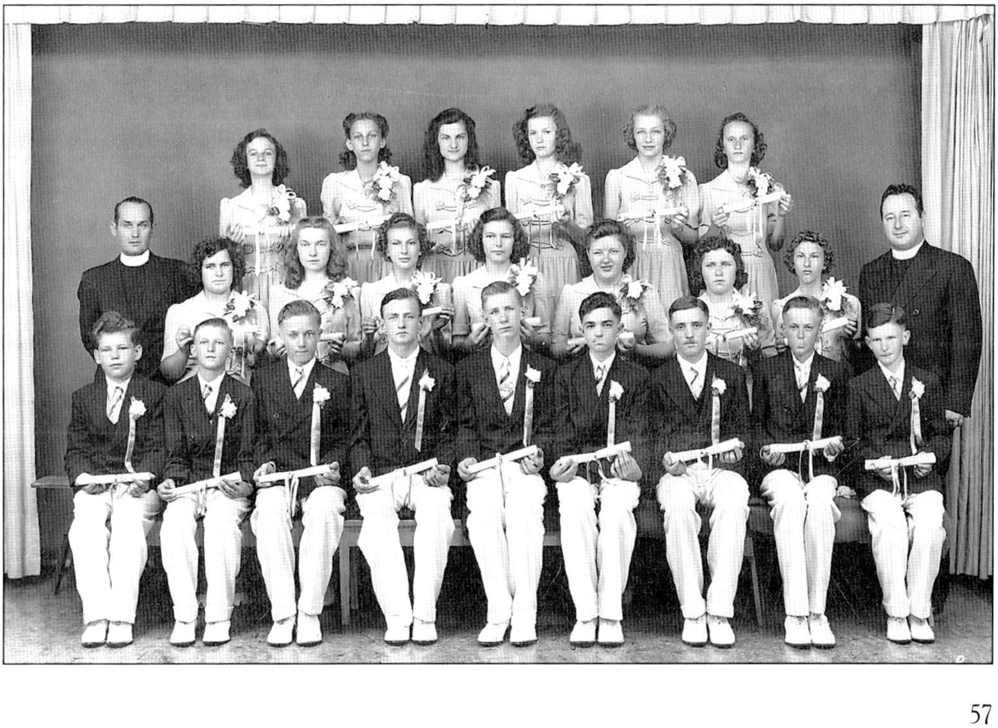

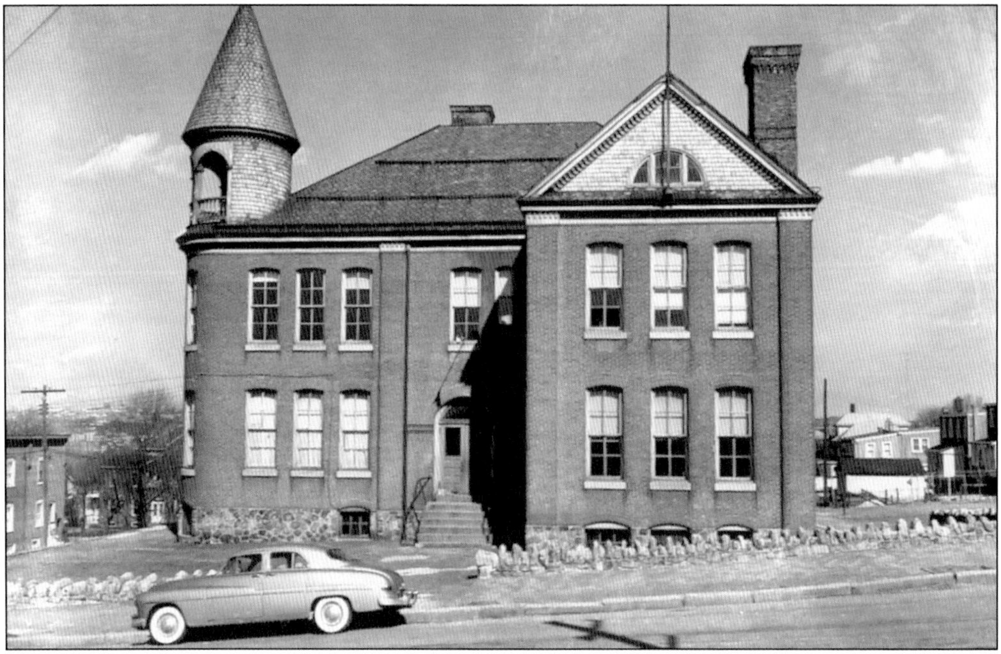

In 1892, the borough's population was nearing 3,000 residents and a high school was needed. A year later in 1893 the Union Avenue School building located at 381 Union Avenue opened as the Bridgeport High School. Thirty years later in 1923, a modern-day high school was built at Seventh and Ford Streets and the Union Avenue School served as an elementary school. A new elementary school opened in 1951, replacing the Union Avenue School that was later demolished. (Bridgeport Hall of Fame.)

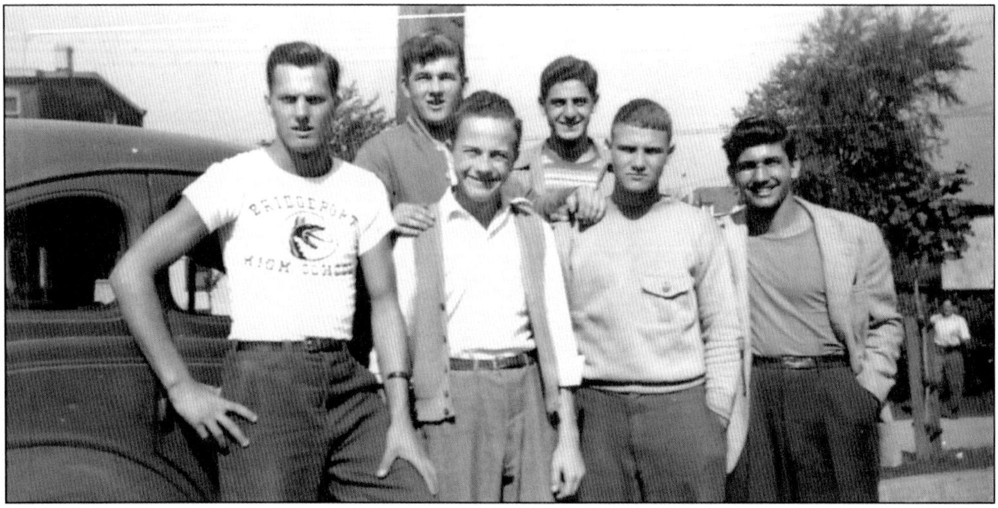

In the spring of 1946, these young lads were busting out of Bridgeport High School just in time to celebrate the postwar economy. It was in 1946 that the Flamingo Hotel opened in Las Vegas, the CIA (Central Intelligence Agency) was formed, and Harry S. Truman was president of the United States. Students at Bridgeport High School in 1946 were listening to Sammy Kaye, Perry Como, the Ink Spots, and Dinah Shore on the car radio. Down at the Broadway Theatre on Dekalb Street *The Best Years of Our Lives*, *Song of the South*, and *It's a Wonderful Life* were just a few of the movies out in 1946.

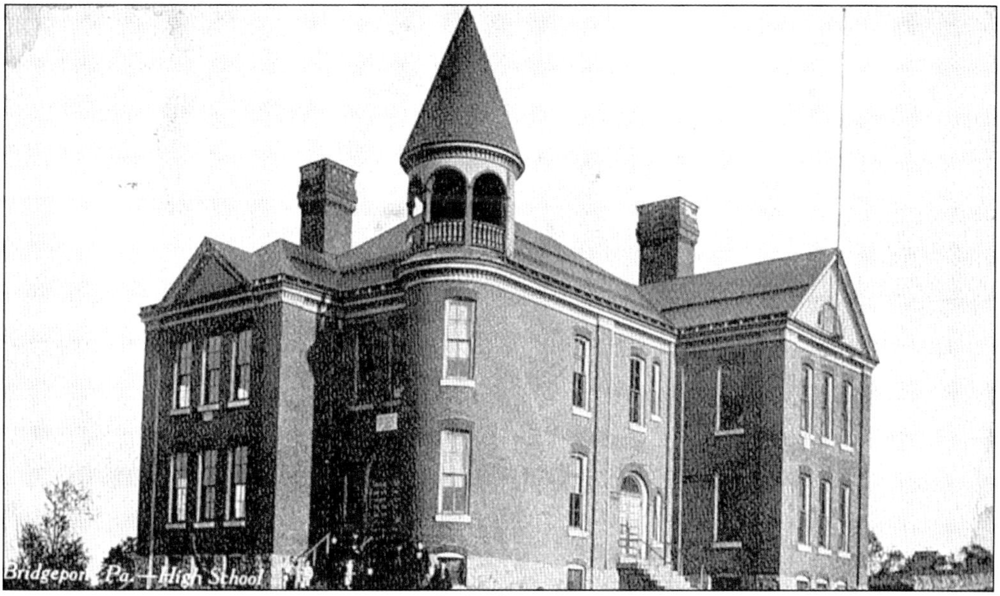

The Bridgeport High School was originally built as the Union Avenue School once located at 381 Union Avenue and served for a time as both a grade school and a high school. By 1910 when this photograph was taken, it became evident that the borough needed a new high school with the town's population swelling to more than 4,000 residents. The new high school was erected at Seventh and Ford Streets and opened in 1923 as the town's population reached 5,000 residents. Bridgeport's high school closed its doors in 1966, when a state mandate forced the merger with Upper Merion Township. (Phil and Sharon Welsh collection.)

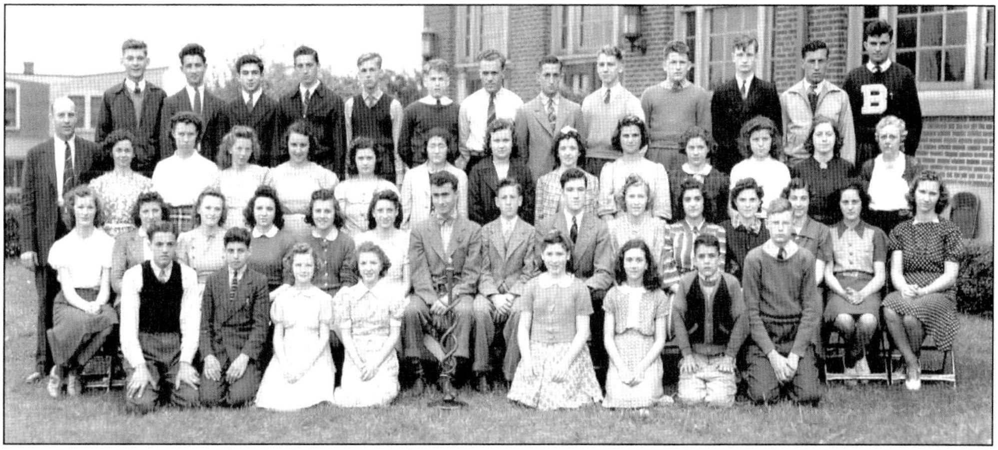

Members of the Bridgeport High School Student Association and the activity they represented during the 1939–1940 school year pose for a group photograph outside Bridgeport High School. Notable in the photograph are school principal Norman W. Katz standing in the second row on the far left, and next to him is Virginia McIntyre, one of the sponsors. A few of the other students in the photograph include, in no particular order, Joe Denczi, Al Fingo, Connie Eliff, Marie Bateman, Francis Chiccarine, John Brennan, Sal Carfagno, Caroline Nowicki, and Mary Zocco. While this class graduated in peacetime, a number of men and women from this graduating class, and class members over the next five years, found themselves on foreign soil fighting in World War II. Many of Bridgeport's sons and daughters sacrificed their lives during the war effort.

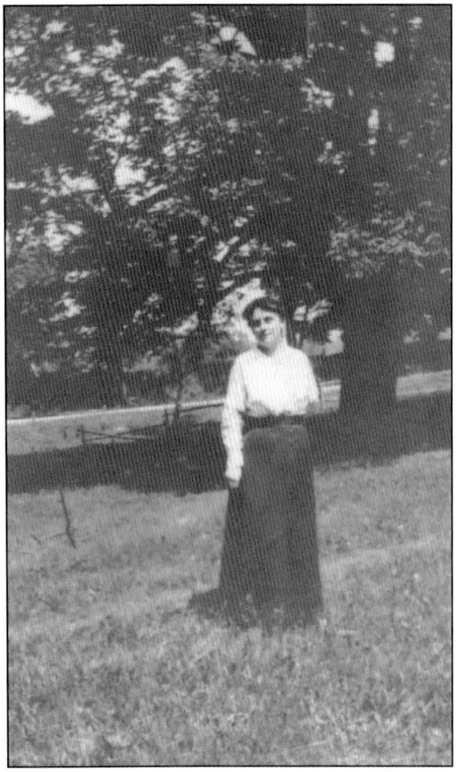

Teachers from the Union Avenue School included Agnes Kriebel, left, and Miss Shiele. In 1917, when these photographs were taken, Bridgeport had three public schools and one parochial school. The Union Avenue School was built in 1893 as a high school and became an elementary school in 1923, when the new high school was built at Seventh and Ford Streets. In 1917, the Union Avenue School graduated eight students, including Helen Star, Berth Milligan, Earl Kutz, Robert Irwin, Harry Whitman, William Whitman, Myer Garber, and Dominic Tufillaro.

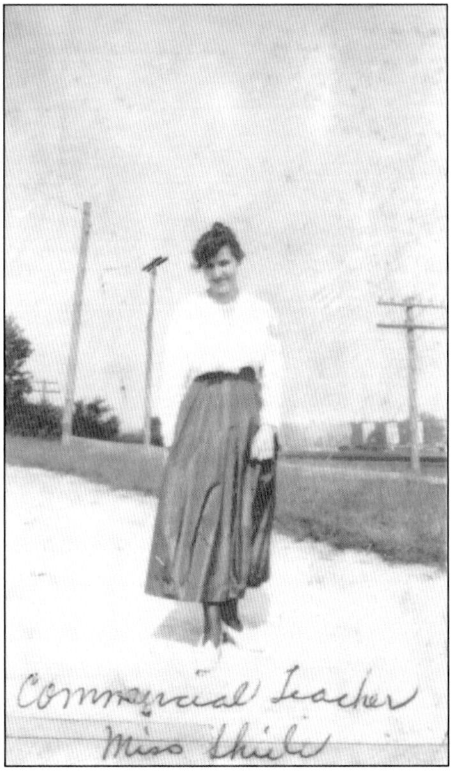

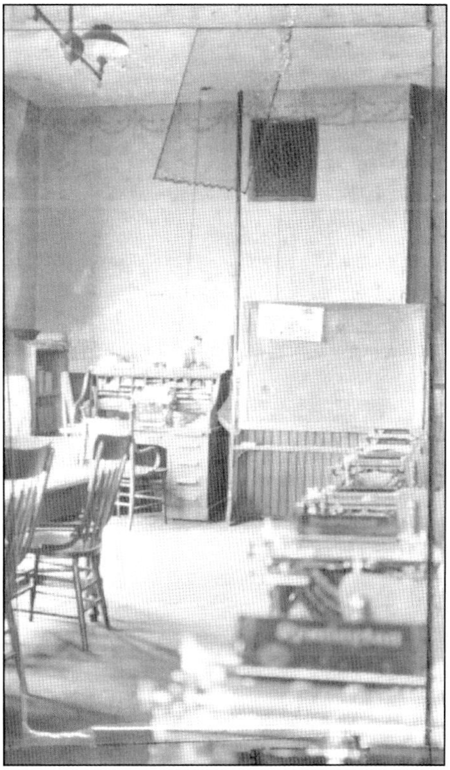

This rare interior view of the Union Avenue School shows the commercial classroom and the school's library. The school was built in 1893 and was serving as the borough's high school when these photographs were taken in 1917. In 1917, the borough's population was just over 4,000 residents, and 20 years later in 1937, the school district was at its peak with 1,250 students enrolled, with more than 700 of them attending the high school located at Seventh and Ford Streets.

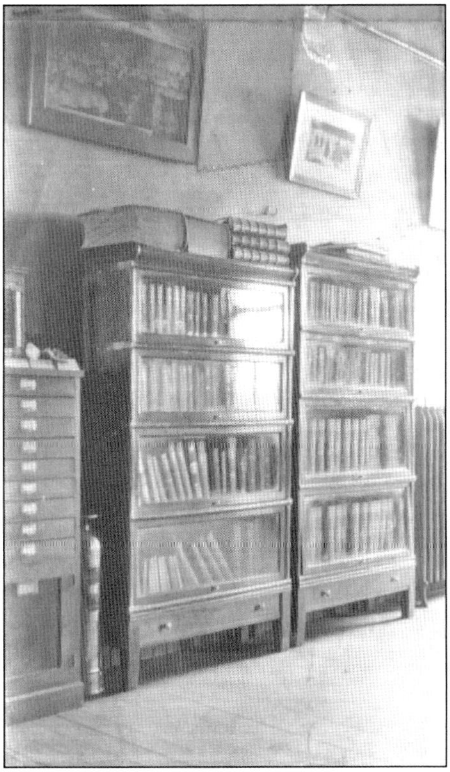

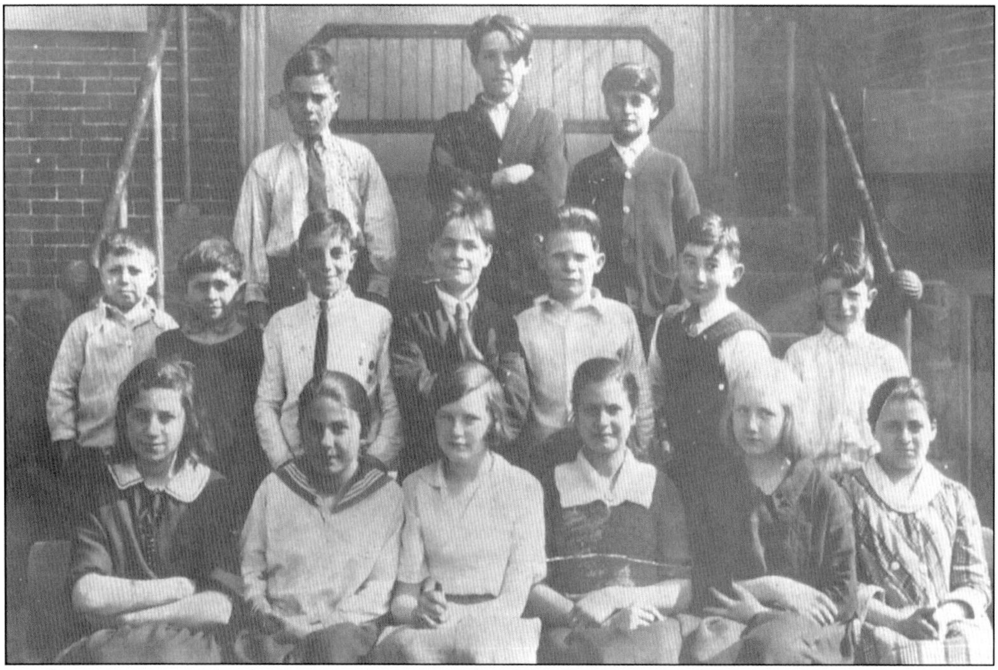

Students pose outside the Union Avenue School back in 1922. The school was the borough's high school but served all grades at the time. Plans were already well underway for a new high school to be constructed at the corner of Seventh and Ford Streets. The new high school opened in 1924 and served as the borough's high school until 1966, when the State of Pennsylvania mandated that any schools under a certain enrollment would be forced to merge, as Bridgeport did with Upper Merion School District in the fall of 1967. (Bridgeport Hall of Fame.)

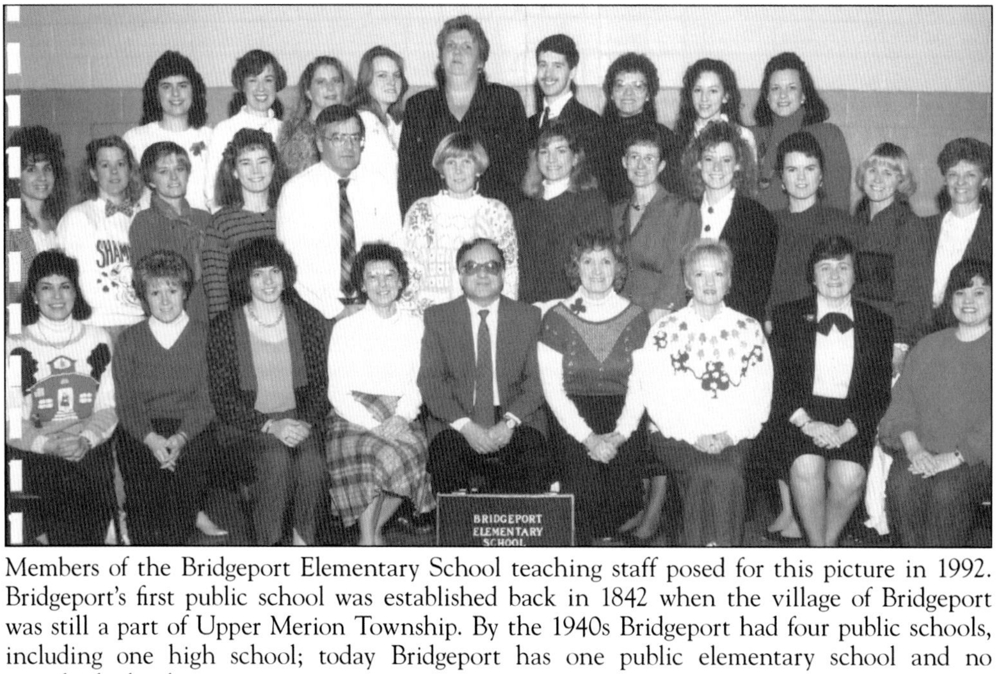

Members of the Bridgeport Elementary School teaching staff posed for this picture in 1992. Bridgeport's first public school was established back in 1842 when the village of Bridgeport was still a part of Upper Merion Township. By the 1940s Bridgeport had four public schools, including one high school; today Bridgeport has one public elementary school and no parochial schools.

Four

TRANSPORTATION

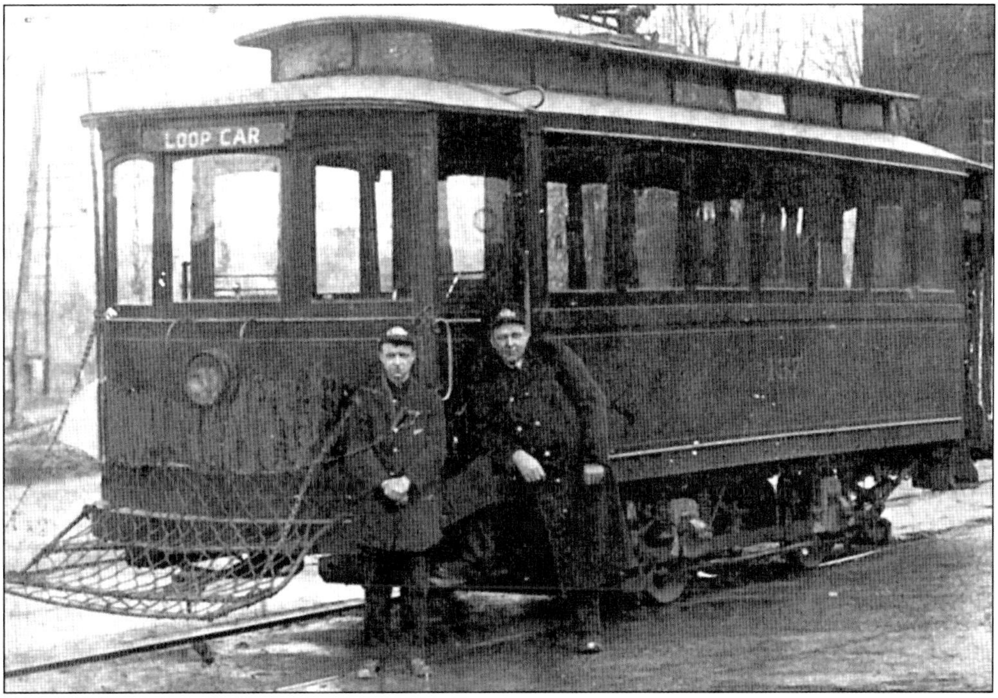

The clanging of trolley cars could be heard in Bridgeport from 1893 until 1933, when a bus service was put in place. The conductor and ticket taker can be seen here posing with car No. 137 on Fourth Street. Notice the net on the front of the trolley known as a cow catcher, or in some cases people catcher.

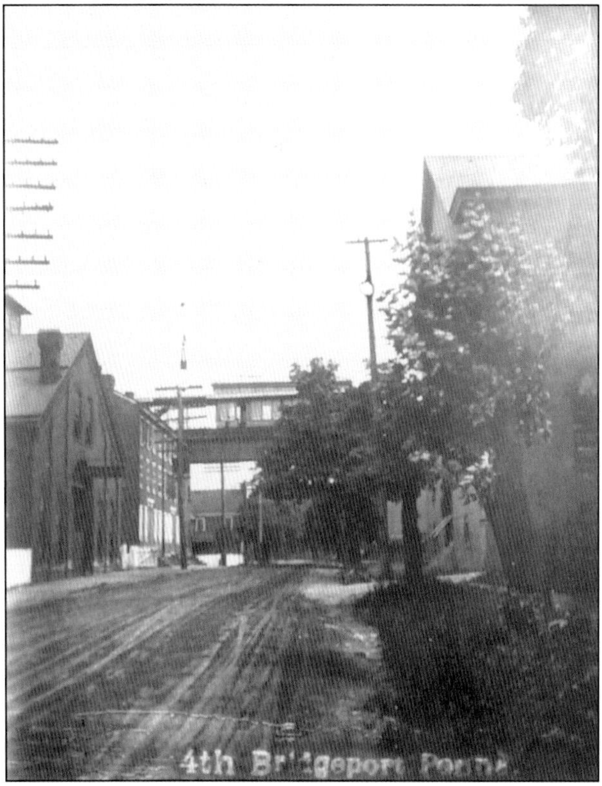

In 1911, Bridgeport's borough council passed ordinance No. 67 authorizing the Philadelphia and Western Railroad (P&W) to construct a high-speed trolley line through Bridgeport, the trolley line expanded the area Bridgeport residents could travel to. The new trolley line went from Norristown to Sixty-ninth Street in Philadelphia. The photograph at left shows the Bridgeport P&W station when it was located at Fourth and Merion Streets back in 1912, and a photograph of what they called the bullet car, seen below at the Bridgeport station in 1976. (Bridgeport Hall of Fame.)

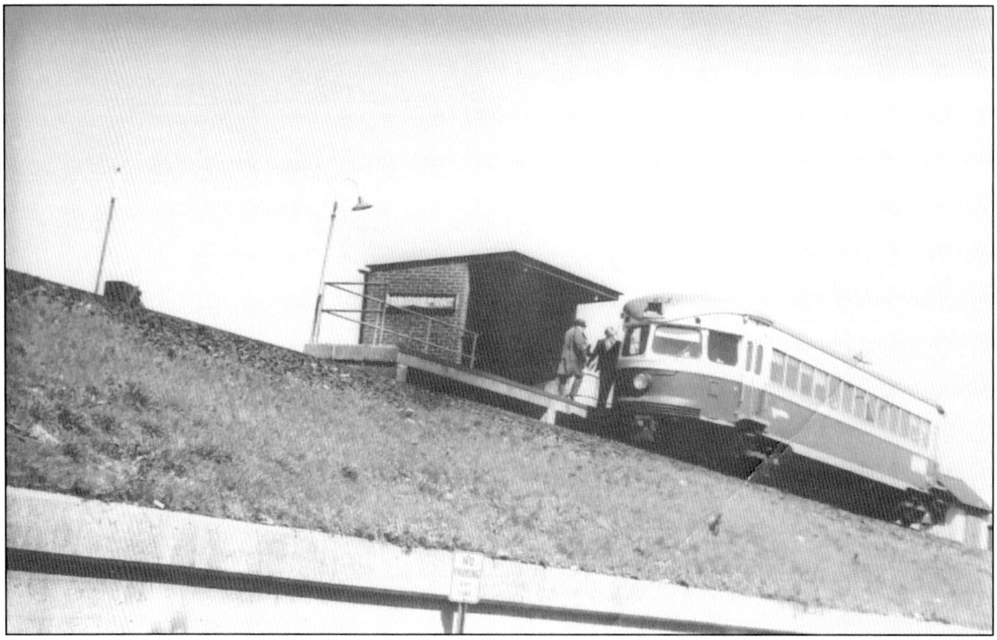

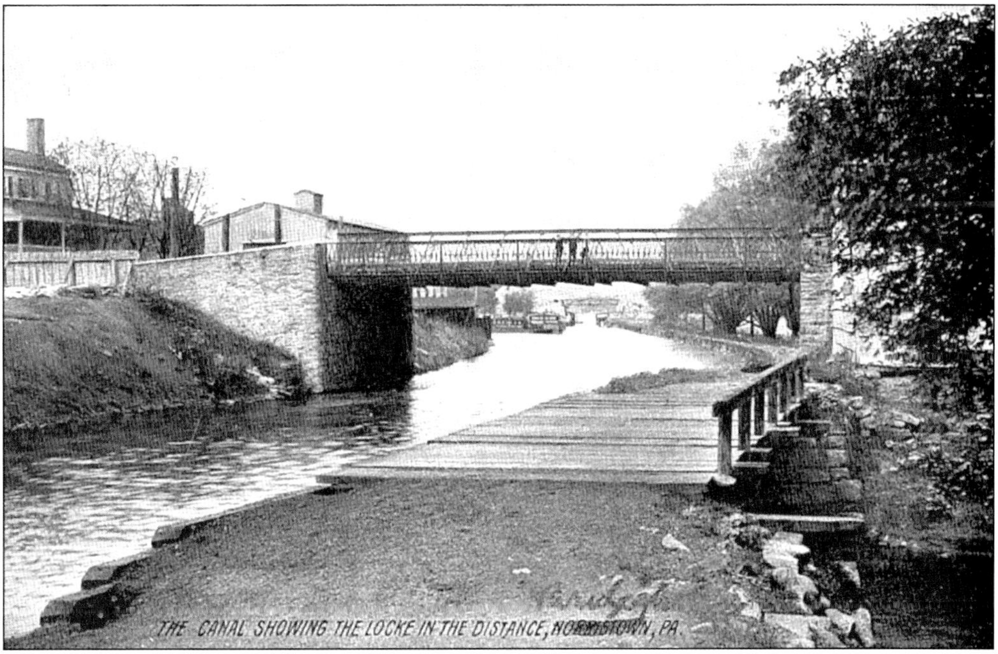

Work on the Schuylkill Canal began in 1816, and nearly eight years later Bridgeport had the canal pass through its town, bringing jobs to the tiny village. Immigrants from other countries became life-long residents because of the canal. By the time Bridgeport was incorporated in 1851, the canal experienced traffic jams navigating nearly 75 boats per week in and out of the port. Goods from the Bridgeport mills and factories were often shipped into Philadelphia, and from the City of Brotherly Love those goods were then shipped throughout the world. Notice the horse and wagon on the towpath where mules often pulled the barges loaded with goods. (Phil and Sharon Welsh collection.)

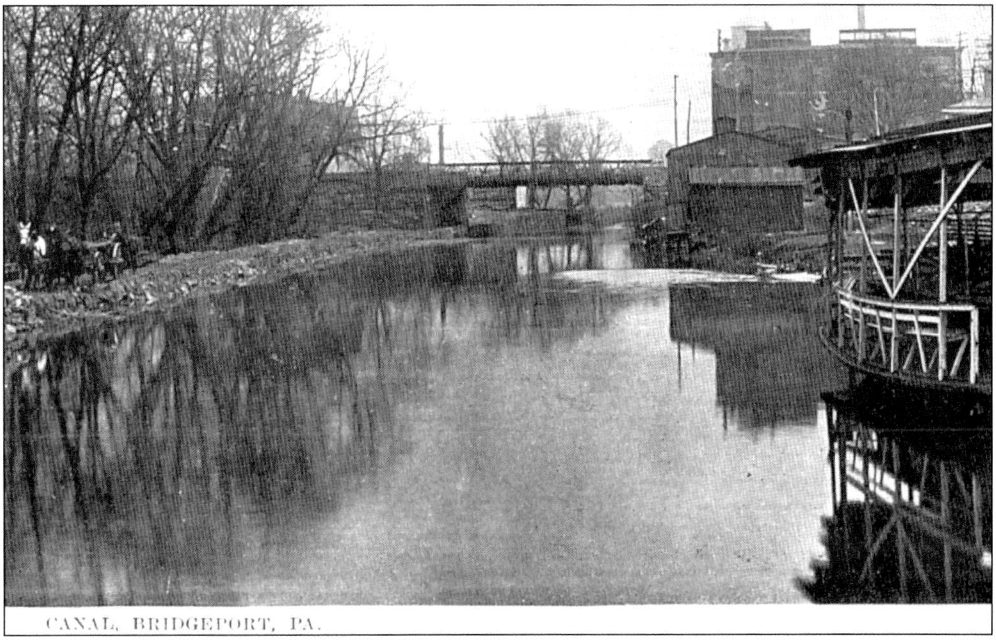

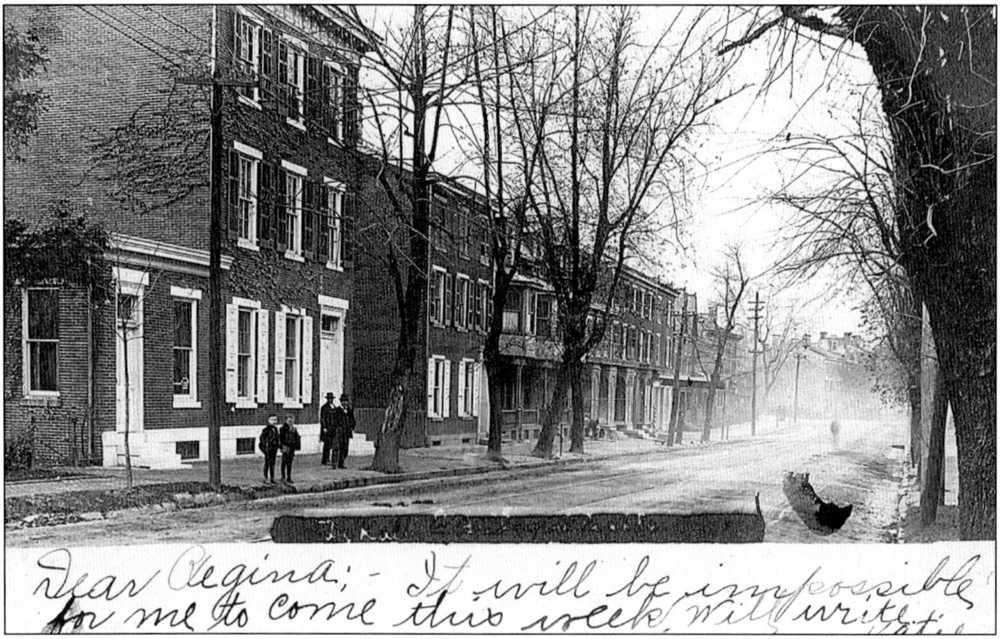

Here are two very rare postcard photographs from the collection of Phil and Sharon Welsh of Dekalb Street in Bridgeport. The photograph above shows trolley tracks running down Dekalb Street. Trolleys ran in Bridgeport from 1893 until 1933, when a bus service went into effect. The photograph below shows a horse and wagon going down Dekalb Street, and notice the lamp hanging in the middle of the unpaved road. In the early 1900s most Bridgeport residents worked at the mills along the Schuylkill River.

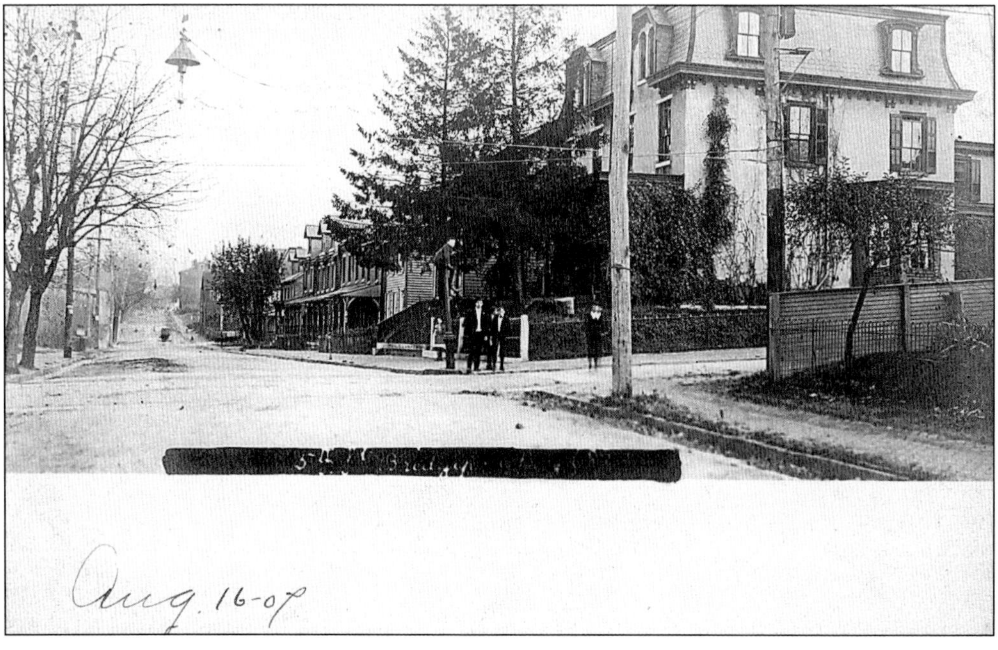

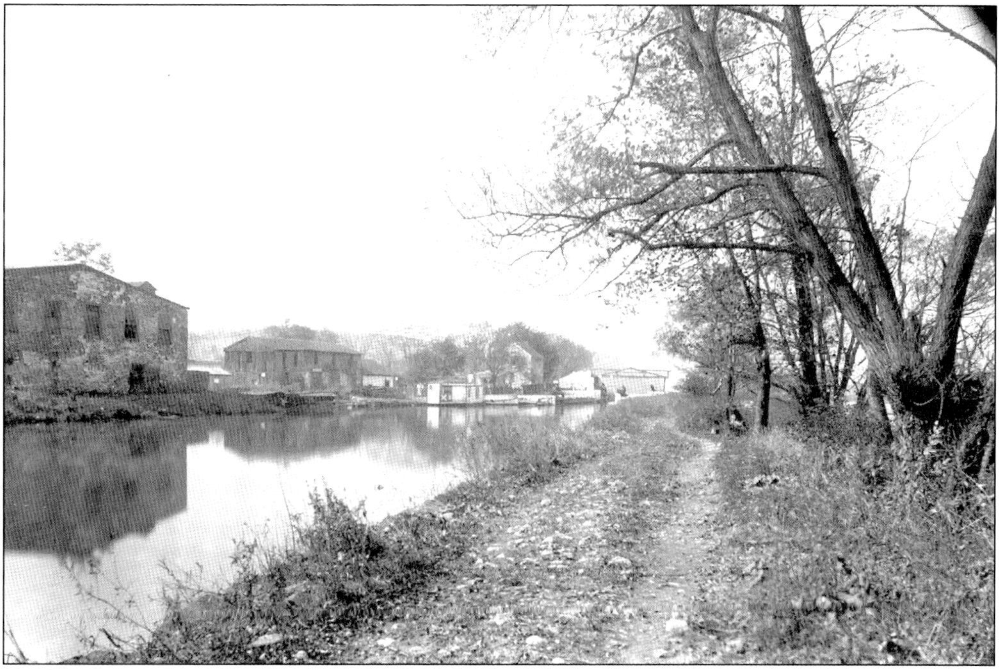

Work began on the Schuylkill Canal back in 1816, 35 years before the town of Bridgeport was incorporated as a borough. In 1816, the village of Bridgeport had less than 50 residents. By 1824 work on the canal was completed. Industries like the ones seen in these photographs included the Bridgeport Paper Mill (above) seen in 1910 before the construction of the P&W trolley line. In the photograph below, the back side of the meat factory can be seen on the left, as well as the Jones and Wright, formerly Jones and Stokes, flour mill. (Historical Society of Montgomery County.)

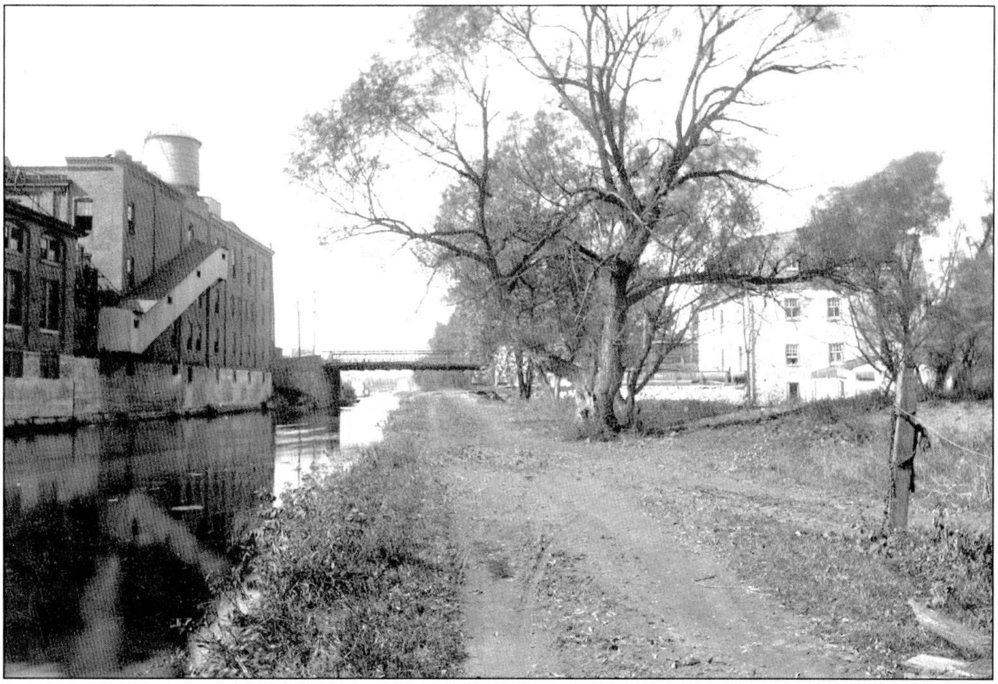

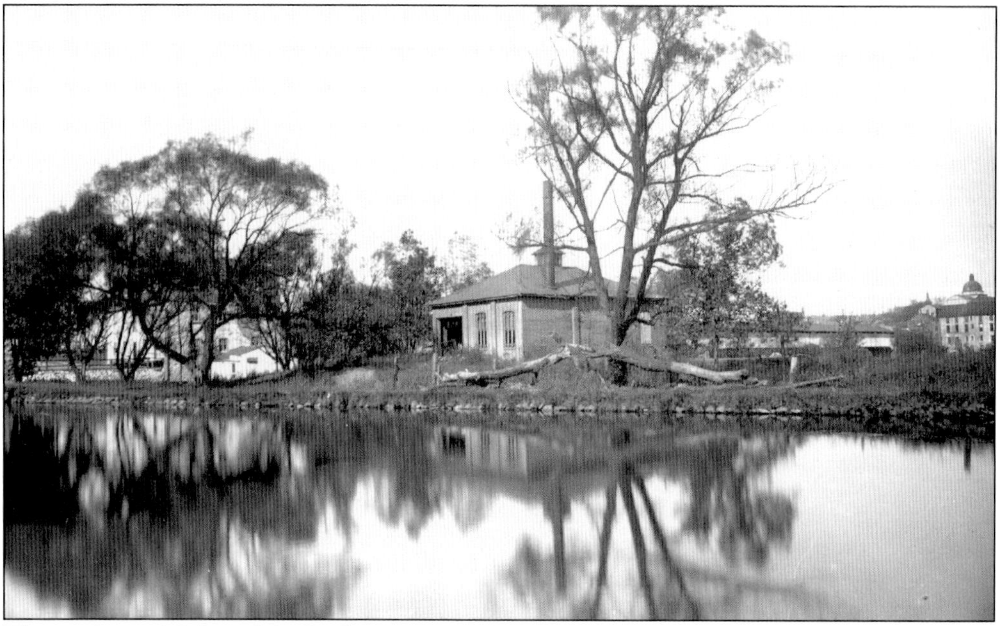

This is a beautiful shot of the Bridgeport Canal back in 1900, when the town's industry depended on the waterways to move goods out of Bridgeport into Philadelphia. The canal, built back in the 1820s, gave life to towns like Bridgeport, Swedesburg, and Conshohocken. Notice the covered bridge to the right of the photograph with Norristown in the background. The covered bridge was a toll bridge back then, costing a pedestrian a penny to cross, or more if one had a horse or sheep.

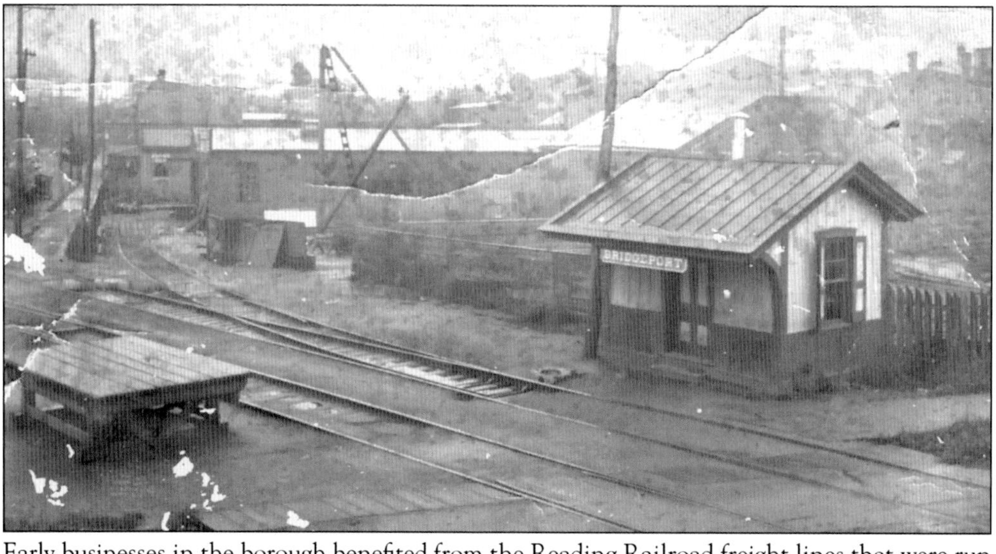

Early businesses in the borough benefited from the Reading Railroad freight lines that were run through the riverside town back in the early and mid-1830s. The railroad played a major part in the success of the James Lees Carpet Mill, Andrew's Brick Yard, Eureka Mill, I. F. March and Sons, and so many other mills that have employed residents of the community over the years. This was a typical scene at that time, with railroad tracks running off the borough's streets into factories to load and unload goods. Notice the horse and wagon to the far left of the photograph on Bridgeport's unpaved streets. (Bridgeport Hall of Fame.)

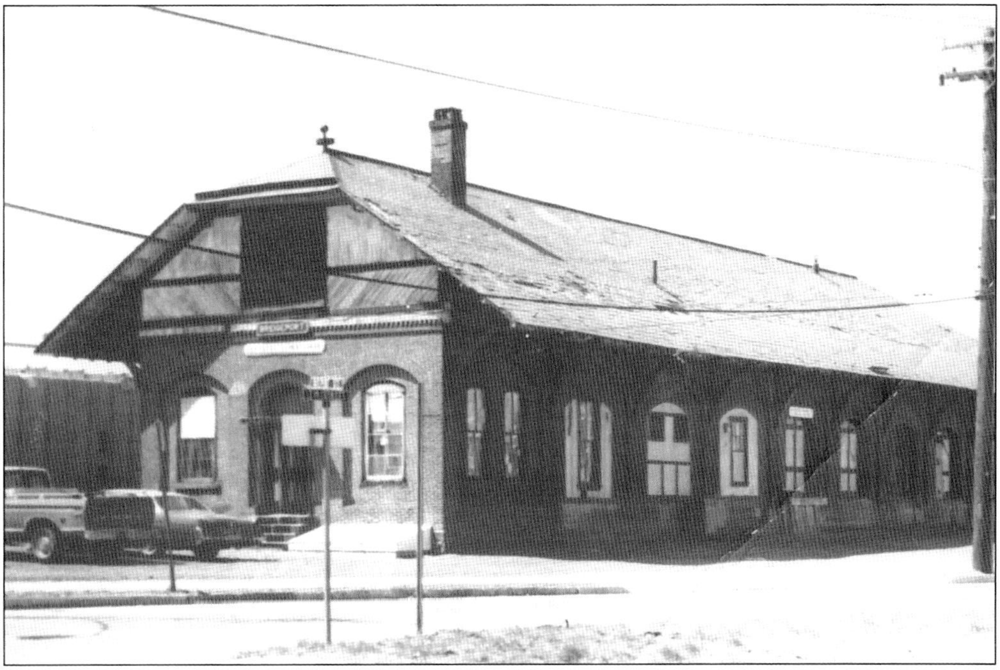

Shortly after the Bridgeport Canal was completed in 1824, the railroad came through Bridgeport in the mid-1830s with passenger service available as early as 1833. But the freight trains and tracks were a true blessing for the industry of the port, putting companies in a position to ship faster and cheaper. The former freight station of the Reading Railroad Company was located at Second and Depot Streets and was constructed in 1882 and became one of Bridgeport's oldest buildings. The photograph below shows the station in recent years; it is currently occupied by John Deere Landscapes. (Bridgeport Hall of Fame.)

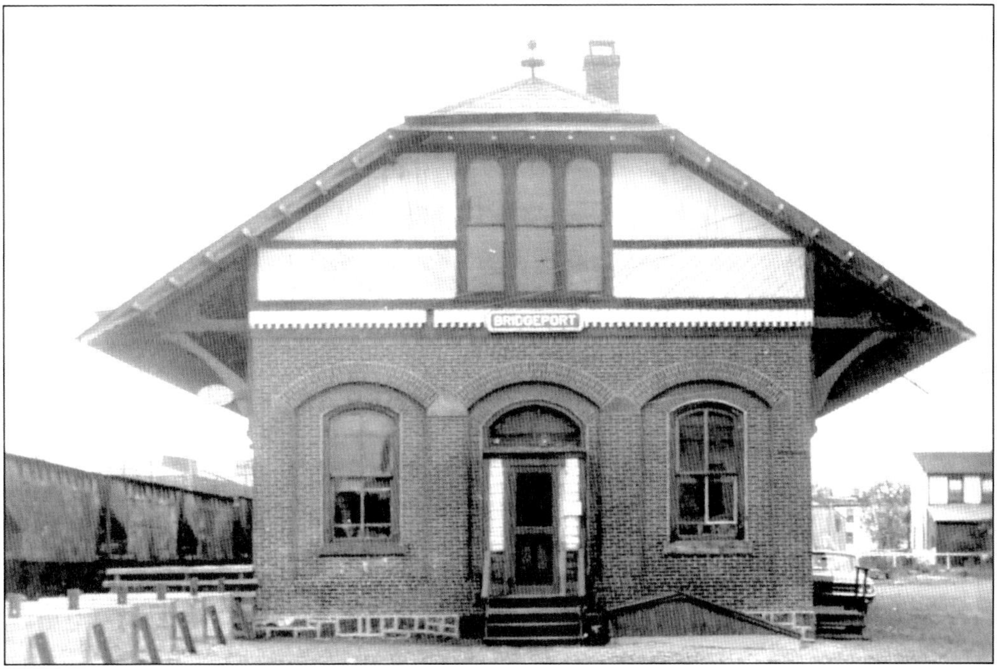

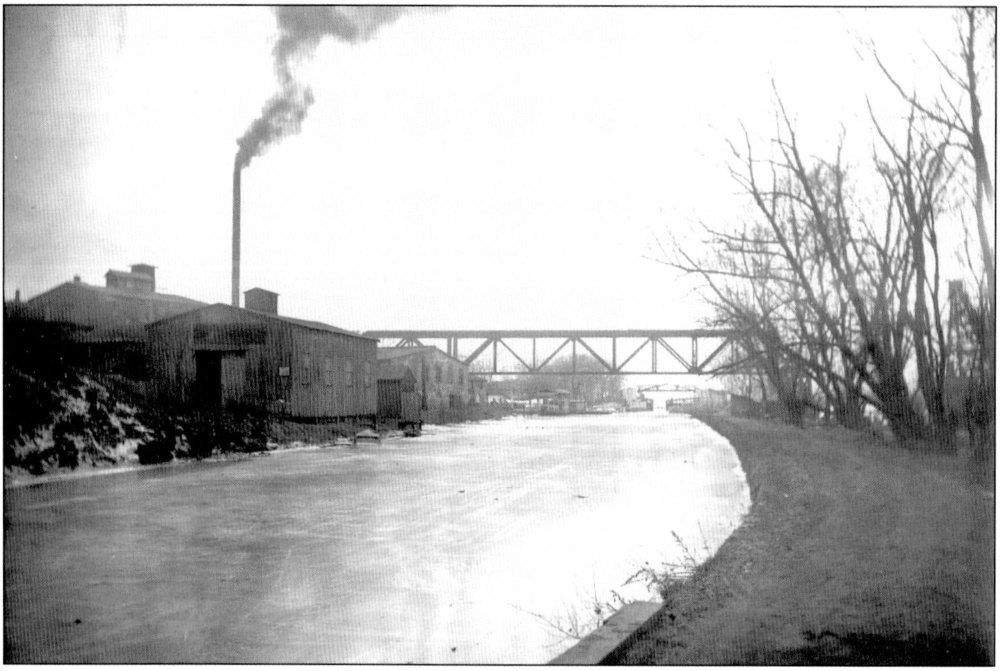

The canal in Bridgeport created the birth of industry in the tiny borough, and that industry brought people long before 1850. In the winter of 1912, when this photograph was taken, Bridgeport had already been incorporated for more than 60 years and industries like Lee's Carpet, I. F. March Sons Company, Bridgeport Wire and Iron Works, and Diamond State Fibre Company allowed families to open small businesses like Marinelli's Grocery Store, Marchese Boot and Shoe Dealer, and Craven's Drug Store. While much of the industry is gone today, family businesses continue to thrive in Bridgeport. (Historical Society of Montgomery County.)

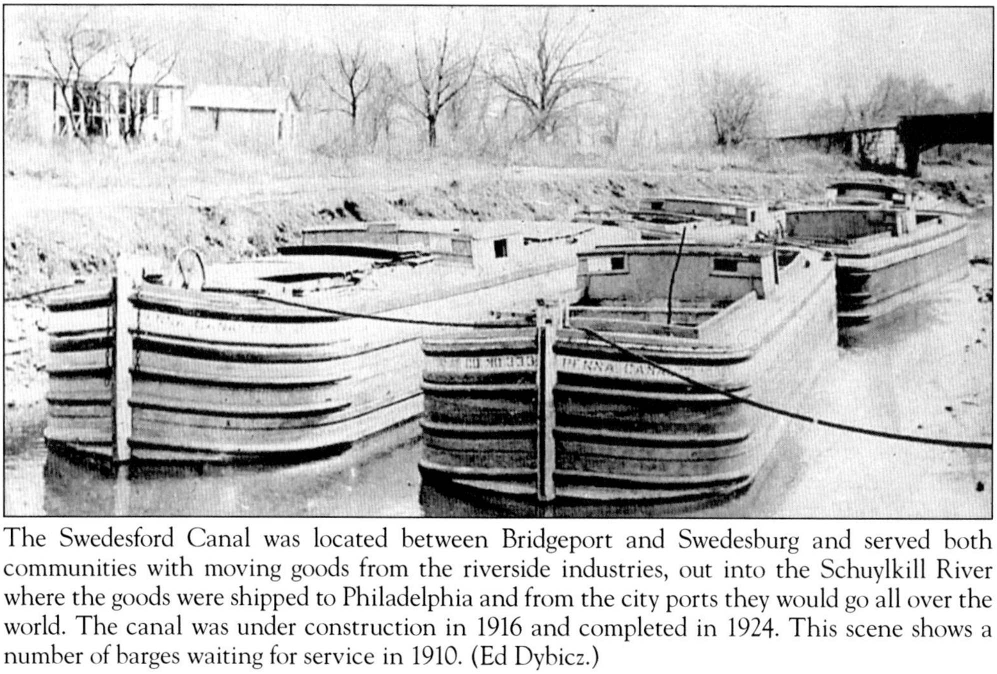

The Swedesford Canal was located between Bridgeport and Swedesburg and served both communities with moving goods from the riverside industries, out into the Schuylkill River where the goods were shipped to Philadelphia and from the city ports they would go all over the world. The canal was under construction in 1916 and completed in 1924. This scene shows a number of barges waiting for service in 1910. (Ed Dybicz.)

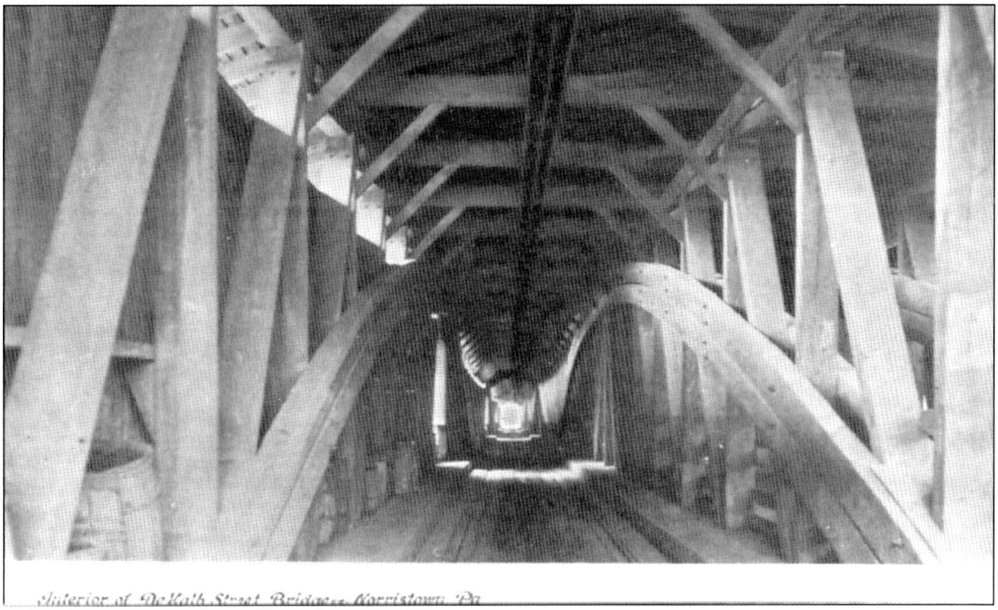

This rare interior view of the covered Dekalb Street bridge spanned the Schuylkill River and was completed in 1830. The bridge was privately owned and was maintained and paid for by tolls paid by pedestrians crossing, pedestrians with sheep and cattle crossing, and horse and wagons moving goods between Bridgeport and Norristown. When the automobiles arrived early in the 20th century, cars would cross one at a time, but a build up of gas and oil on the wood decking led to a massive fire when a car backfired and ignited a blaze that destroyed the wooden bridge in 1924.

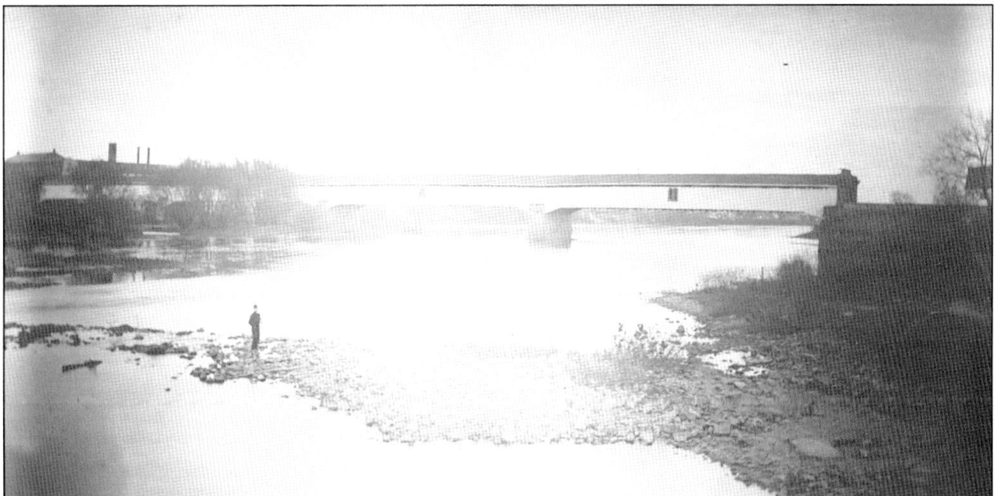

The Dekalb Street bridge, seen here from the Bridgeport side of the Schuylkill River, was constructed in 1829 and opened for business in 1830. The privately owned bridge charged tolls for crossing, and the fees covered the construction and maintenance cost of the bridge. During the 1870s Bridgeport resident William Rennyson led a movement that was in favor of free bridges. With the help of Dr. Charles Mann, Dr. Joseph Lees, Joel Andrews, and Hugh McInnes, following a fire in 1883, the Dekalb Street bridge was freed in October 1884. (Historical Society of Montgomery County.)

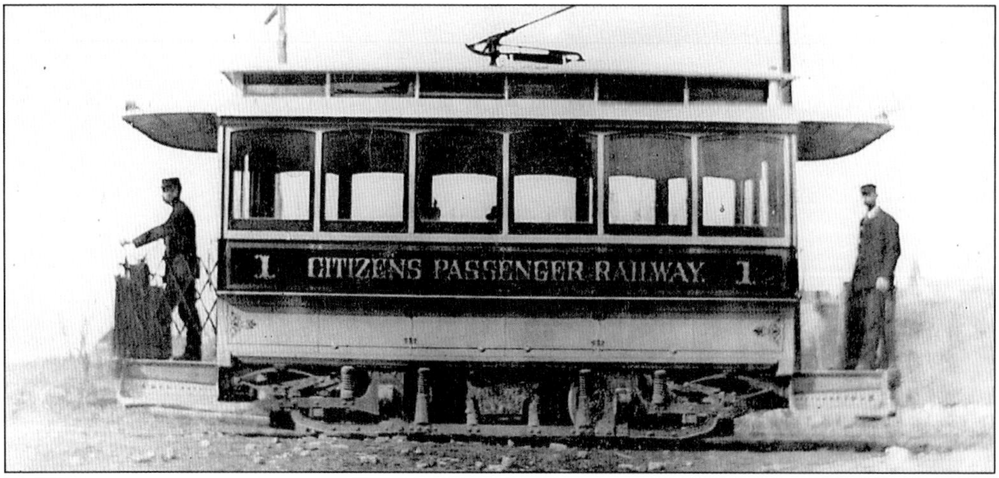

In the early days, several attempts were made to establish a horse-drawn trolley service, but it was not until 1893 that tracks were laid and an electric trolley line ran through Bridgeport. The Citizens Passenger Railway line was established and served the borough for 40 years, the final trolley running on September 9, 1933. The Southeastern Pennsylvania Transportation Authority (SEPTA) introduced bus service in the borough, but the buses did not run on Sundays and holidays. Bridgeport later added a taxi service in 1947, when Russell Light drove a cab out of West Fourth Street. (Ed Dybicz.)

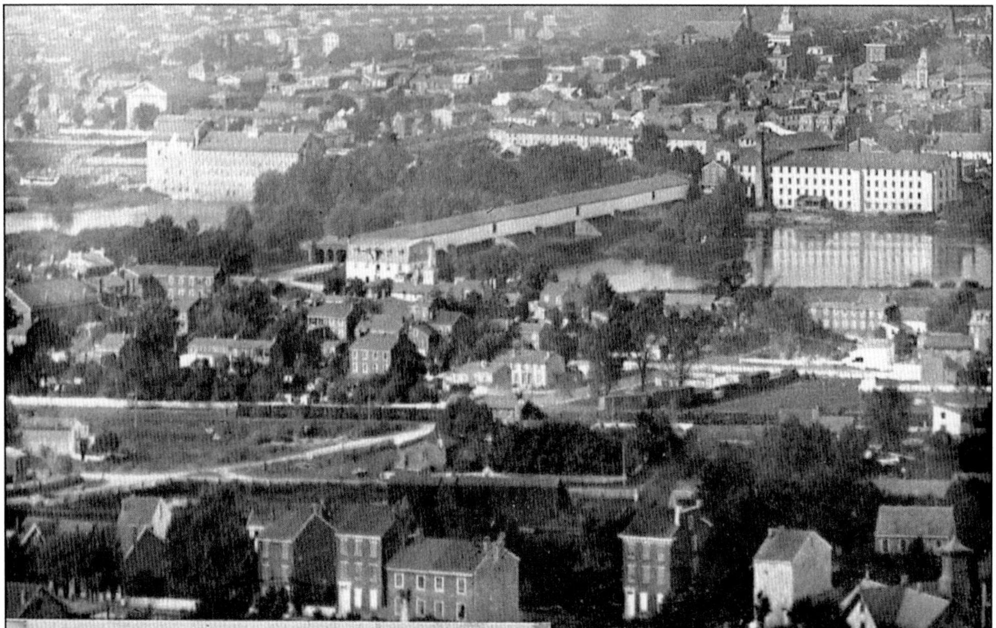

This is a rare view of the old covered bridge taken in 1924 from the Bridgeport side of the river showing Norristown in the background. The covered bridge was constructed in 1829, and the collection of tolls started in 1830 as the bridge was privately owned. The bridge was rebuilt in 1861 as dividends as high as 13 percent a year were paid back on stock. Pedestrians were charged a penny, for up to six animals the cost was 4¢, a herd of sheep or horse and wagons cost more. This bridge burned into the river in 1924, and a concrete bridge replaced the wooden structure. (Ed Dybicz.)

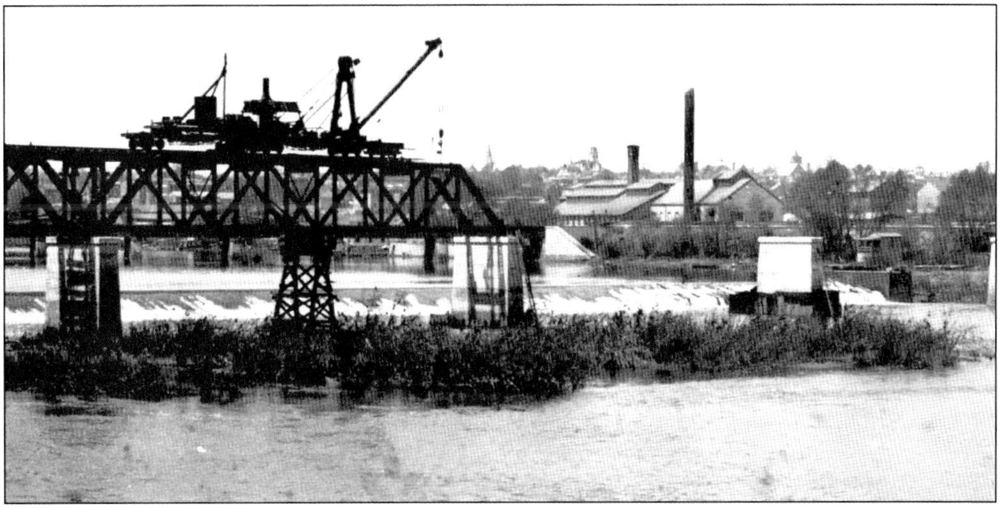

The Bridgeport Town Council passed a borough ordinance on October 11, 1911, to authorize the construction of a branch line of the P&W Railway through the borough of Bridgeport leading into Norristown. This rare photograph shows the construction of the P&W rail line out over the Schuylkill River leading from Bridgeport to Norristown just in front of the dam. In the early days of the trolley service in Bridgeport the passenger station was located at Fourth and Merion Streets. Following World War II the station was moved to its current location on Merion Street between Fifth and Sixth Streets. (America Responds with Love, Inc.)

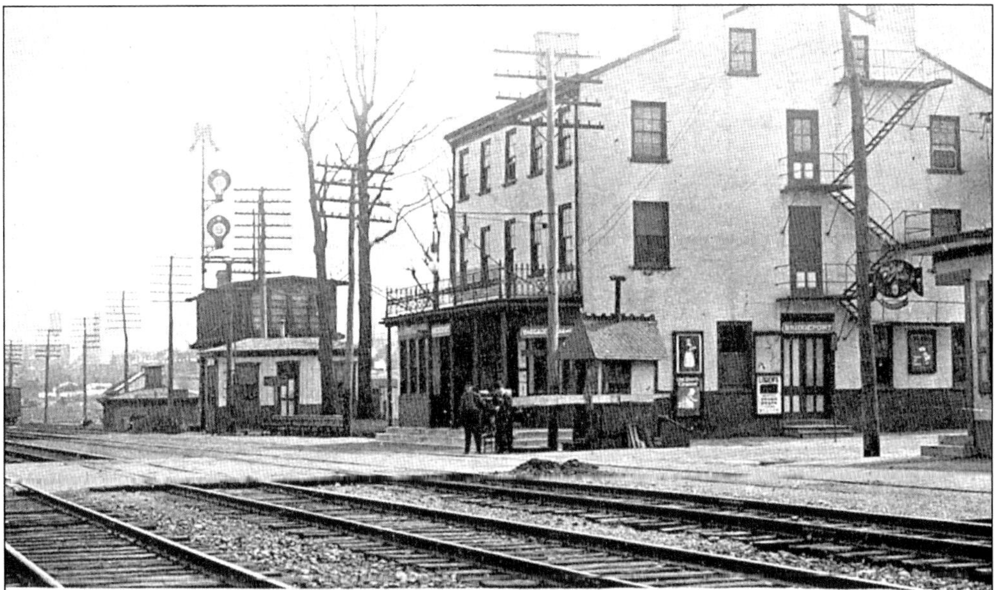

PASSENGER STATION, BRIDGEPORT, PA.

This postcard shot of the Bridgeport passenger railroad station back in 1914 shows the Dewan Hotel in the background. Bridgeport has had railroad passenger service since 1833, and 60 years later in 1893, a trolley service was introduced to the residents. In 1914, Bridgeport was a thriving borough with 4,000 residents and five hotels. Beside Dewan's, other hotels included Barrett's, Barry, Dillon, and Hotel Bridgeport. The borough also had three druggists, 21 grocers, and five barbers. (Phil and Sharon Welsh collection.)

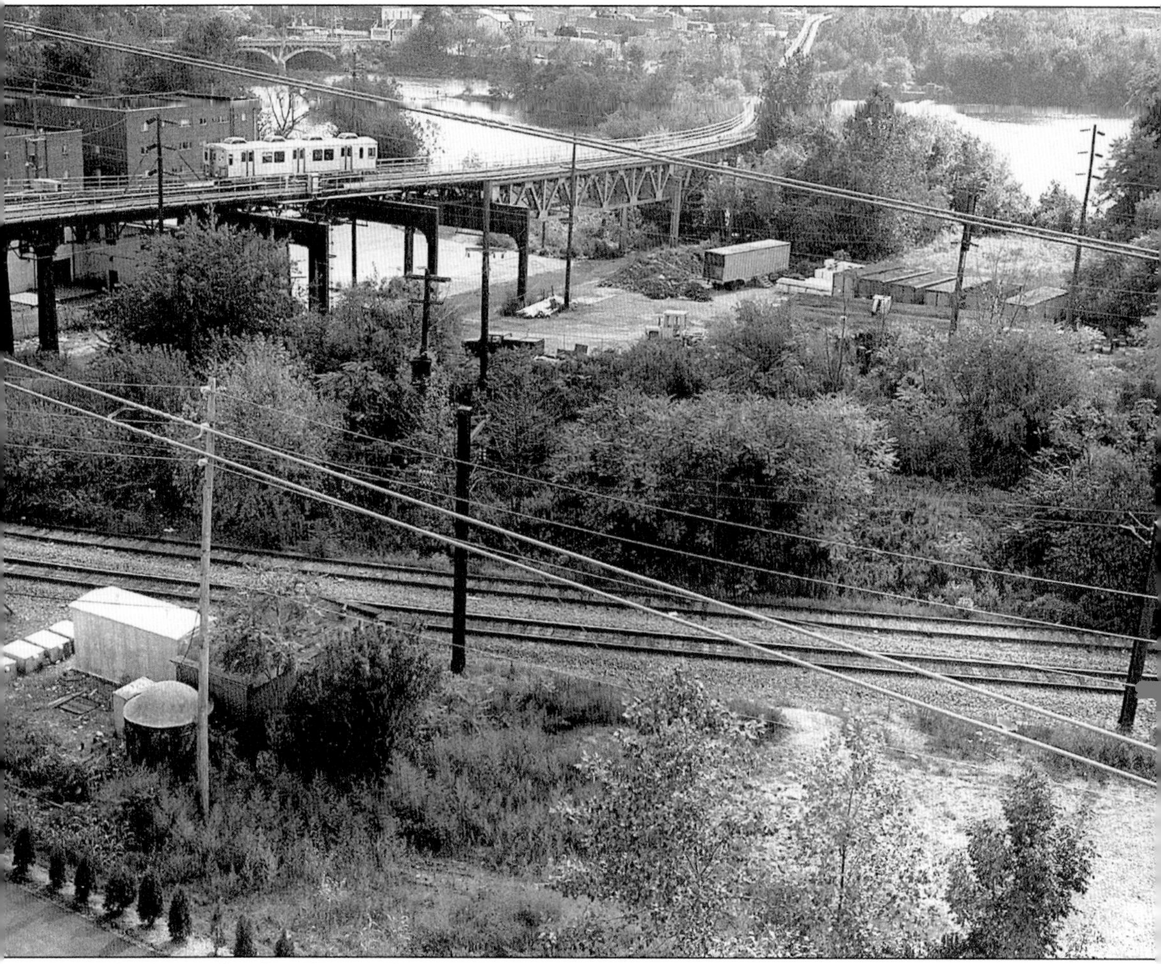

The borough of Bridgeport has come a long way since its incorporation back in 1851. Today 4,500 people call Bridgeport home. The borough also serves as a gateway from King of Prussia to Norristown, Blue Bell, and beyond. This photograph shows the P&W trolley crossing the river from Bridgeport into Norristown and the DeKalb Street bridge in the background. Bridgeport is a town in transition with promising development along the waterfront.

Six

BUSINESSES

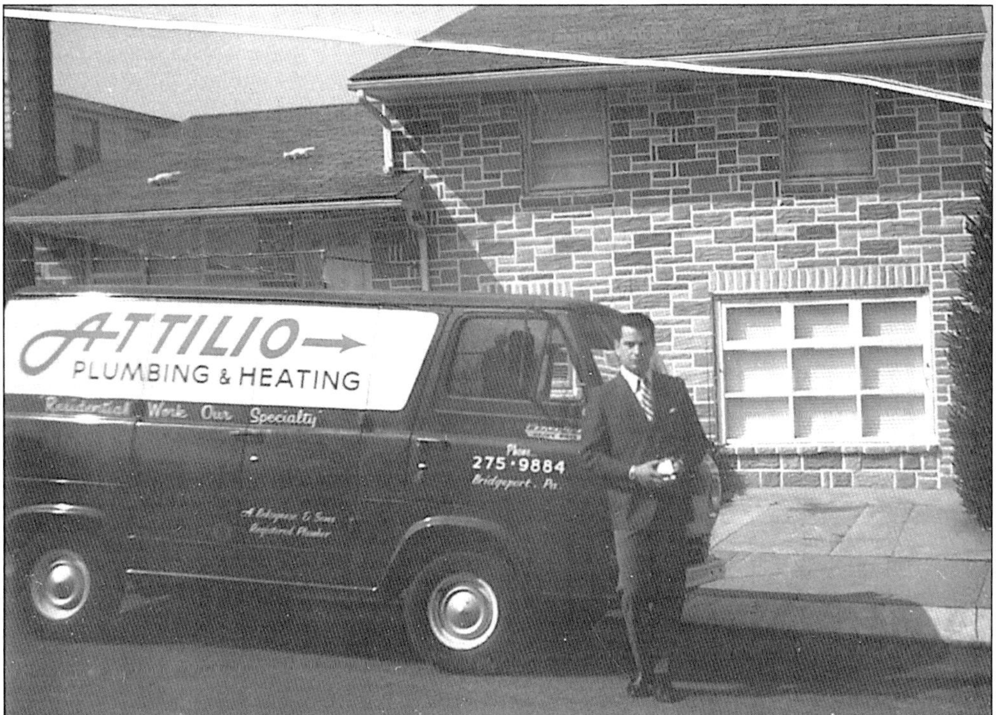

Attilio Bolognese poses with his plumbing van outside his house at 643 Bush Street in Bridgeport back in 1967 when he started his plumbing business. While family-owned businesses seem to have been reduced in recent years, Bridgeport had 77 retail outlets registered in the borough back in 1967 and another 50 service establishments. Almost all of the businesses were family owned and operated, and many of them are still in business today. Over the years Attilio's plumbing and heating business has expanded, thanks in part to his right-hand man, Patrick Bolognese. Attilio can be grateful to the town fathers back in 1927, when the borough council adopted an ordinance to install a sewer system.

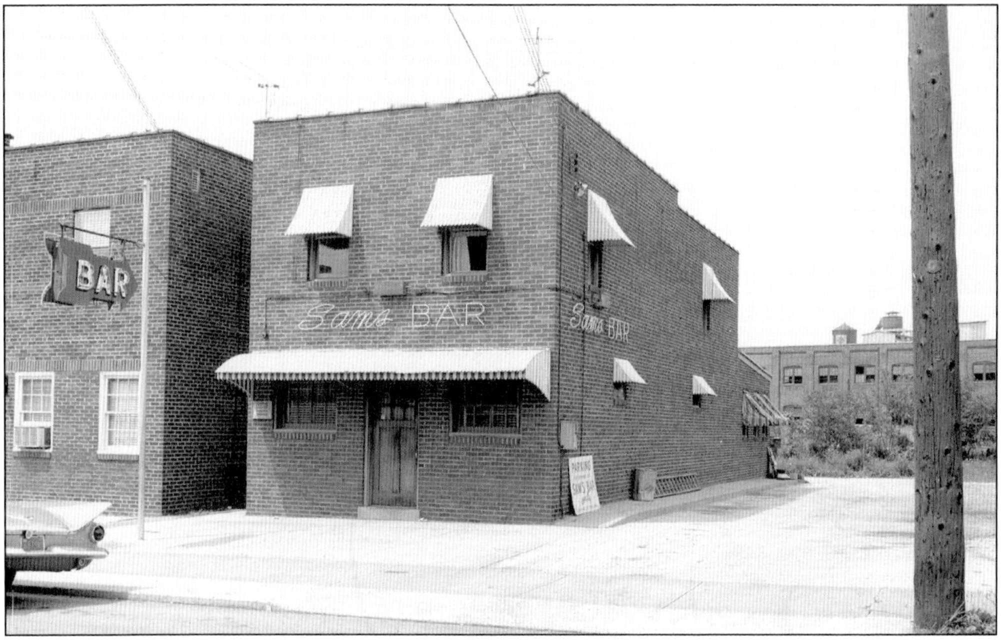

At any given time the borough of Bridgeport was home for up to a dozen drinking establishments like Sam's Bar located at 69 Fourth Street, seen here back in July 1960. Bridgeport was home for dozens of family-owned businesses in 1960 like Maslanka's Groceries, Susy Jo Donuts, Desimone's Cafe, Bridgeport Bowling Lanes, Nadwodny's Market, and Danny's Diner. The building is currently occupied by Christine's Salon.

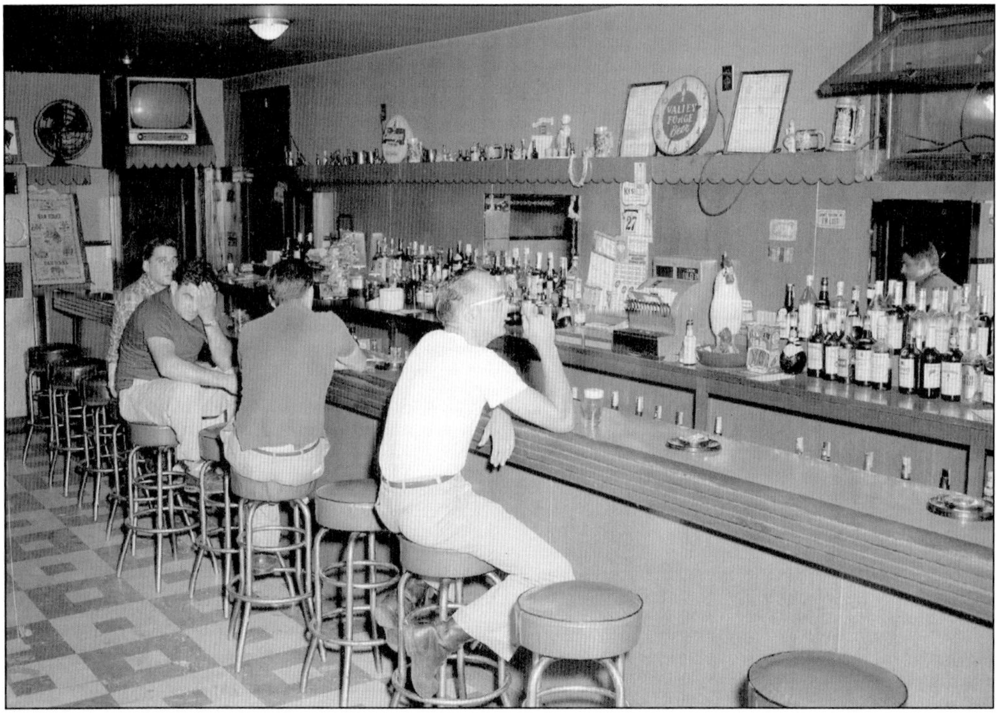

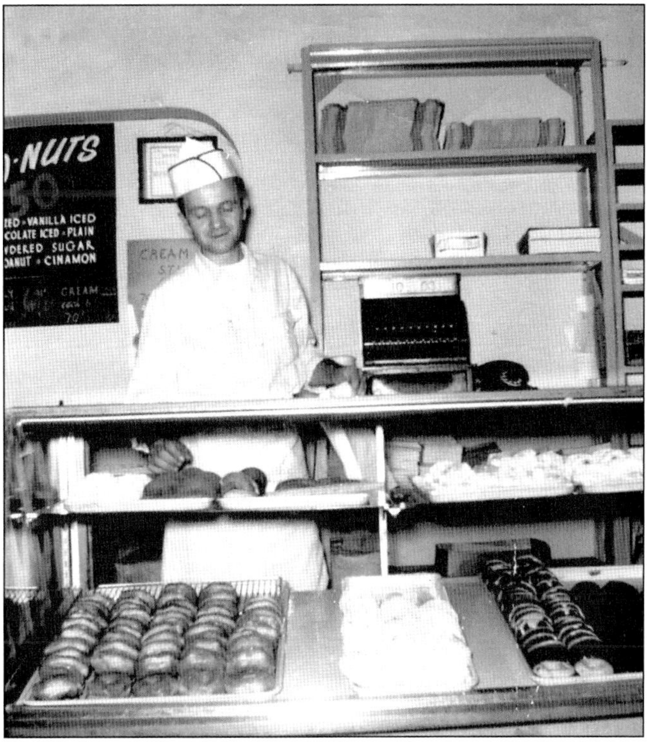

Suzy Jo Donuts has been pumping out the best donuts in Montgomery County for more than half a century. Joe and Betty Davis opened up a donut shop on Seventh Street back in 1955. The couple relocated to Fourth Street in 1962 and have remained there since. The Davises had two daughters, Suzanne and Joanne, hence the name Suzi Jo's. Joe Davis is seen behind the counter back in the old days when donuts could still be had for 50¢ per dozen.

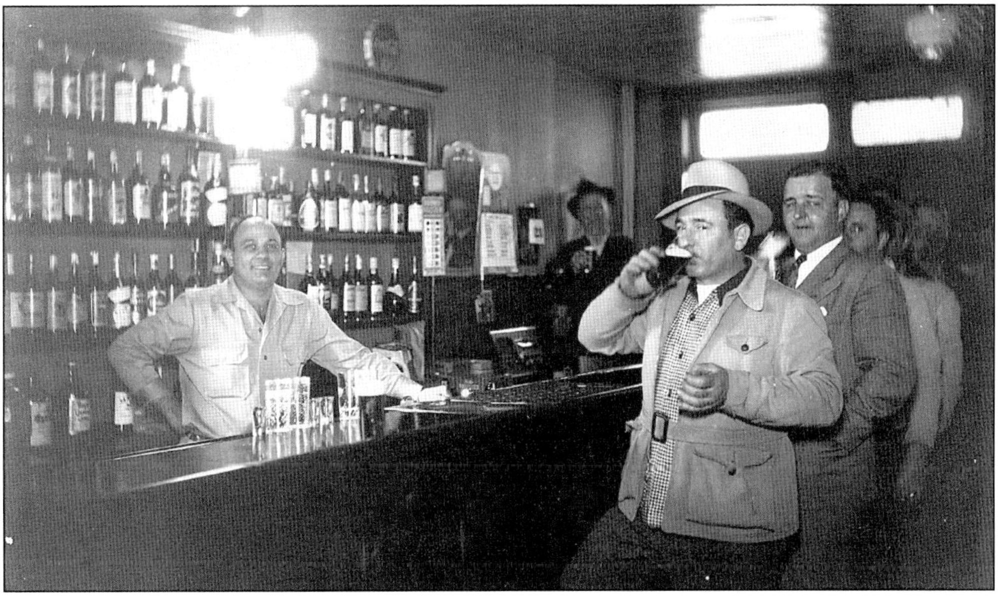

In the late 1930s, the country was slowly putting the Great Depression behind, and Bridgeport residents were once again finding work and opening up small businesses. With seven saloons and beer joints already in operation, Carmine DeSimone Sr. decided there was plenty of room for another taproom. DeSimone opened his taproom on the corner of Prospect and Holstein Avenues in the summer of 1938 and has passed the business to family members, including Edward and Carmen Jr., standing behind the bar in 1950. The two brothers passed the business in 1977 to Carmen, David, and Russell, who continue to run the operation. (DeSimone's Café.)

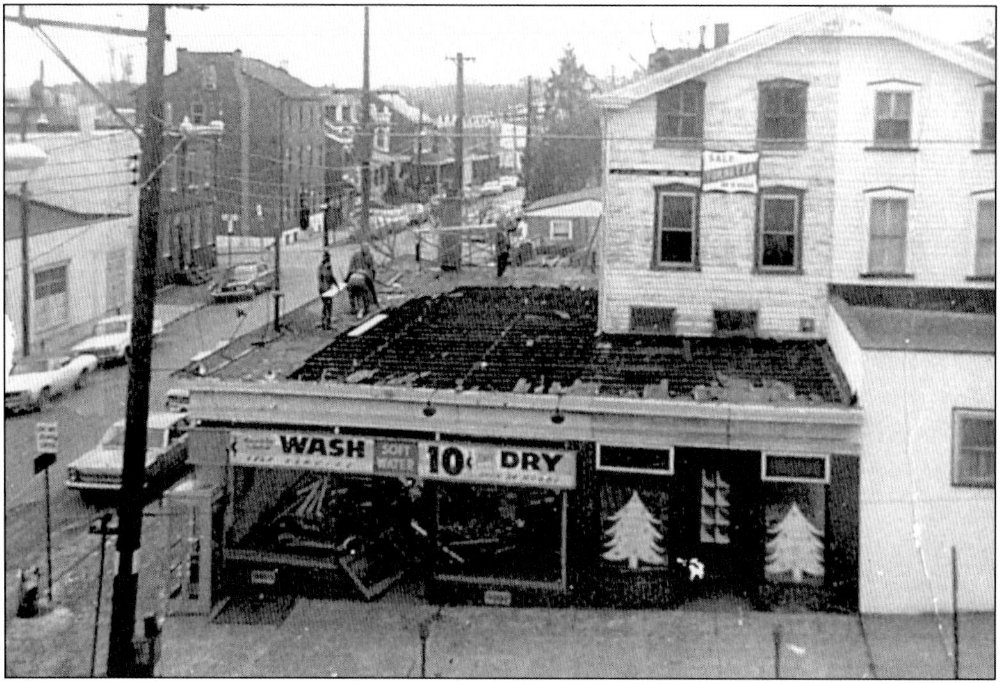

Back in 1955, when Mickey DeJohn opened his pizza business on Dekalb Street, Bridgeport was full of family businesses. Bridgeport had 70 family businesses operating in 1955, including Danny's Diner, Desimone's Cafe, Friendship Grill, Iacovelli's Grocery, and Susy Jo Donuts. In 1968, a Pennsylvania state highway project forced DeJohn's to move slightly uptown two blocks where demolition began on a former laundromat to construct the new DeJohn's, which was renamed Franzones Pizzaria when it reopened in 1970. (The Franzone family.)

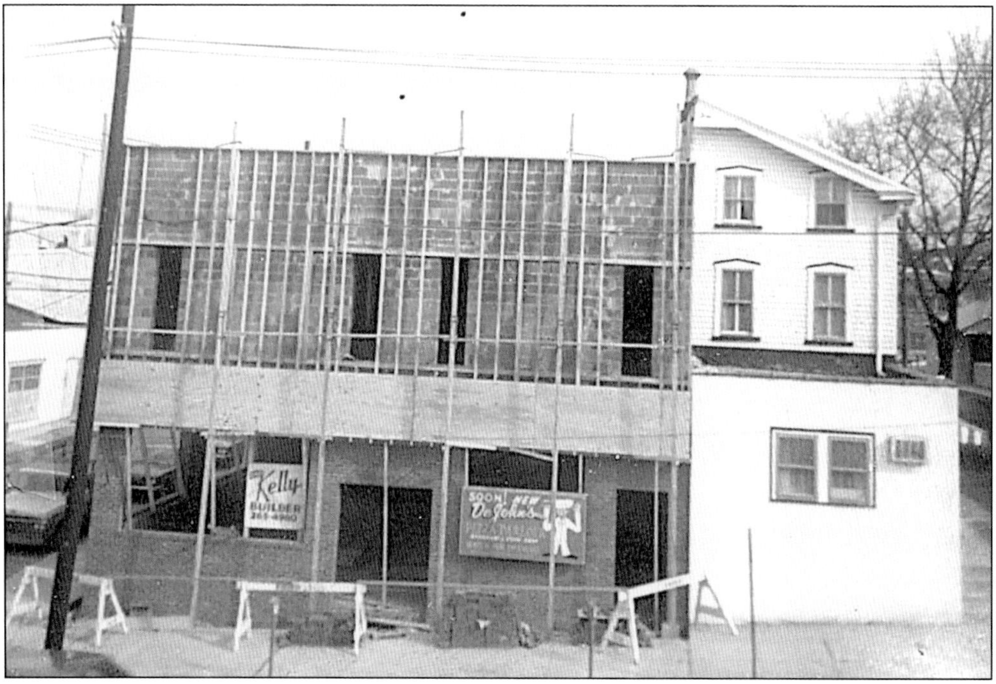

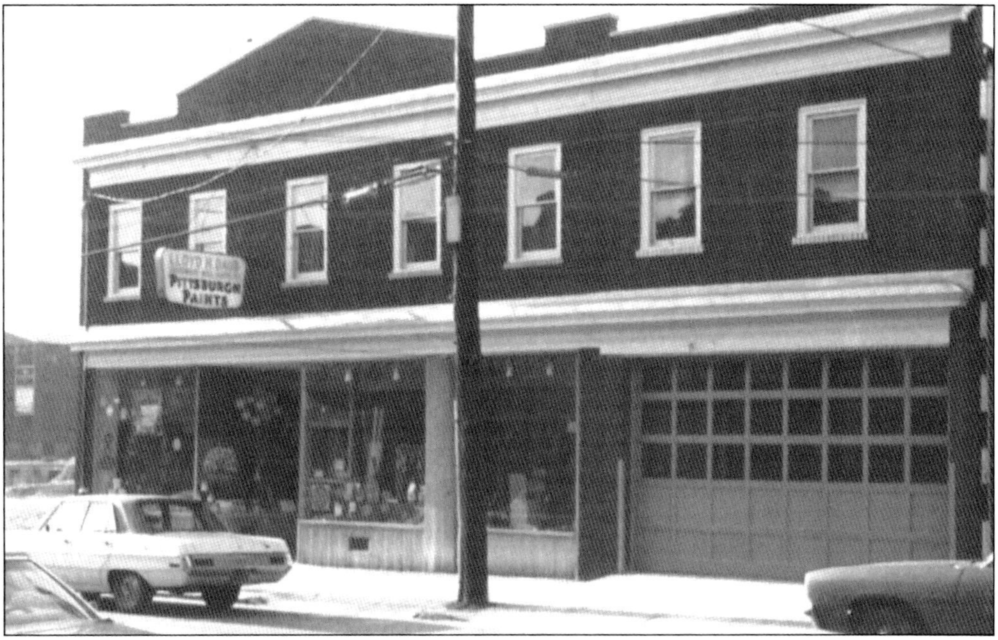

When Daub's Hardware Store closed in 1986, many Bridgeport residents were sorry to see it go, but few people realized the long history of the business. Lloyd Daub learned the business at Quillman's Hardware Store in Norristown. When Daub started his own business in September 1922, he was working out of two small rooms in a house he purchased, along with a plumbing business from Samuel Coates. By the late 1920s Daub razed the house to construct this building and started a second store in Norristown. The business took in all of $8 on the first day of business in 1922, and by 1951 Daub employed 28 local residents.

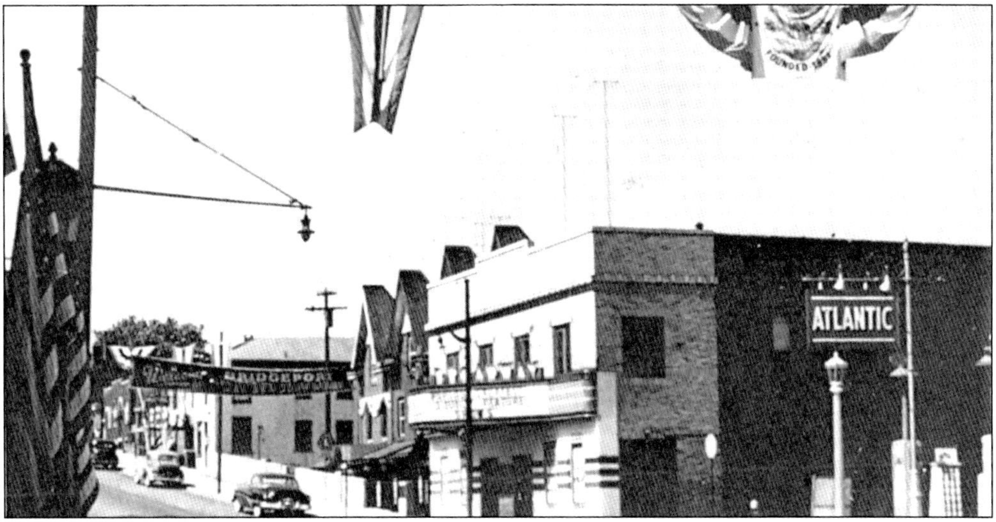

Bridgeport was decked out in the spring of 1951 in honor of the borough's centennial celebration. Bridgeport was incorporated on February 27, 1851, with 422 acres and 572 residents. This photograph was taken at Second and Dekalb Streets, notice the Atlantic Service Station on the far right of the picture and the Broadway Theatre in the center. The Broadway Theatre opened in 1928 and delighted Bridgeport residents with first-run movies until the theater closed its doors for good in December 1951.

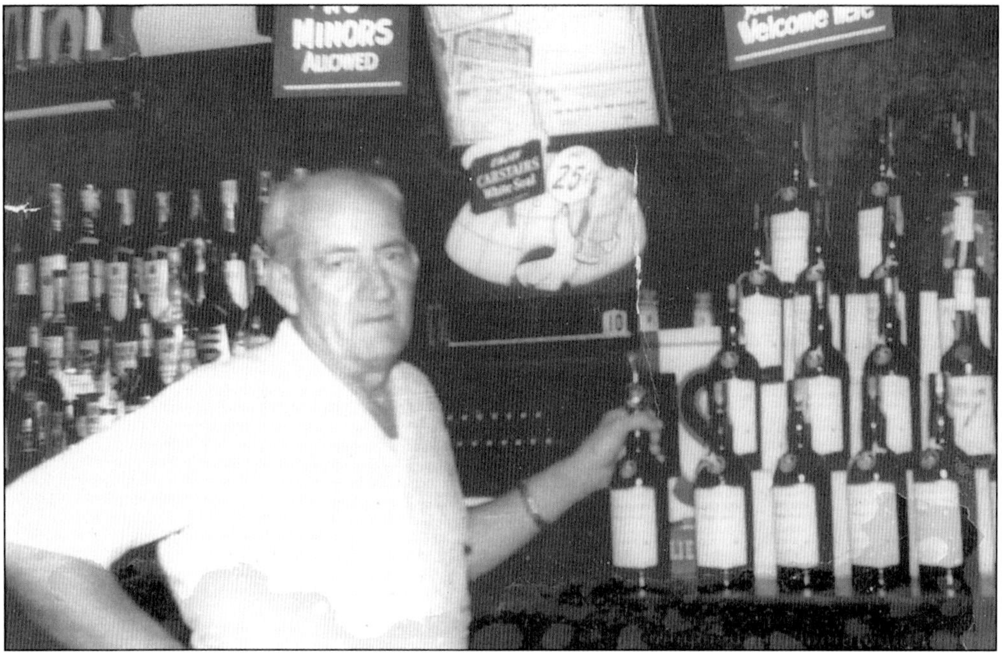

Louis Chiccarine, founder of Chick's Bar located at 233 East Fourth Street, stands behind the bar back in 1952. Louis changed the name of the Walnut Shade Inn to Chick's Bar in 1933. In later years Louis purchased a barbershop at 235 Fourth Street and added a dining room onto the bar. Louis passed the business onto his son Pete, and Pete worked the business until his son David took over. David currently runs the operation of the business. (The Chiccarine family.)

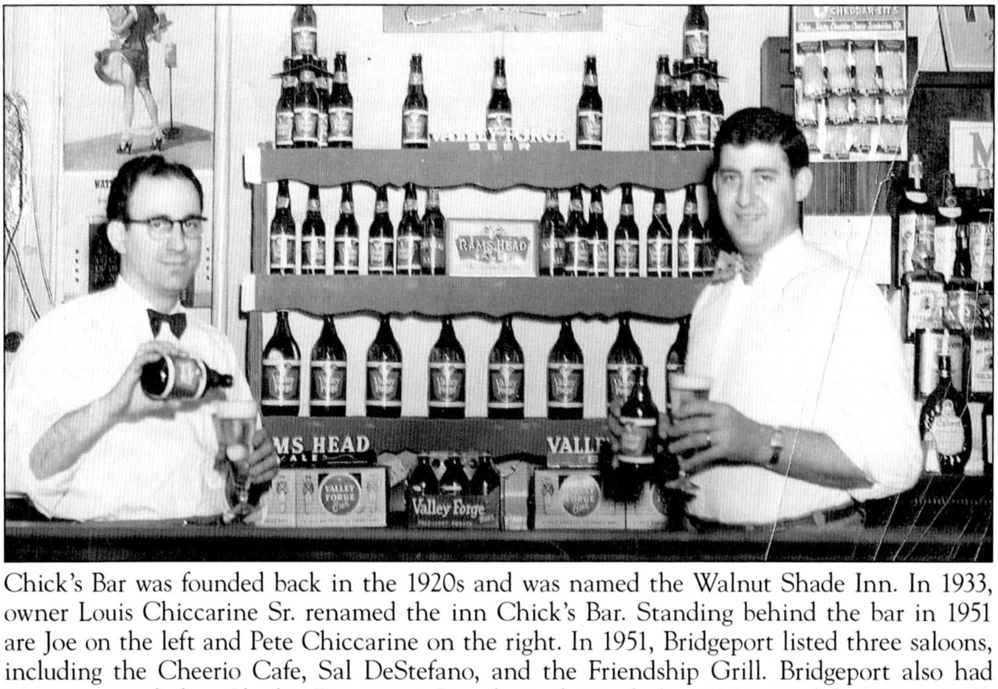

Chick's Bar was founded back in the 1920s and was named the Walnut Shade Inn. In 1933, owner Louis Chiccarine Sr. renamed the inn Chick's Bar. Standing behind the bar in 1951 are Joe on the left and Pete Chiccarine on the right. In 1951, Bridgeport listed three saloons, including the Cheerio Cafe, Sal DeStefano, and the Friendship Grill. Bridgeport also had 12 taverns, including Chick's, Desimone's Bar, the Lark Hotel, the 201 Bar, and the Depot Grill, just to name a few. (The Chiccarine family.)

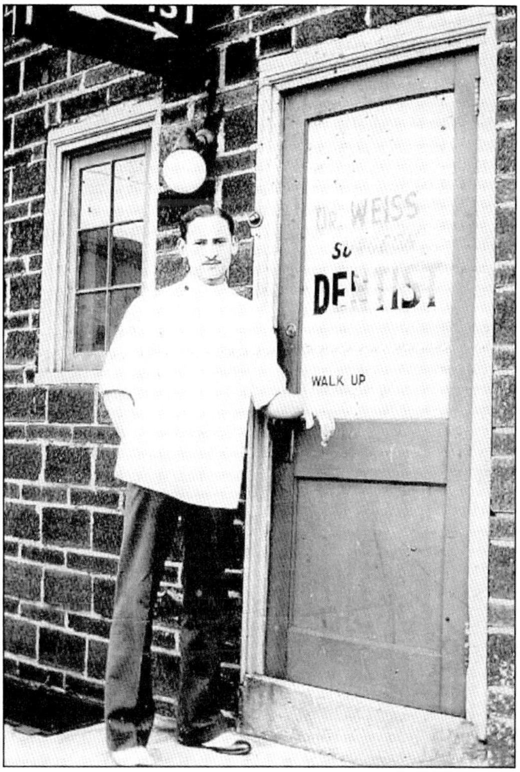

Dr. Samuel Weiss was one of three dentists practicing in the borough of Bridgeport back in 1938 when these photographs were taken at his office located at 312 Dekalb Street. Weiss is seen standing at the front door of his office just a block up from the Broadway Theatre, and (below) working on a patient. Weiss practiced dentistry for years.

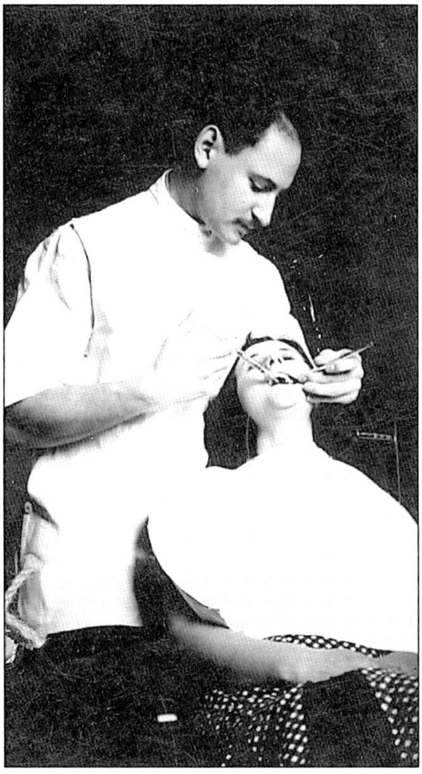

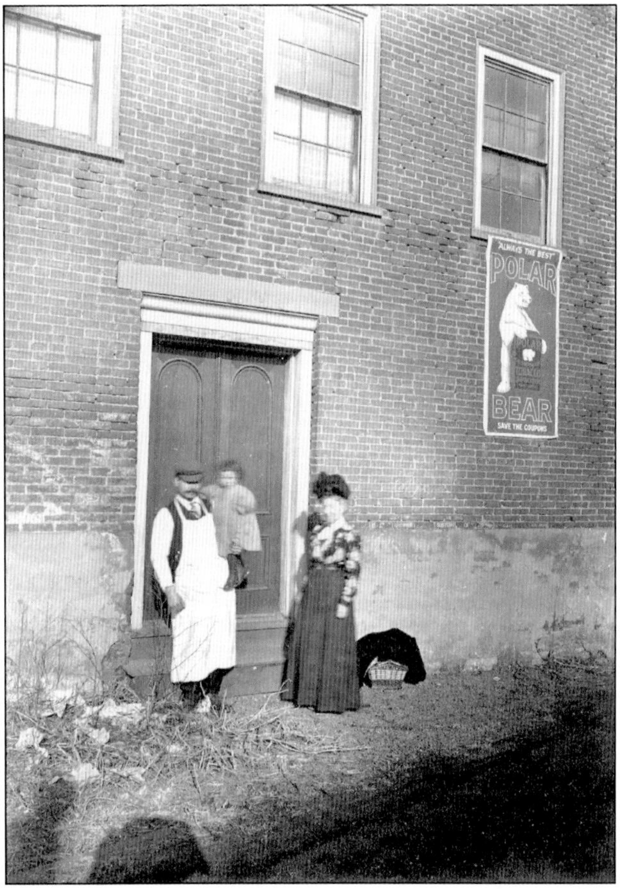

The Marinelli family poses outside their grocery store once located at Fourth and Depot Streets. Mr. Marinelli purchased the corner store in 1905 from members of the Patton family and is seen in the photograph at left posing with his mother and daughter behind the store. The photograph below shows Mr. Marinelli with his daughter, wife, and mother. For 25 years the Marinellis supplied residents with groceries, cigarettes, meats, and tobacco. In 1930, the business was sold and renamed Demetris Uptown Market, and members of the Demetris family continue to sell everything from groceries to cigarettes, meats, and tobacco, pretty much as it was a century ago. (Historical Society of Montgomery County.)

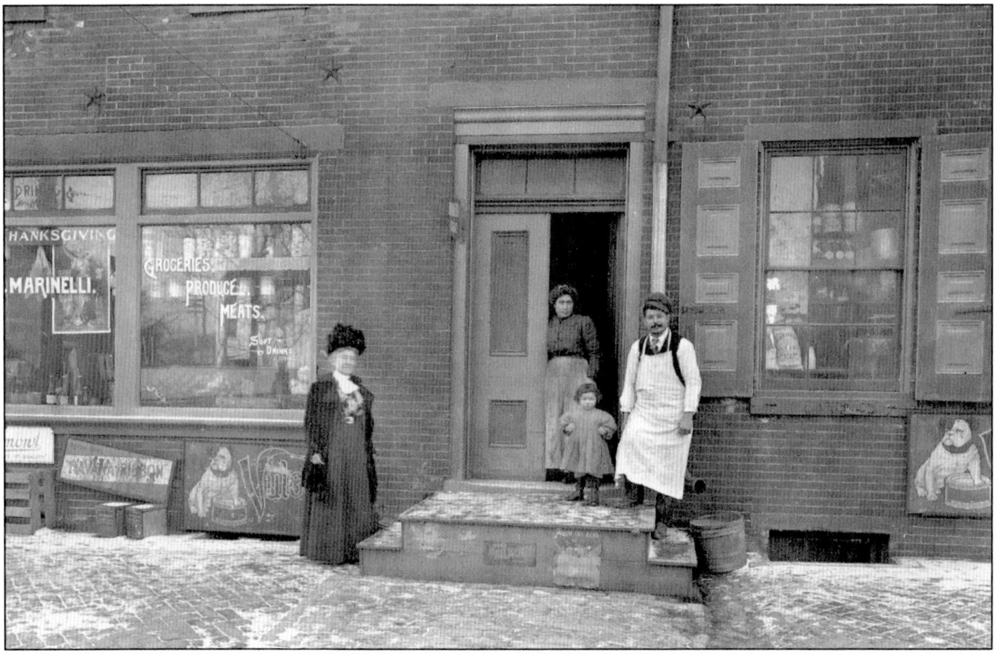

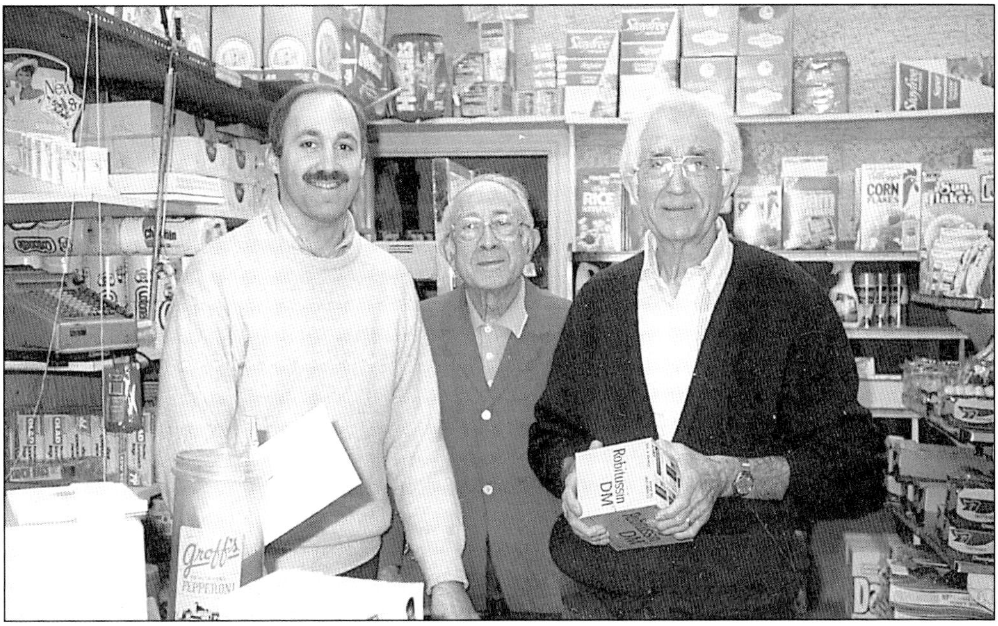

The Demetris Uptown Market has been owned and operated by members of the Demetris family for more than 70 years. The store can be traced back to the Patton family back in 1899. The Marinelli family purchased the store in 1905 and for 25 years provided residents with day-to-day needs. The Demetris family purchased the business during the storm of the Great Depression and carried a number of families through the hard times. Current owner Dennis Demetris can be seen in the photograph above standing next to former owners of the store, his uncle Tom, who passed away in 1989, and Dennis's father, Jack. In the photograph below, Dennis is seen outside the store with his father.

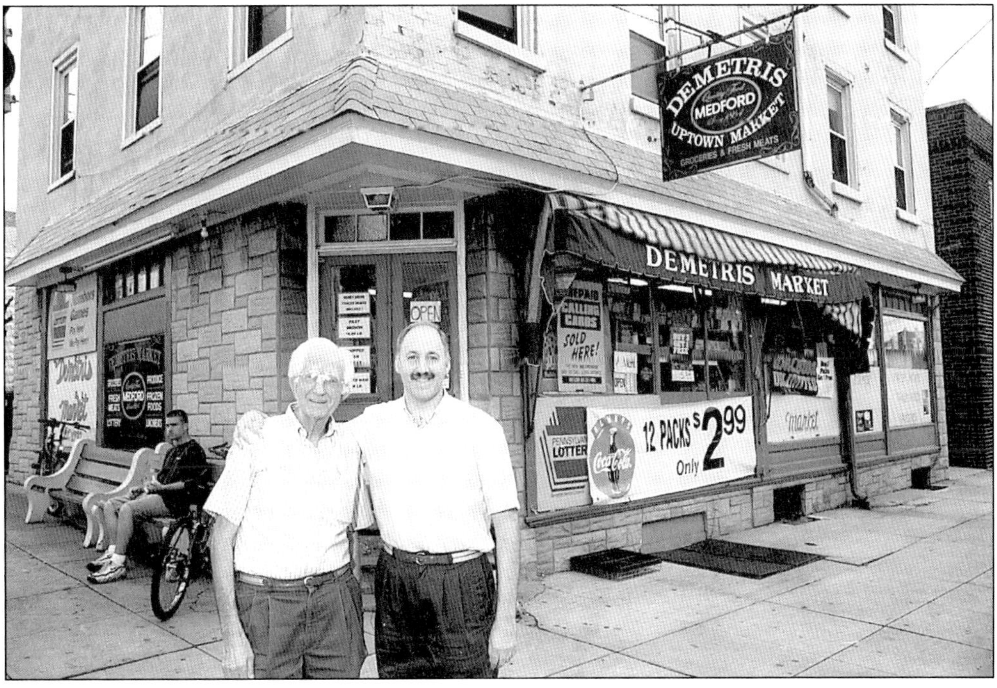

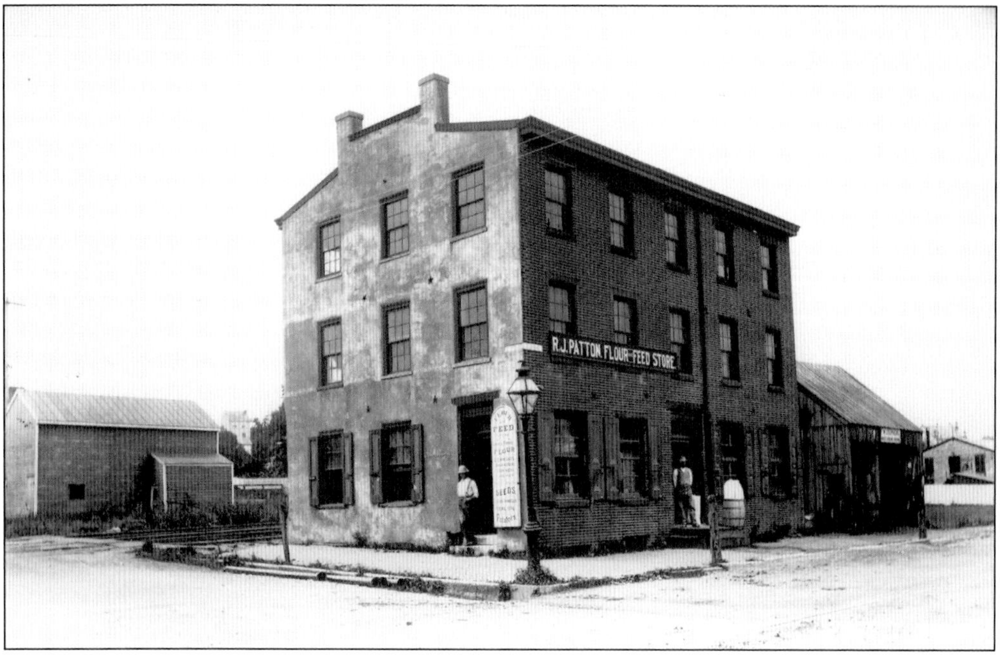

The R. J. Patton Flour and Feed Store once located at Fourth and Depot Streets was established in 1899 and for six years supplied the local neighborhood with its daily needs. Patton sold the store in 1905, and the store continued as Marinelli's Grocery. More than 100 years later the corner store still serves the community out of the same building as Demetris Uptown Market.

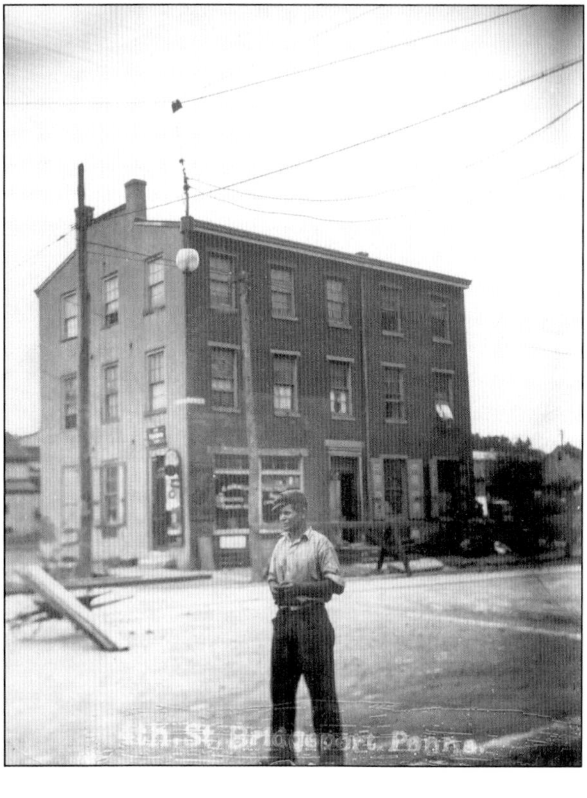

Marinelli's Grocery Store is seen in this 1907 postcard photograph located at Fourth and Depot Streets. Notice the electric streetlight hanging in the middle of the intersection. Bridgeport installed 10 gas streetlamps in 1870, and Levi Emery was hired to light the lamps each night at dusk and was paid $6 per month. Electric streetlamps were introduced in Bridgeport in 1899 when Norristown Electric installed 39 electric lights, and a month later the gas lamps were removed. (Historical Society of Montgomery County.)

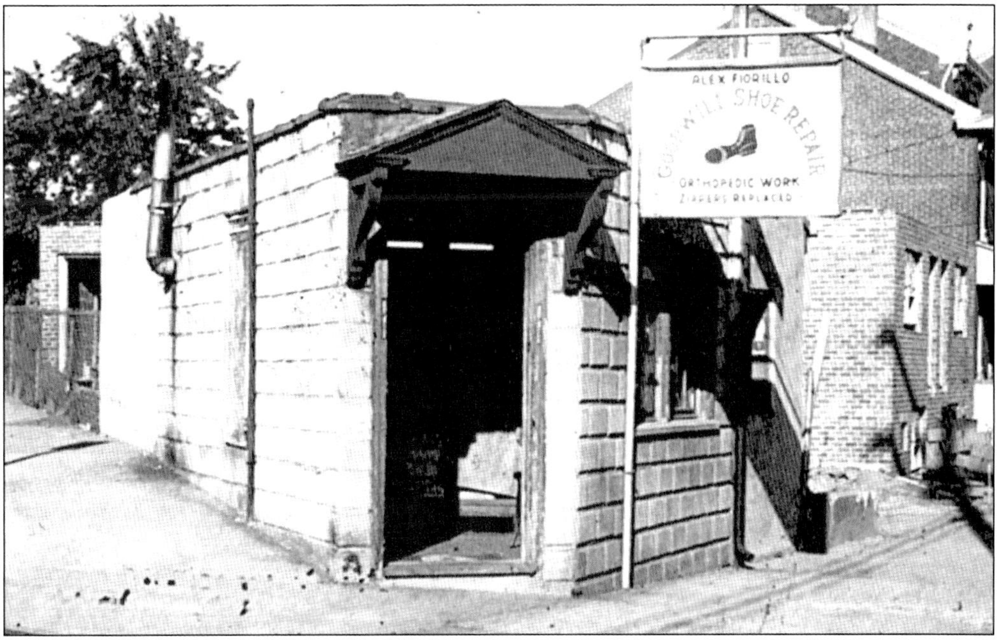

Alex Fiorillo's shoe repair shop was located for many years at the corner of Fourth and Bush Streets. Back in the 1930s, when this photograph was taken, Bridgeport never had less than five shoe repair shops in the borough and sometimes more. Visitors passing the corner of Fourth and Bush Streets today will find a more modern structure and Chuck's Hot Dogs store in its place.

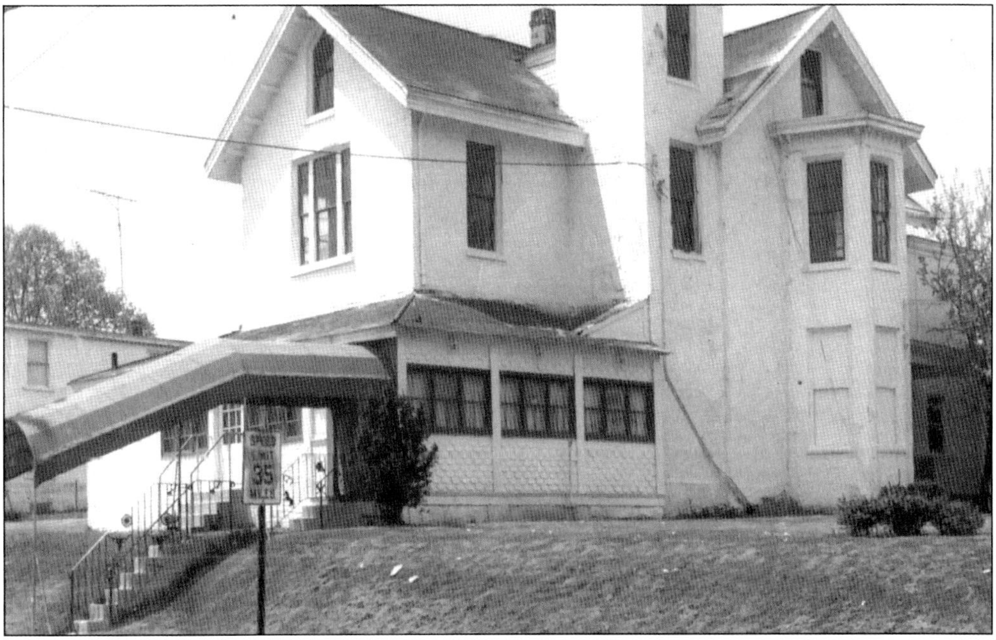

The former Tarlecki homestead was one of the oldest buildings in Bridgeport before it was razed in 1976 to make way for a nine-unit apartment building with a storefront that currently houses Studio 8 Color Specialist. The building was located at Fifth and Ford Streets, across from Our Lady of Mount Carmel Church. Over the years the restaurant was called the Model "T" Tavern, the Burgundy Inn, and the Cheerio Cafe. (Bridgeport Hall of Fame.)

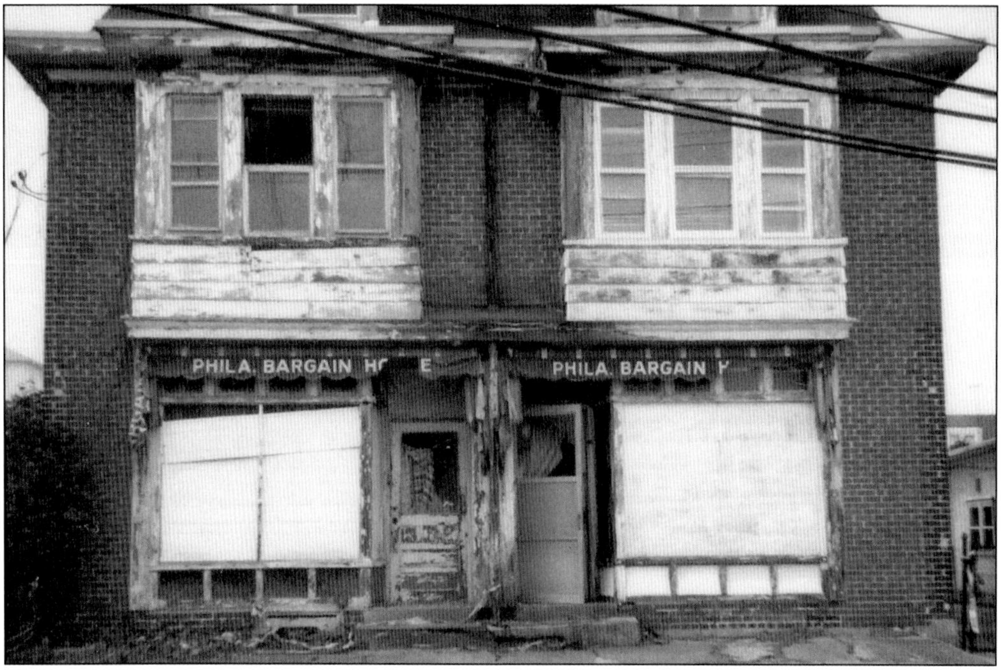

When the Philadelphia Bargain Store opened on East Fourth Street near Coats in Swedesburg back in 1933, the country was coming out of the worst depression ever. That depression, however, did not deter Bridgeport residents from opening small businesses. That determination was the heart and soul of the town and the spirit of the residents. In 1933, the Friendship Grill opened, as did Demetris Uptown Market and Chick's Bar. The Philadelphia Bargain Store closed its doors in the 1970s, and the building was demolished in the 1990s. (Ed Dybicz.)

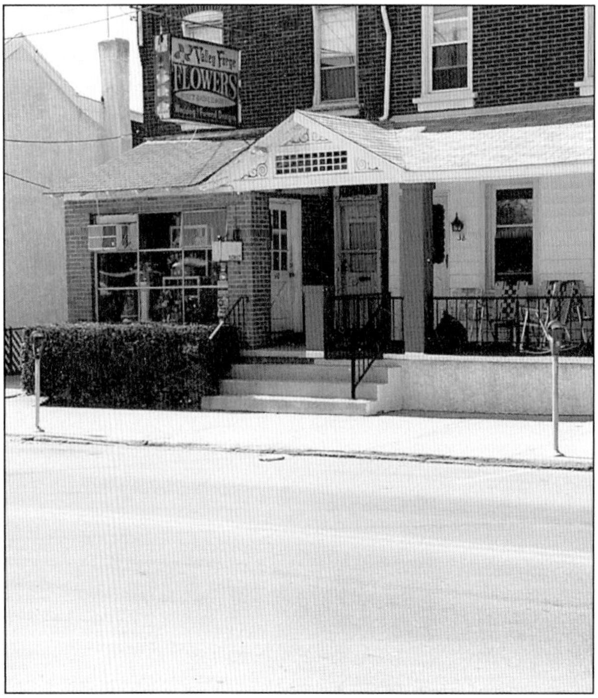

The Valley Forge Flower Shop located at 40 East Fourth Street has been adding color to the Bridgeport area for nearly 40 years. Jack and Barbara Hedgecock opened a flower shop in 1969 on Fourth Street and by 1975 purchased the building at the current location. In 1969, Bridgeport's economy took a hit when Lee's Carpet moved to Valley Forge Park. However, the retail, wholesale, and service establishments showed a slight increase in 1969 over recent years, indicating family businesses like Valley Forge Flower Shop were thriving in Bridgeport.

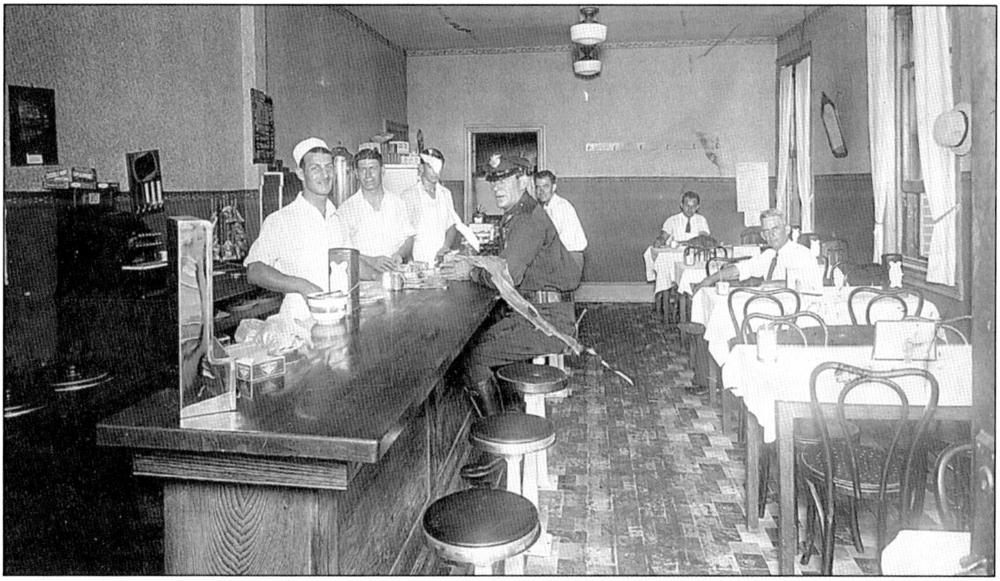

George's Diner opened in 1932 and was once located at 338 Dekalb Street, next to Ide's Drug Store. Standing behind the counter on the left is a young Danny D'Orzio, who later owned and operated Danny's Diner. Danny's brother Mike is standing in the middle, and Slim Lux is on the right. The Bridgeport police officer is Benny Waters, who was seen for many years directing traffic at Fourth and Dekalb Streets just outside the diner, and an unknown customer sits next to him. George Aumann, owner of the diner, is sitting at the back table, and John Kinnane is sitting at the near table. (Bill Danitz.)

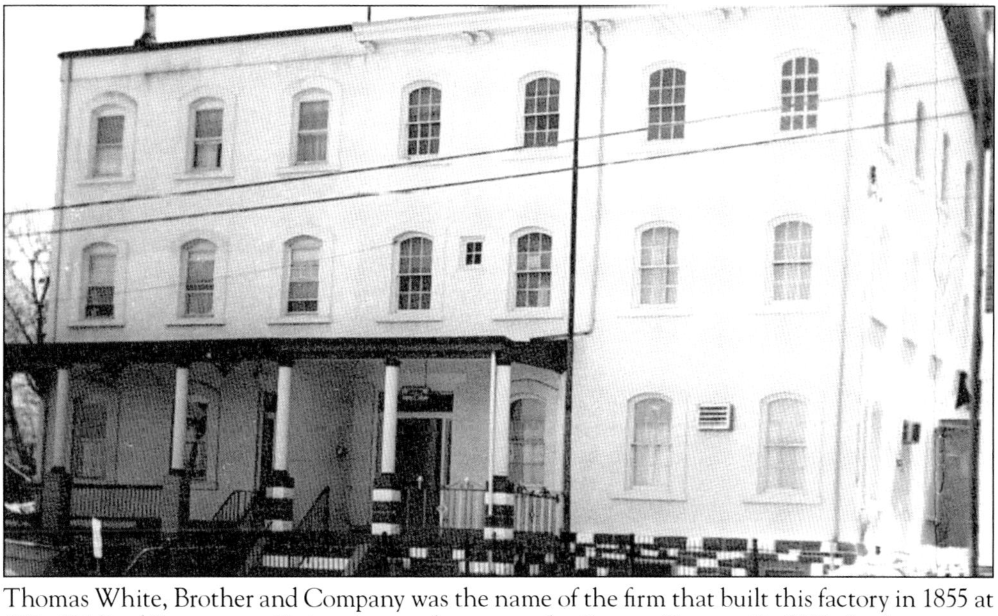

Thomas White, Brother and Company was the name of the firm that built this factory in 1855 at 492–494 Ford Street near Union Avenue known as the Bonnet Factory. By 1858 the factory was the largest manufacturer of women's headgear in Pennsylvania; in spite of this, the factory closed its doors before 1860. The Bonnet Factory later became the temporary church and rectory for the new St. Augustine Parish, which celebrated its first mass to more than 300 Catholic families on July 18, 1892. (St. Augustine Church.)

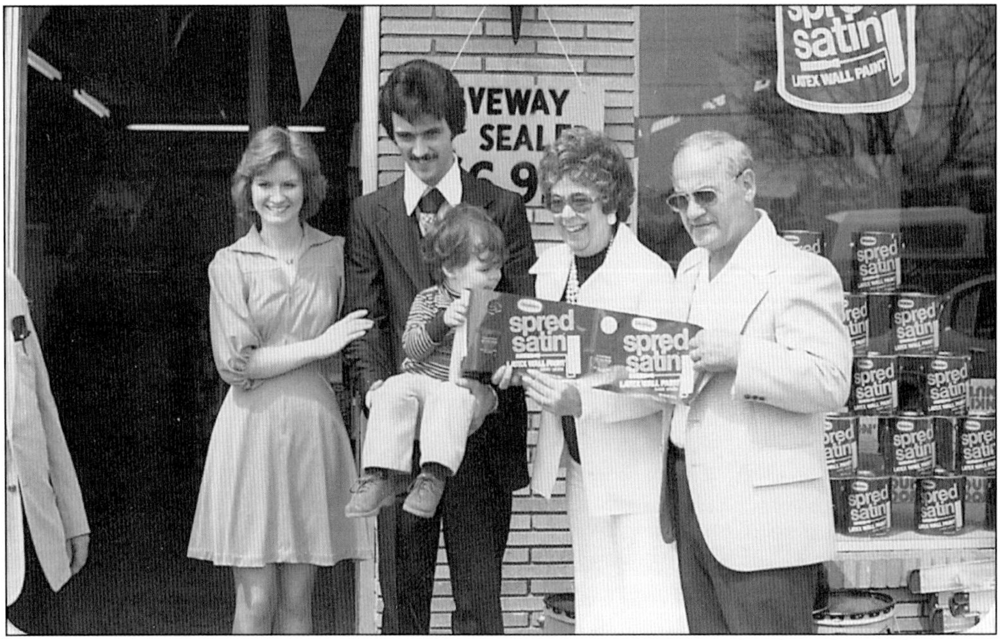

It was a grand opening for Bridgeport Paint Center back in 1979 as Richard Sterley and Thomas Dallesandro began their careers in Bridgeport with Glidden Paints. Posing with his family at the grand opening is Thomas with his wife, Louise, and his son Sean, along with his mother and father, Rose Marie and Tom Sr. The business partners' slogan back in 1979 was "they believe in good old fashion service," and more than 25 years later the pair still gives good old-fashioned service. (Bridgeport Paint.)

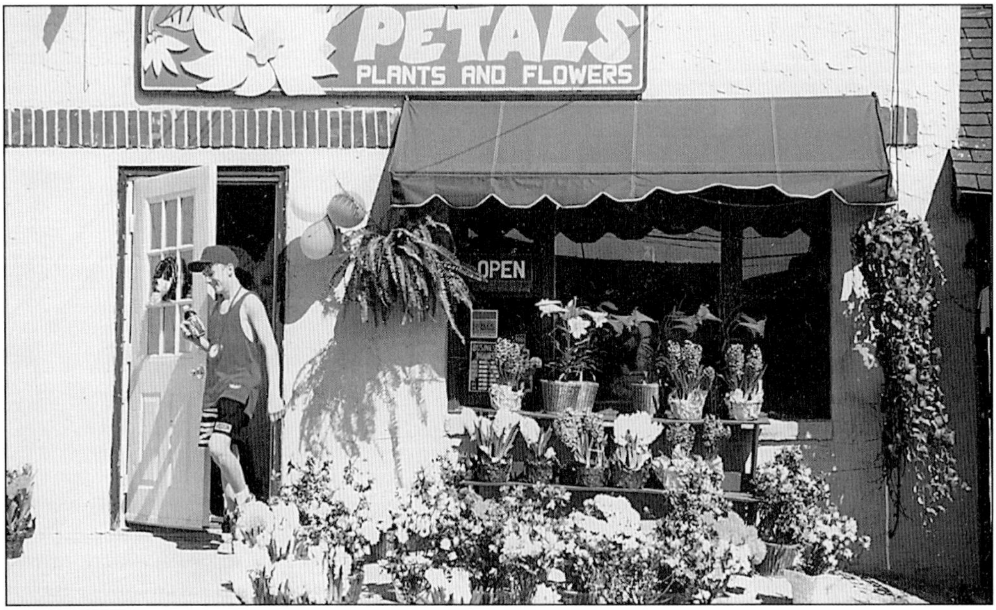

Tommy Strouse is seen outside his former flower shop once located on the corner of Crooked Lane and Ford Street, behind the King Manor Cafe. Strouse started out selling Christmas wreaths and poinsettias in a parking lot 20 years ago and has moved to a spacious store located at 1170 Dekalb Pike. Strouse's former flower store is now part of the Bridgeport Rib House.

Seven

EVENTS

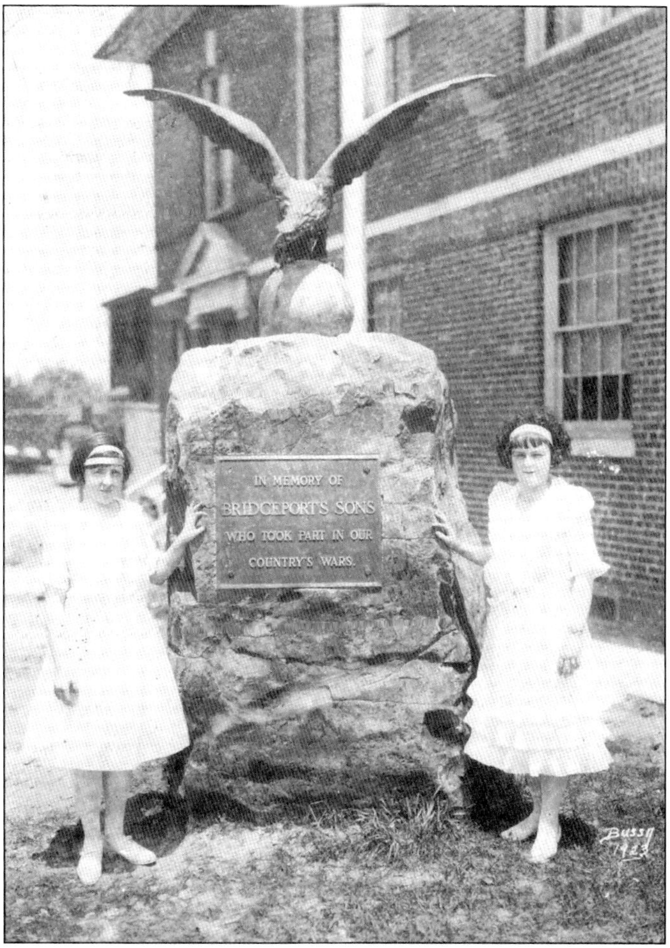

George "Buck" Zaehringer hauled this stone weighing more than a ton from Gulph Mills to the newly erected Bridgeport Borough Hall located at Fourth and Mill Streets in 1923. The country was still recovering from World War I, and many of Bridgeport's sons and daughters served. The stone monument that still graces the borough hall is in memory of residents who served in all the wars. On May 30, 1923, Katherine Wafer, on the left, and Ethel Coats unveiled the monument and presented it to the town as a gift from the citizens. The memorial was received by burgess Richard Welsh. (Bridgeport Hall of Fame.)

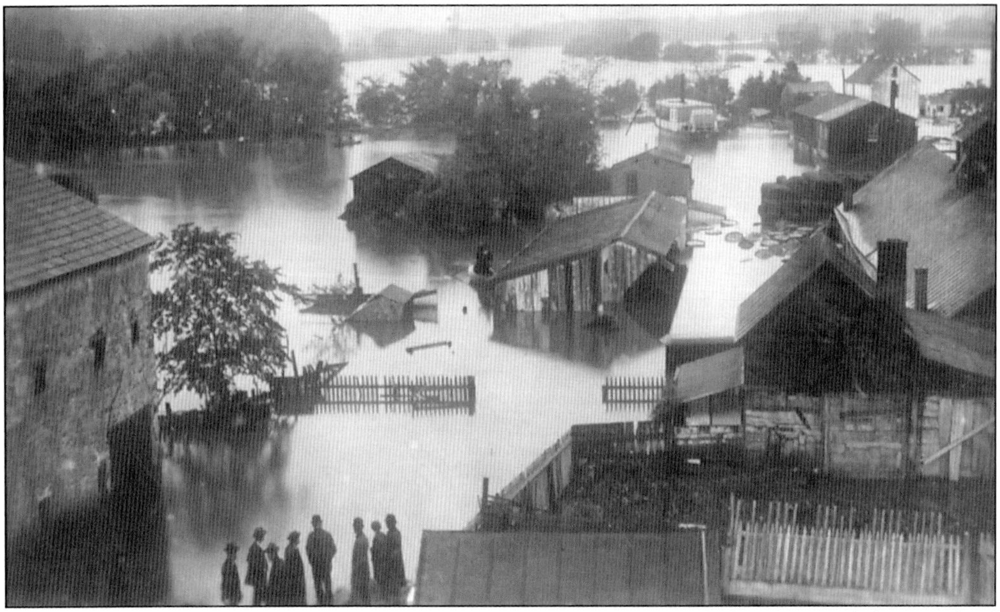

Bridgeport's last major flood happened in 1972 when the river swelled and caused thousands of dollars in damage to the community. But it was nothing like the flood Bridgeport was pounded with back in February 1902. To the left of the photograph, water can been seen submerging the first floor of the Wright's Flour and Grist Mill. The Bridgeport Ferry can be seen in the upper right-hand corner as residents gather at the bottom of the photograph to assess the damage. The photograph was taken from the third story of Evan's Hotel.

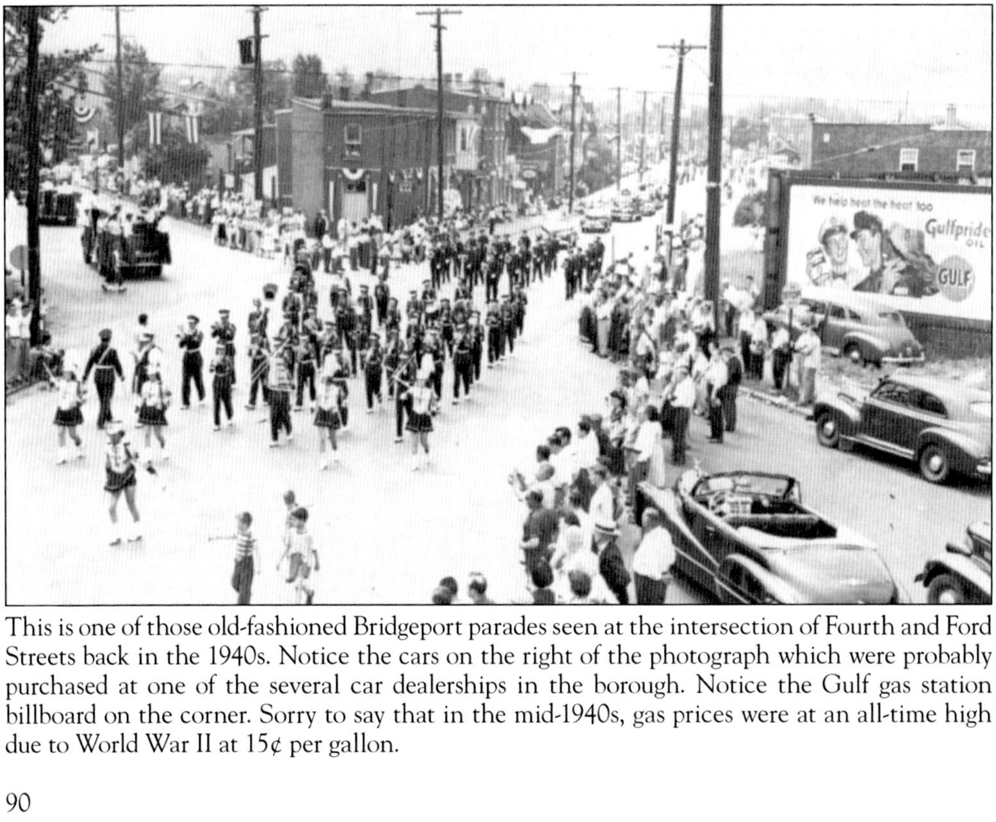

This is one of those old-fashioned Bridgeport parades seen at the intersection of Fourth and Ford Streets back in the 1940s. Notice the cars on the right of the photograph which were probably purchased at one of the several car dealerships in the borough. Notice the Gulf gas station billboard on the corner. Sorry to say that in the mid-1940s, gas prices were at an all-time high due to World War II at 15¢ per gallon.

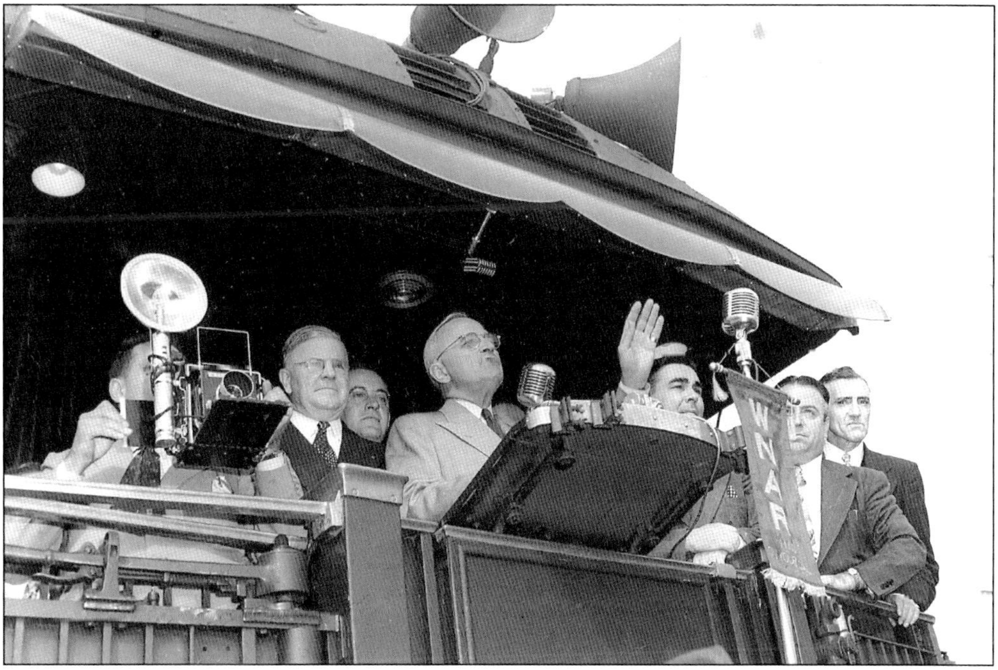

On October 7, 1948, presidential candidate Harry S. Truman's train pulled into Bridgeport on one of his famous "whistle stops" train campaign. An estimated crowd of more than 10,000 residents from Bridgeport and surrounding communities greeted Truman and his wife, Bess. When Truman's train pulled into Bridgeport at 9:37 on that October morning he was behind in the polls. After speaking to the large crowd made up of schoolchildren, union workers, and Democratic leaders, Bess made a brief appearance, and within 10 minutes of stopping, the train was off to Reading. (Bill Landis.)

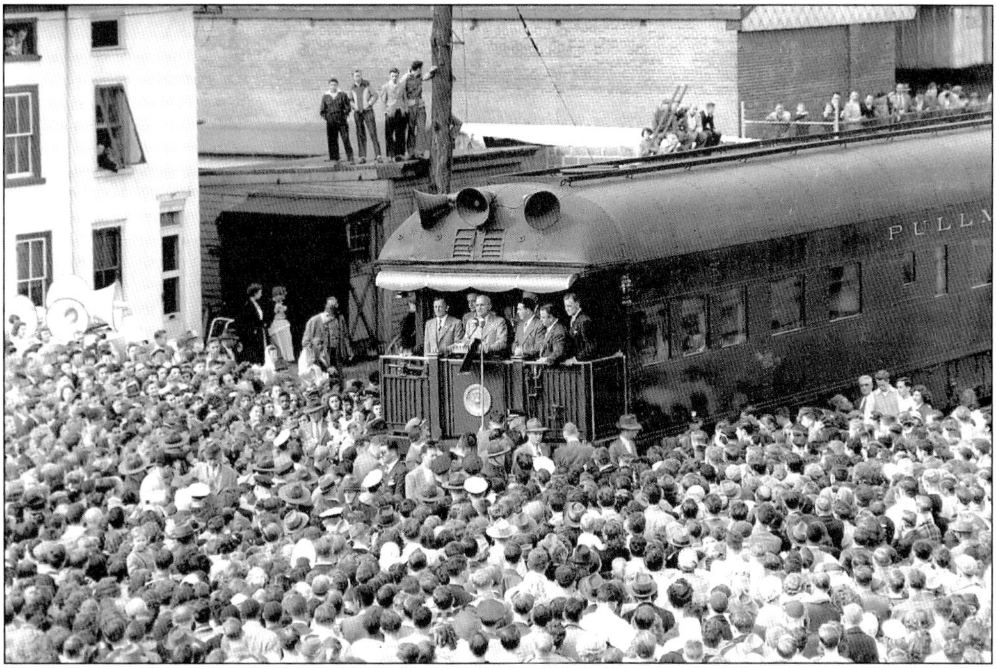

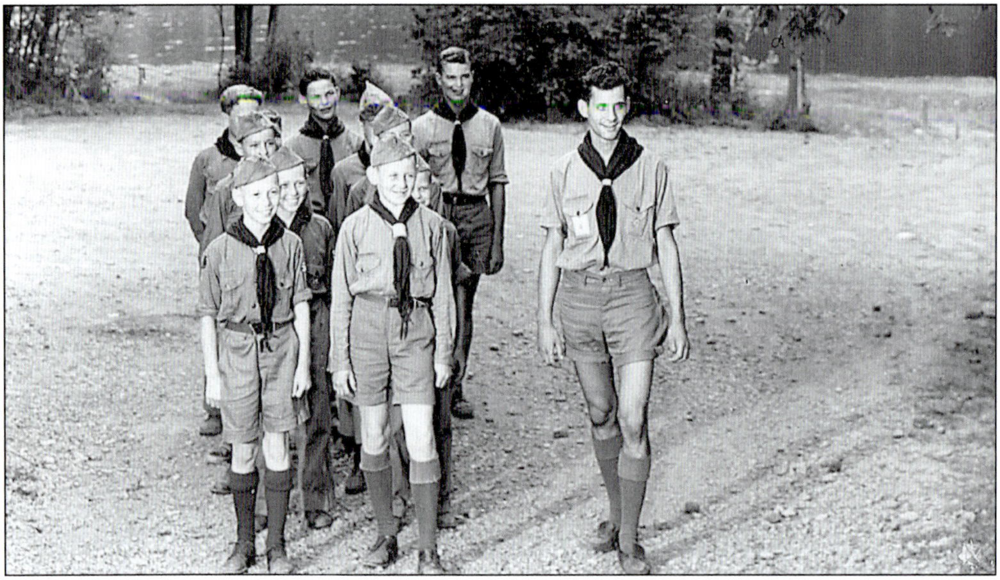

Members of St. Augustine's Roman Catholic Church of Bridgeport Boy Scout Troop No. 5 stroll the grounds of Camp Delmont back in 1947. Members of the troop in the photograph include Charles McQuaid, George Gallagher, James Nash, William Baker, Joseph Tovak, Charles Epright, John Maguire, Gerald Haines, William Malonay, Daniel Malonay, Jerome Grant and Charles Pastonius. (Bill Whitmore.)

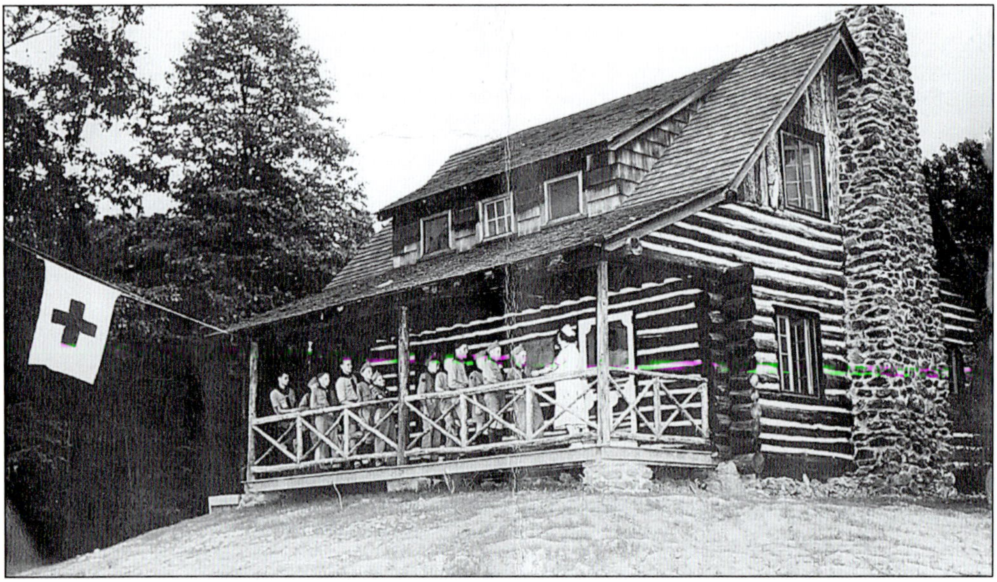

Camp Delmont is a national retreat site for the Boy Scouts of America, and back in October 1946, St. Augustine's Roman Catholic Church of Bridgeport applied and was granted a charter from the National Boy Scouts of America National Council. William D. Gillespie was Troop No. 5's first scoutmaster. Assistant scoutmasters for the troop included James Lawless, Joseph Turley, William Bard, and William McGough. The troop committee consisted of Rev. William Scully, Patrick McGee, Joseph McQuaid, Joseph McGee, John McNeill, and Albert Wagner. This photograph, taken in the summer of 1947, shows members of Troop No. 5 at the Red Cross Treatment Center at Camp Delmont. (Bill Whitmore.)

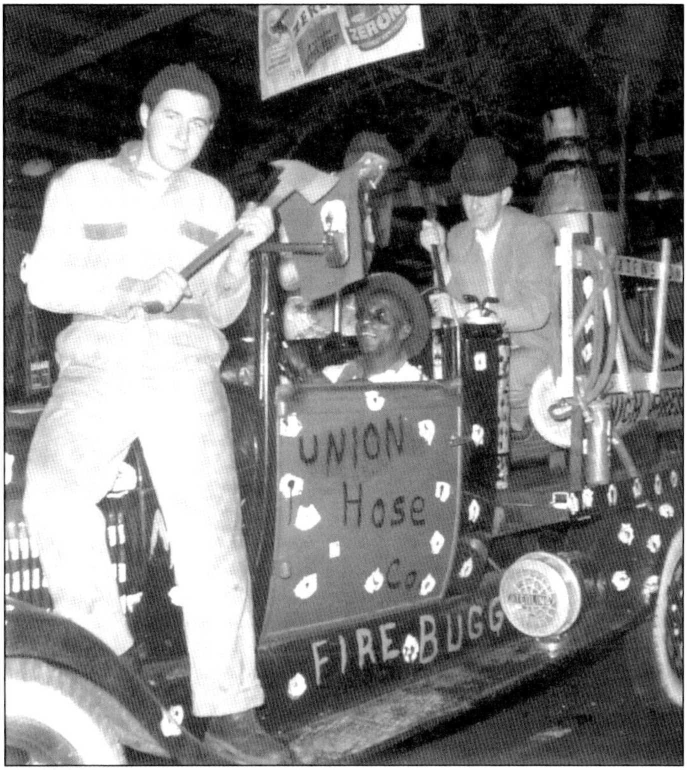

Four local guys were caught hamming it up back in 1952 with a decorated truck waiting to participate in the Philadelphia Mummers Day Parade. Standing on the fender with an ax is Rocky Pignoli, sitting in the driver's seat is Larry Livers, standing above Larry with a cigarette in his mouth is Chappy Hastings, and on the back is Joe Homa. The photograph was taken in a garage on Dekalb Street. (Rocky Pignoli.)

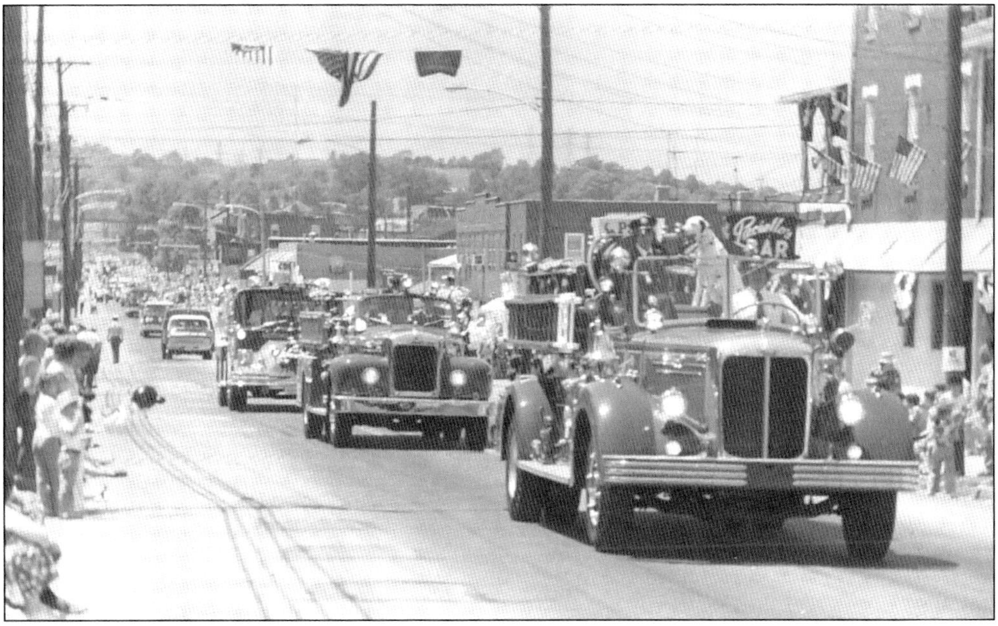

More than 20,000 spectators lined Fourth Street in Bridgeport on Saturday, June 5, 1976, to view and enjoy the Bridgeport Firemen's Centennial Parade. The parade was sponsored by the Good Will Fire Company, seen in this photograph, and involved 87 fire companies from all over the state of Pennsylvania along with a number of marching bands and floats. Mayor Daniel DeOrzio and council president Samuel Santoro praised the efforts of the fire departments.

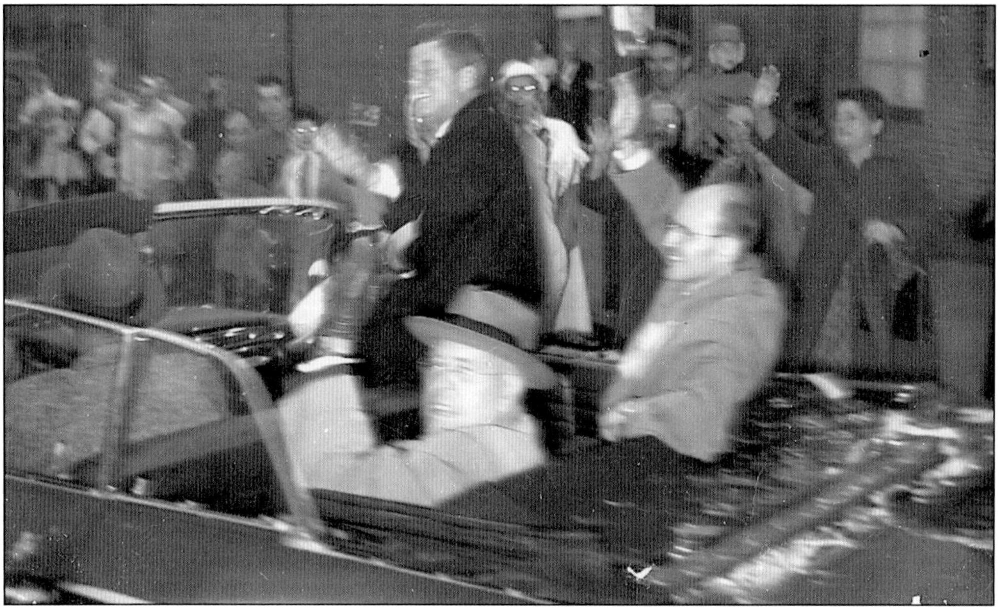

This blurry photograph was captured by photographer Ed Dybicz as Sen. John F. Kennedy rode through Swedesburg and into Bridgeport on Saturday, October 29, 1960. Kennedy was on a whirlwind tour of Montgomery County and traveled along River Road into Bridgeport where the senator traveled Fourth Street to Dekalb Street and into Norristown, where thousands of voters greeted him at Roosevelt Field. Notice Pennsylvania governor David L. Lawrence in the foreground riding in the back seat. On this rainy October Saturday, Kennedy rode with the top down and made a couple stops in Swedesburg and Bridgeport to accept flowers and other assorted gifts. (Ed Dybicz.)

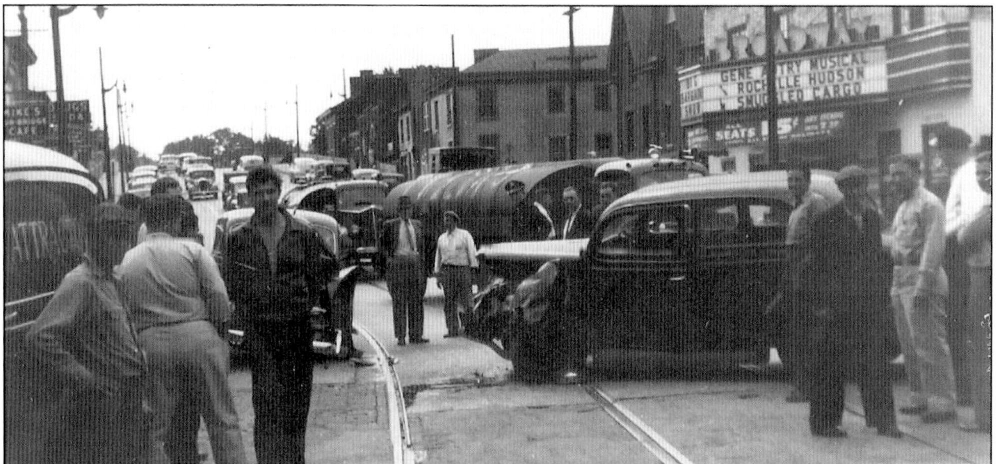

This accident located at Second and Dekalb Streets back in the mid-1930s shows the Broadway Theatre in the background attached to two private residences. Gene Autry and Rochelle Hudson were featured on the marquee. On the far left of the photograph, signs for Mike's Cafe and Hurz Drug Store are visible. The Broadway Theatre opened to the delight of more than 5,000 Bridgeport residents back in 1928, just as talkies hit theaters across America. The Broadway showed first-run movies until December 1951, before closing its doors to become a warehouse. (Van Weiss.)

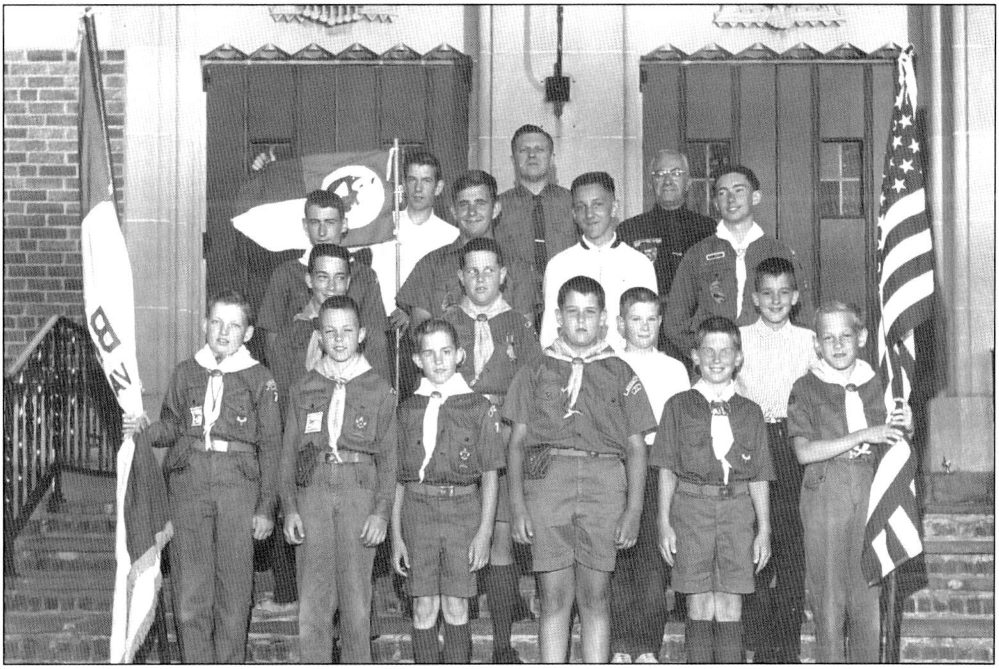

Members of St. Augustine's Boy Scout Troop No. 73 line up for a picture back in 1964 on the steps of St. Augustine's Church on Ford Street. The two scoutmasters in the back row are Bill Whitmore and Mike Ercole. Other scouts in the picture include Billy Palmer, Bob Schaff, John Gavin, Jim Willikson, Mike Sheenan, Bob Cooke, Charlie Gavin, Ed Dunn, and Bill Murray. (Bill Whitmore Sr.)

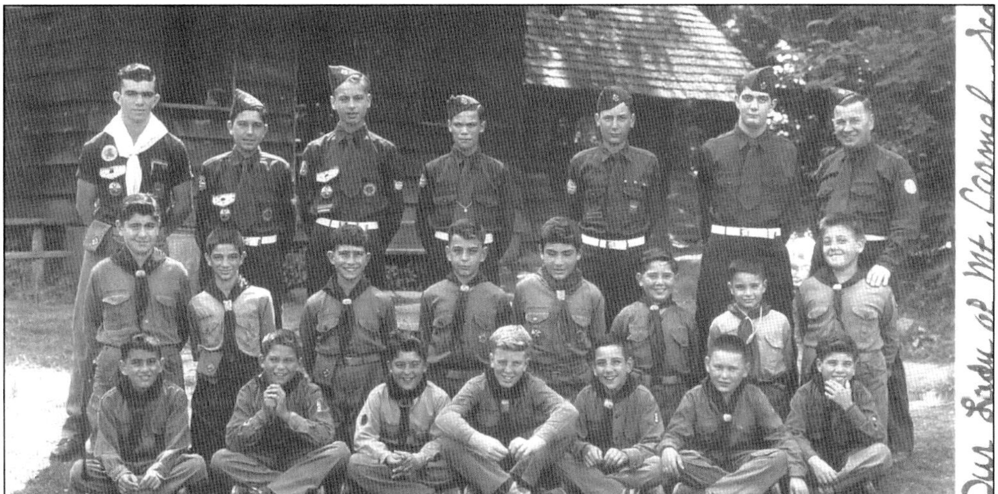

The Boy Scout Troop from Our Lady of Mount Carmel Church and its leaders can be seen in this group photograph taken back in the summer of 1952 at Camp Delmont. The Boy Scouts of Our Lady of Mount Carmel was just one of many organizations from within the church, especially back in the early and mid-1950s when the school's population was at an all-time high. Both St. Augustine's Church and Our Lady of Mount Carmel Church chartered Boy Scout troops in the late 1940s as a way to reach out and offer more to the children of their parishes. (Bridgeport Hall of Fame.)

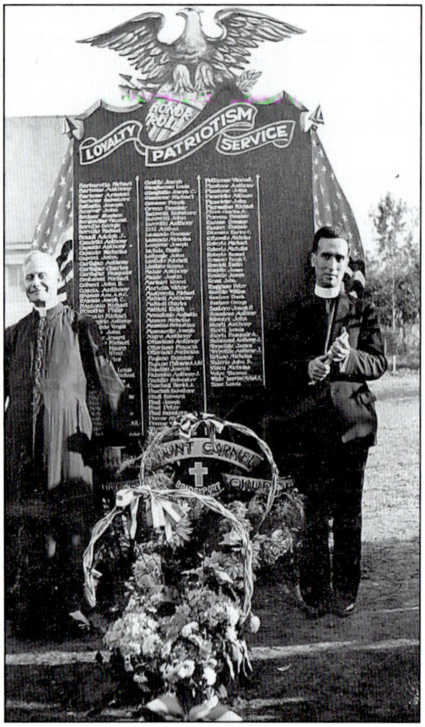

This picture taken on October 11, 1942, served as a tribute to all the Bridgeport sons and daughters serving their country during World War II. The list grew to include more than 400 Bridgeport residents serving in the war from 1941 through 1945. World War II came to an end on May 8, 1945, in Europe and August 14 in the Pacific. World War II involved 57 nations, and more than 55 million people died. Fr. Rosario Sciarrone and Fr. Joseph Megna pose with Bridgeport's honor roll. (Rose Gentile.)

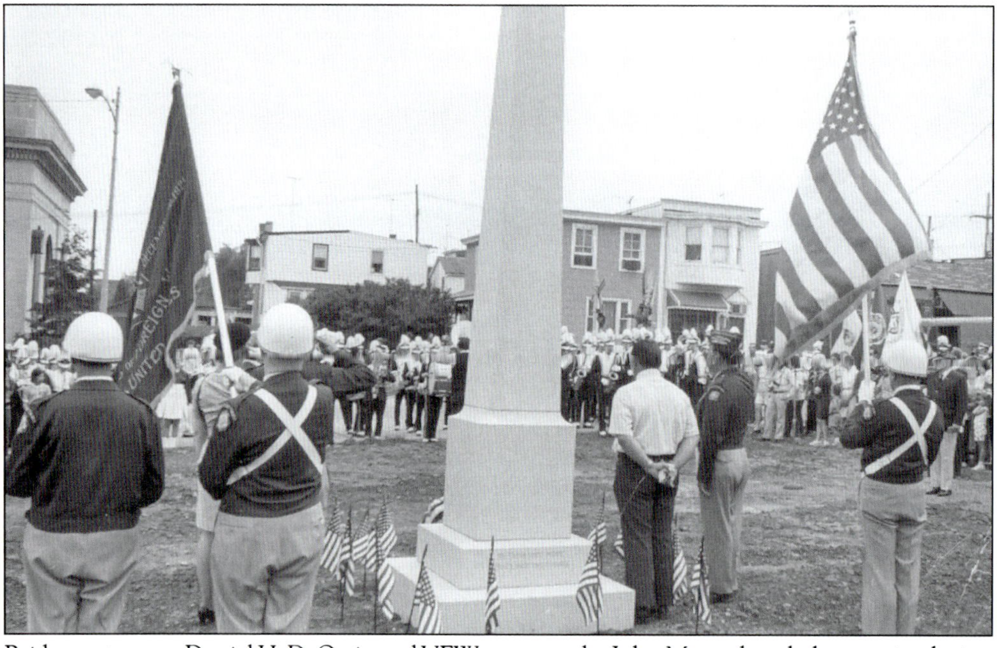

Bridgeport mayor Daniel H. DeOrzio and VFW commander John Moran handed out praise during the dedication of the bicentennial monument and senior park located at Fourth and Dekalb Streets. Members of the Bridgeport Coates-Wafer and Gladwyn Posts, VFW, are seen standing at attention during the dedication services on Memorial Day 1976. Other officials present for the unveiling included Anthony Chiccino, Samuel Santoro, John Lattanze, Philomena Pagano, Joseph Homa, and police chief Joseph Daloisio. (Bridgeport Hall of Fame.)

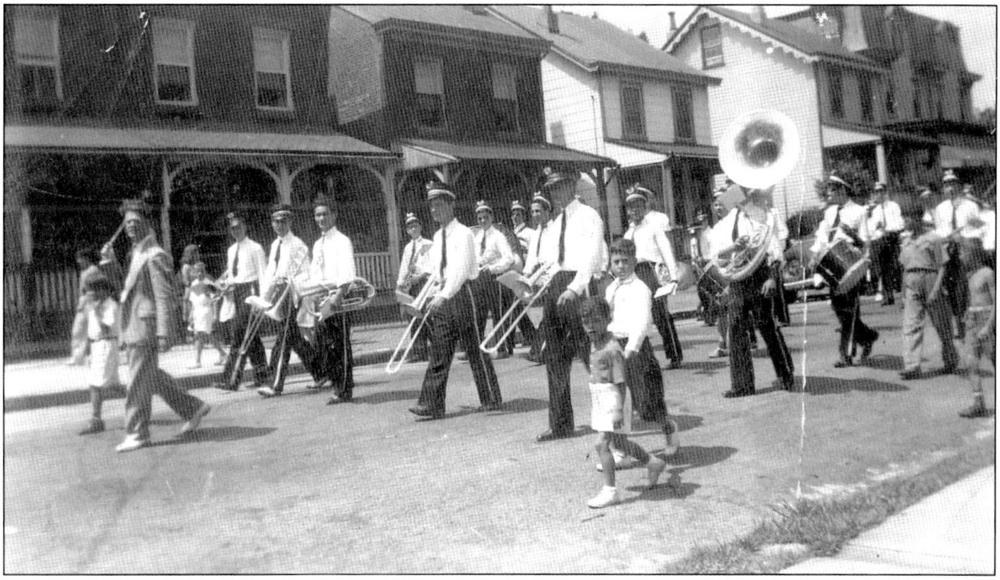

Area children marched along with members of the Bridgeport High School band back in the fall of 1940. The future was bright for the high school students as the borough of Bridgeport's population was at an all-time high with 6,000 residents. Some of the students dreamed of working at one of the two car dealers in town or one of the four gas stations. The Pink Haven Hotel, I. F. March's Lumber yard, and the Broadway Theatre were a few of the other businesses operating in the borough in 1940. (Rose Valerio.)

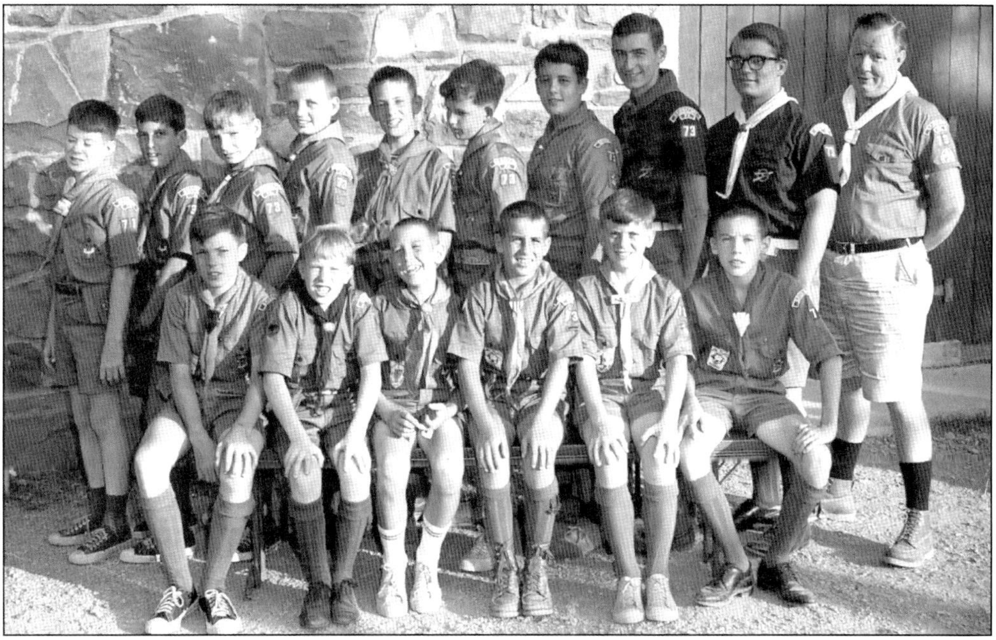

Members of Bridgeport Boy Scout Troop No. 73 take time out at the scouting summer retreat Ressica Falls back in 1965 to pose for this photograph that included, from left to right, (first row) Bob Schaff, Billy Ritchie, John Doughtery, Ed Ostroski, Billy Whitmore, and Ed Doughtery; (second row) Bob Cook, Jimmy Garvey, Jack Coll, Billy Palmer, Rich Cunnaine, Dan Cannon, Jim Wilkison, Ed Dunn, Lefty Mislayak, and Bob Cook Sr. (Edward Ostroski.)

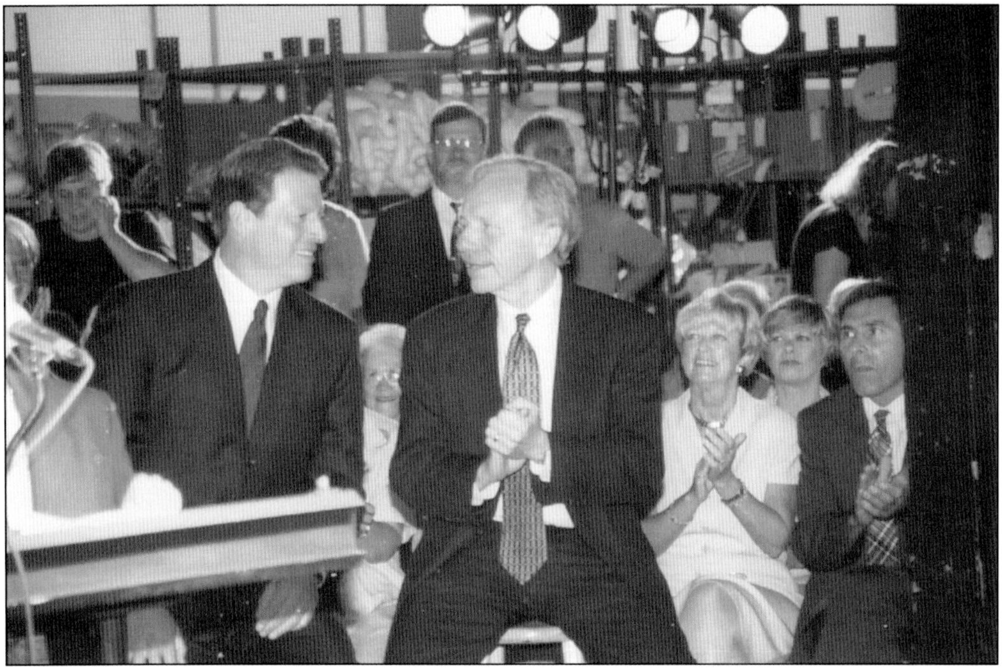

Al Gore, vice president of the United States and presidential candidate back in August 2000, and running mate Joe Lieberman, vice presidential candidate, brought their campaign to Bridgeport to court the labor vote. The pair visited the Little Souls, Inc., Doll Factory in the Continental Business Center located along the river. Gore and Lieberman thrilled the locals in Bridgeport with their appearance but eventually lost their bid for the White House. (Jack Coll.)

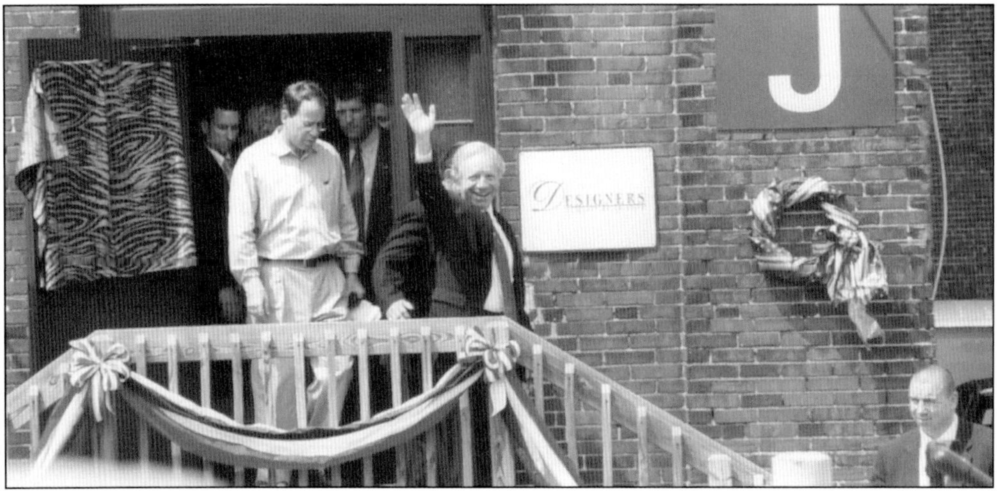

Joe Lieberman, United States senator from Connecticut and a vice presidential candidate back in the 2000 presidential race, waves to the Bridgeport crowd as he leaves the Little Souls, Inc., Doll Factory where he and Vice Pres. Al Gore spoke to an enthusiastic crowd. Lieberman and Gore were in Bridgeport at the Continental Business Center courting the labor vote and promoting female-owned businesses. Nine months after the campaign appearance the Little Souls doll factory along with nearly 48 other businesses in the former industrial complex burned to the ground on Wednesday May 16, 2001, causing more than $10 million in damage and leaving nearly 1,000 workers unemployed. (Jack Coll.)

Eight

RESIDENTS

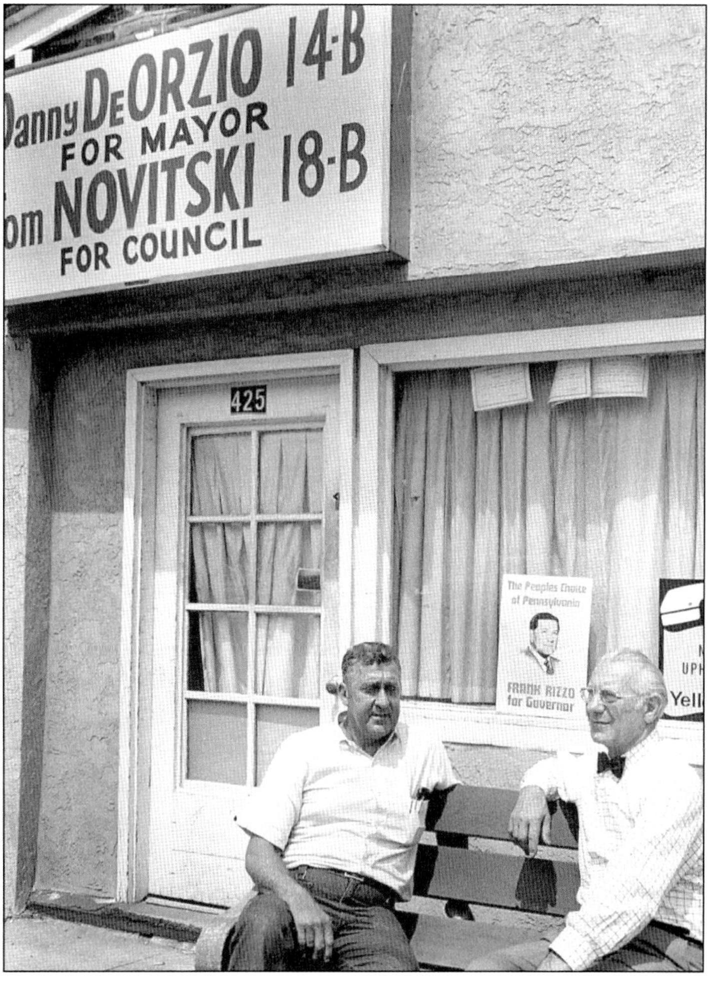

In the early 1970s, Bridgeport borough was feeling a little numb as mill towns along the Schuylkill River, one by one, were packing up and shutting down, leaving a lot of Main Street businesses scrambling to stay open. In 1971, Tom Novitski, sitting on the left, was running for town council and Danny DeOrzio, on the right, was running for mayor of Bridgeport. The two knew all about small businesses as Novitski owned and operated an upholstery shop on Ford Street and DeOrzio owned and operated Danny's Diner on Dekalb Street. Notice the Frank Rizzo for governor sign in the window behind the two men, a true sign of the times. (Nancy Novitski.)

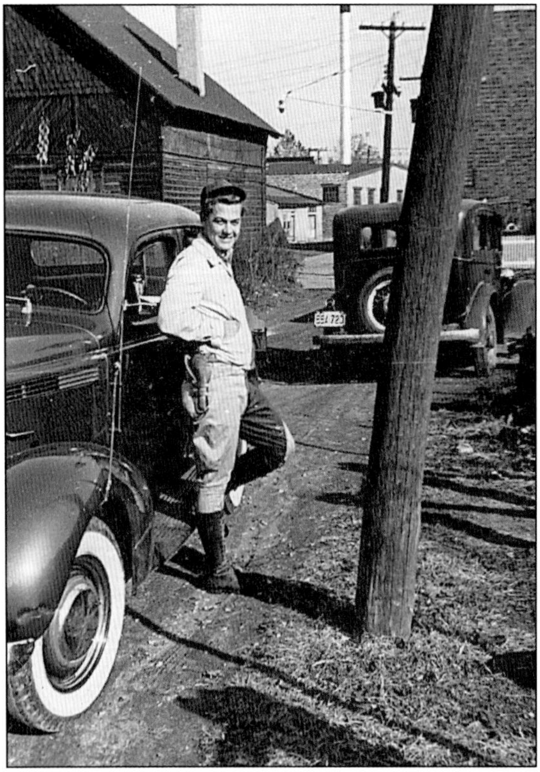

Ralph Fink leans against his car back in 1938, posing in Merion Alley at the rear of the Broadway Theatre. The structure on the left was Bridgeport's official weight station, and Fink is looking toward the paper mill. Back in 1938, Fink would have had to cough up 10¢ per gallon for gas, and a movie ticket to the Broadway would have cost him 25¢. Fink was a 1937 graduate of Bridgeport High School and went on to become a decorated World War II army veteran. Fink was 19 years old when this photograph was taken. (Van Weiss.)

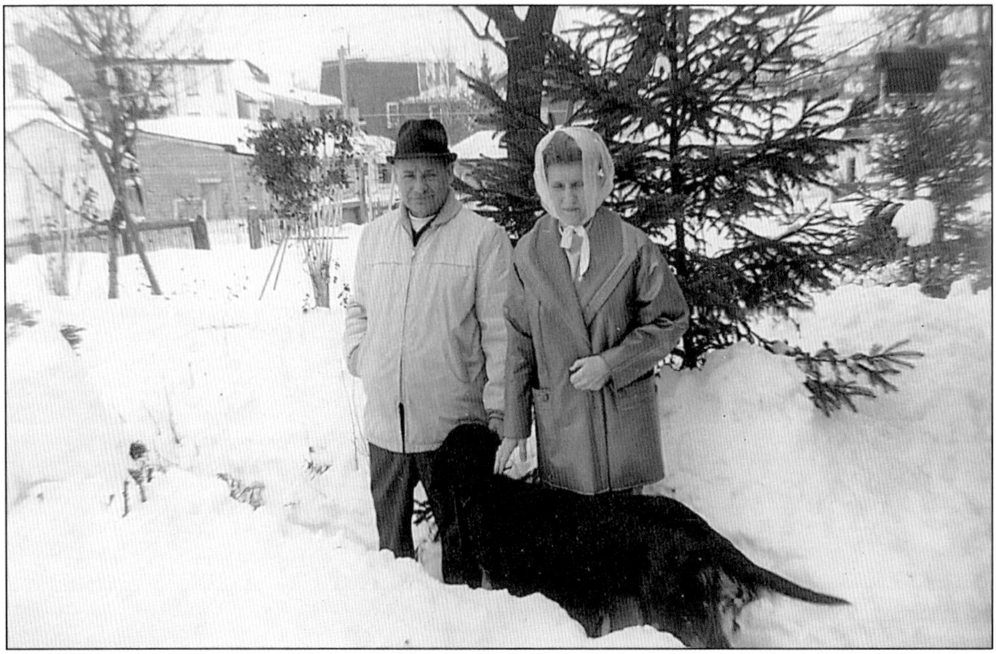

Longtime Bridgeport residents Alex and Florence Hall pose for a photograph in the backyard of their house on Bush Street following a snowstorm in December 1966. The average income for a Bridgeport resident in 1966 was nearly $7,000 a year, and the average cost of a new home was $14,175. (Alex Hall.)

John A. Turley, founder of Turley Insurance Agency back in 1934, poses with his dog Pete behind Bridgeport Borough Hall. Turley started his insurance business at Front and Dekalb Streets before moving to where Bridgeport Trophy is located. He finally moved his business to 123 West Fourth Street where his son John and grandsons John and Robert continue the business. Turley was the borough treasurer for several years and also served as the borough magistrate for more than three decades. This photograph of John and Pete was taken in 1948.

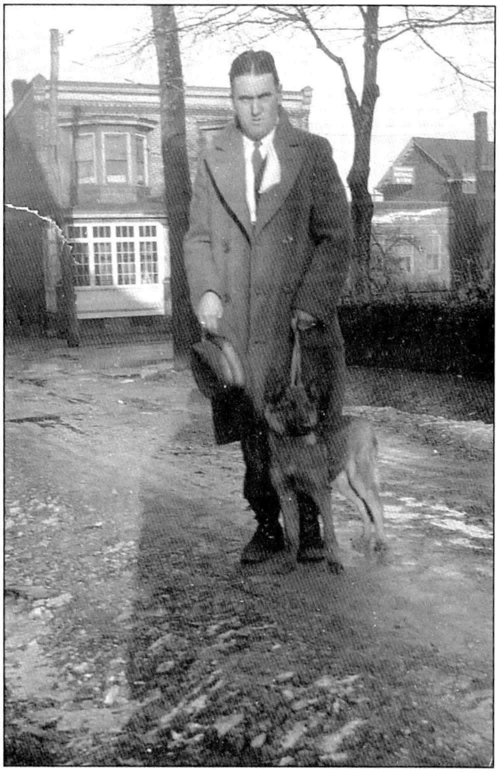

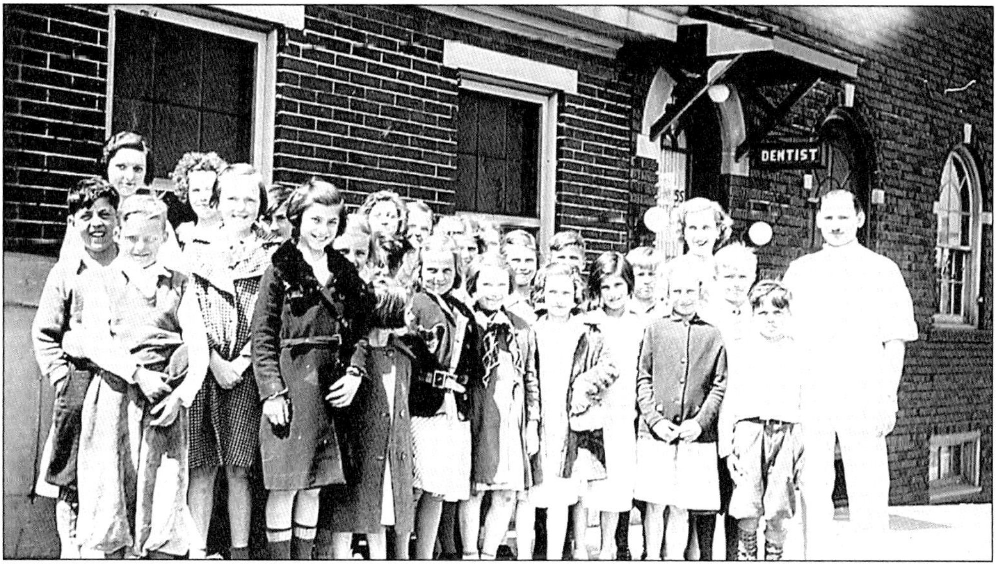

This photograph, taken in the spring of 1938, shows Dr. Samuel Weiss on the far right of the photograph with students from the Upper Merion School District. The students would visit the dentist office, once located at 312 Dekalb Street, for a check-up once a year. It was reported by Dr. Weiss's son, Van, that his father would get 25¢ per student for checkups and cavity fillings. Samuel was one of three dentists with an office in Bridgeport at that time. The other two dentists were Edward Gibbons located at 404 Dekalb Street and Bertram Martin located at 508 Dekalb Street. (Van Weiss.)

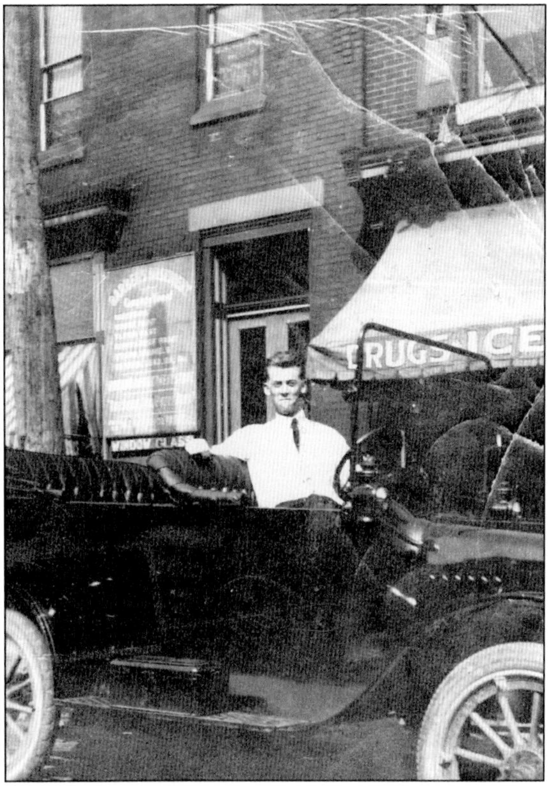

An unidentified Bridgeport resident poses with a late 1920s car outside a store. The sign on the wall reads Garber's Basement, and offers window glass. The sign on the awning reads Drugs, Ice. In 1930 Bridgeport had three drug stores, Atwood Yearkle on Dekalb Street, Green's Drug Store located on the 100 block of East Fourth Street, and Hurst Drug Store, then located at Dekalb and Third Streets. (Bridgeport Hall of Fame.)

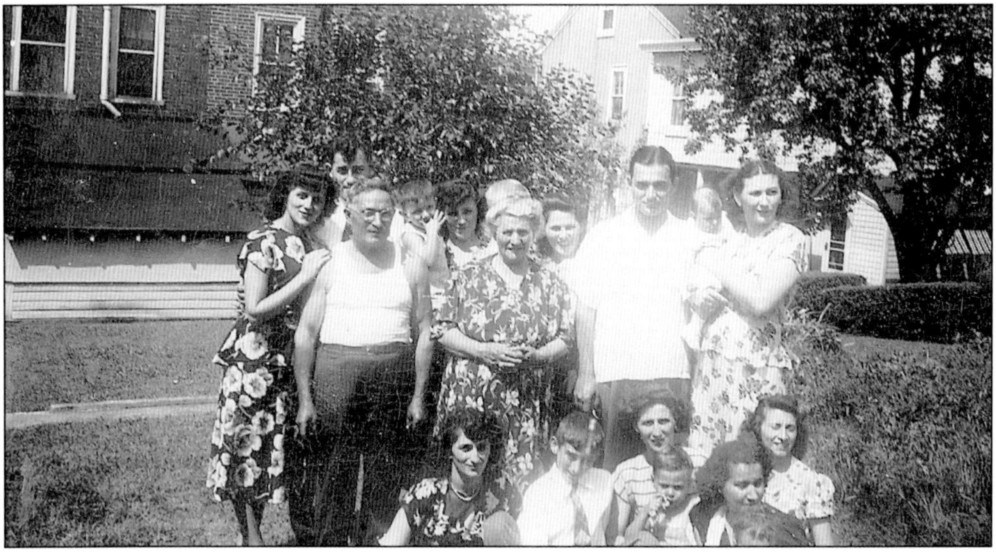

Family members of Gaetano and Maria Pizza, seen in the second row, second and third from left, enjoy a spring get-together in their backyard located on Grove Street. When this photograph was taken in 1949, America was enjoying a postwar spending and growing spree. The minimum wage was raised to 70¢ an hour, a new car from the factory cost on average $1,420, and a movie ticket at the Broadway Theatre jumped to 60¢. But keep in mind that it was still only 3¢ to mail a letter and the average rent was $70 per month. (Phil Johns.)

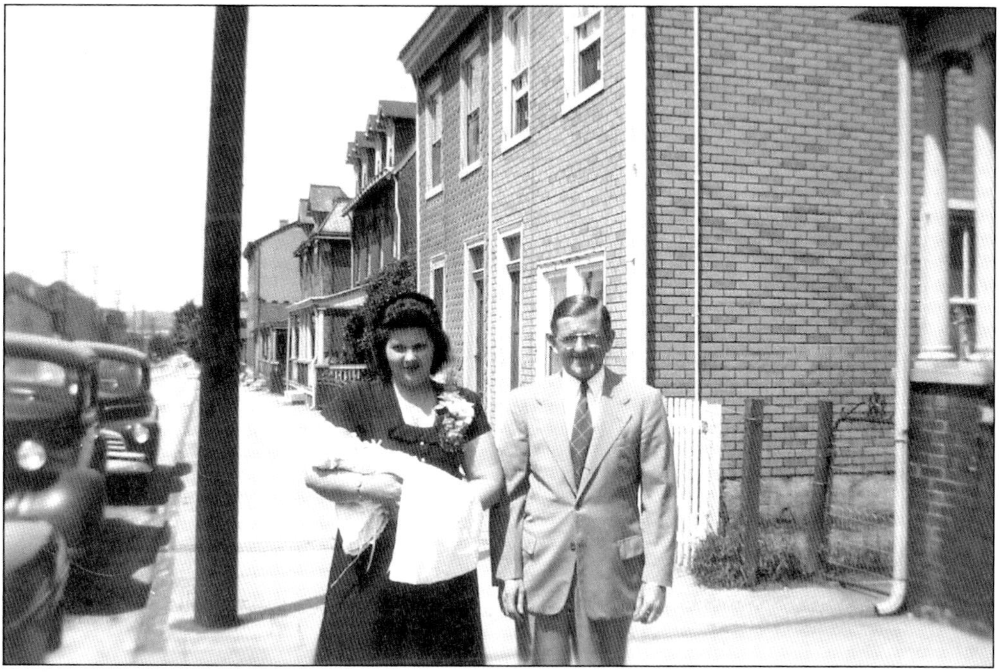

Sophie and Joseph Hasco hold the newborn daughter of their neighbors Earnest and Anna Pignoli. The baby, Ann Pignoli, was born in 1948 at a time when Bridgeport was a very prosperous borough following the war. Industry was up, and many new family-owned businesses were established in coming years, such as Iacovelli's Grocery Store, Danny's Diner (opened in 1944), and Nadwodny's Market (opened the year this photograph was taken). (Rocky Pignoli.)

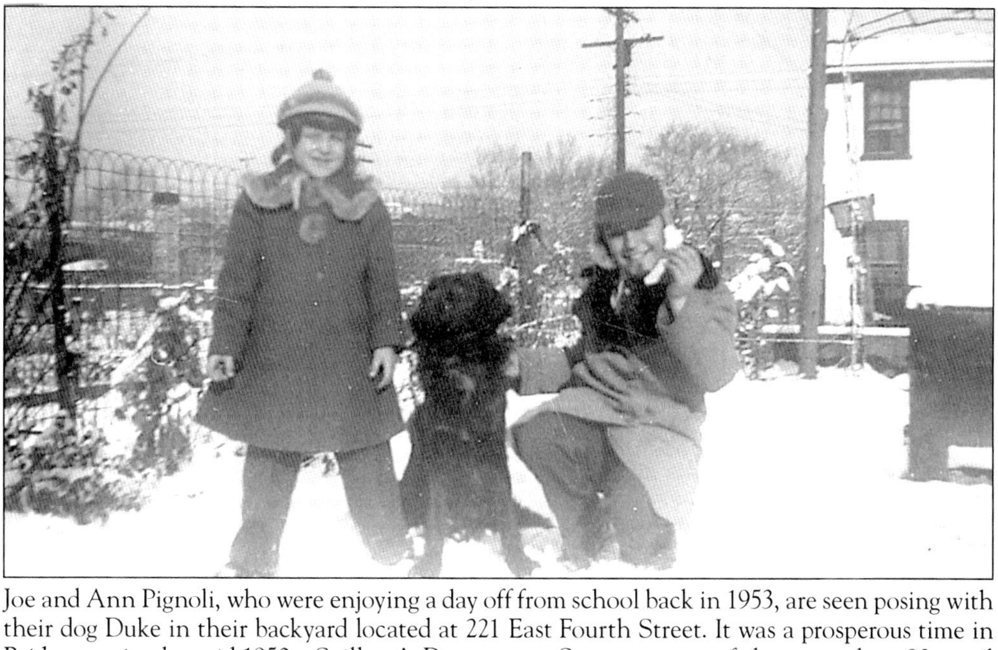

Joe and Ann Pignoli, who were enjoying a day off from school back in 1953, are seen posing with their dog Duke in their backyard located at 221 East Fourth Street. It was a prosperous time in Bridgeport in the mid-1950s; Spillane's Department Store was one of the more than 80 retail shops in the borough, and kids taking a day off from school in February 1953 could go to the movies and enjoy the premiere of Walt Disney's *Peter Pan*. (Rocky Pignoli.)

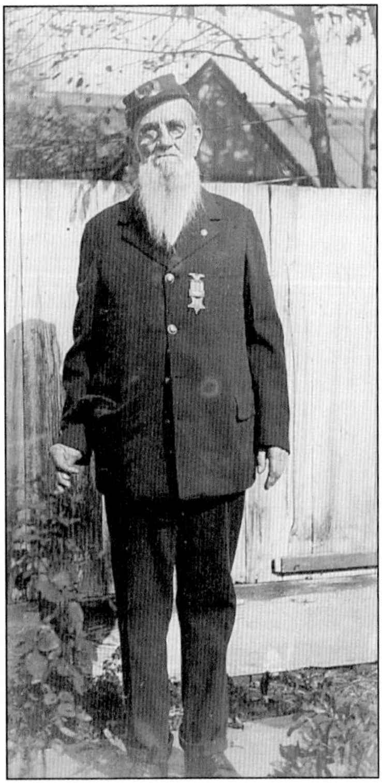

Sam Coats was one of the founding members of the Bridgeport Fire Company when it was formed back in 1891. Coats owned and operated Coats Hardware Store located at 130 West Fourth Street. Coats was a plumber and operated his business out of two old houses located at the site. Over the years Coats started stocking and selling anything related to hardware needs. In September 1922, Coats sold his business to Lloyd H. Daub. Within five years, Daub demolished the two old houses and built his hardware store that served Bridgeport until 1986. (Phil and Sharon Welsh collection.)

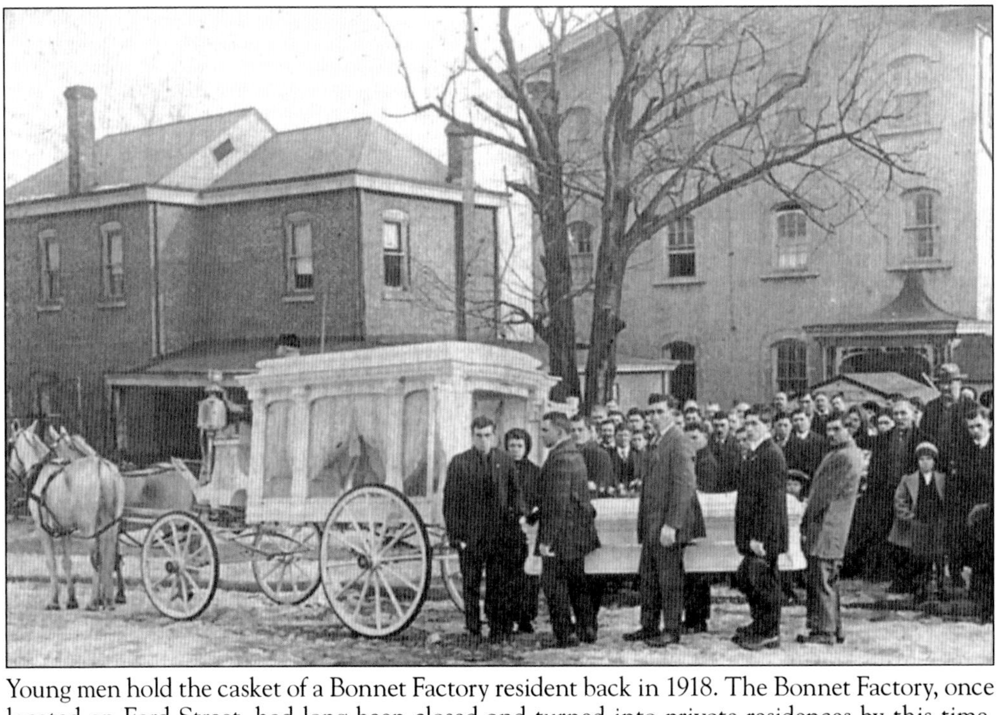

Young men hold the casket of a Bonnet Factory resident back in 1918. The Bonnet Factory, once located on Ford Street, had long been closed and turned into private residences by this time. The funeral procession photograph was taken on Union Avenue near Ford Street following church services. Notice the horse-pulled hearse and that Union Avenue was still a dirt road.

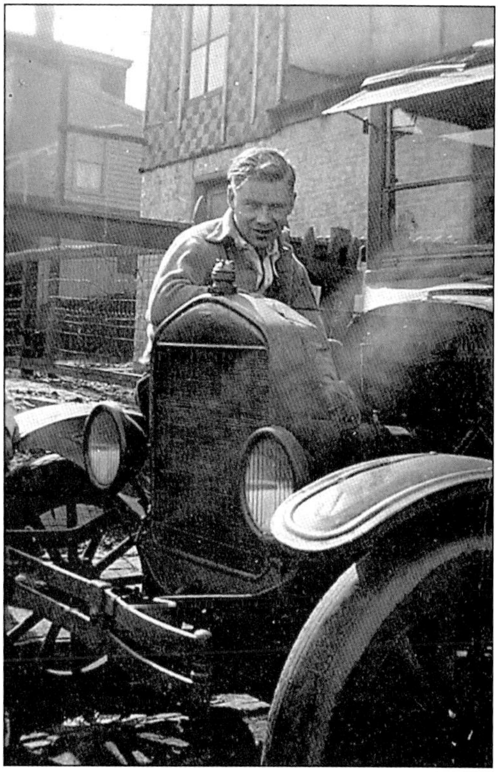

Alex "Ike" Hall is seen here with his car in the alley behind 449 Bush Street back in 1930. According to the 1930 census, Bridgeport had a population of 5,600 residents, with more available jobs than residents. Jobs came easy at James Lees, the C. B. Daring Company, I. F. March Company, A. H. March Packing Company, Protectus Paint Company, and dozens of others. As for Ike, in 1930, he had to contend with the fact that the borough was installing a traffic regulation sign at Fifth and Mill Streets following careful consideration by members of the police committee and other members of the town council. Below is Ike 36 years later in 1966 standing in front of his 1964 Chevy truck on the 400 block of Bush Street. (Alex Hall.)

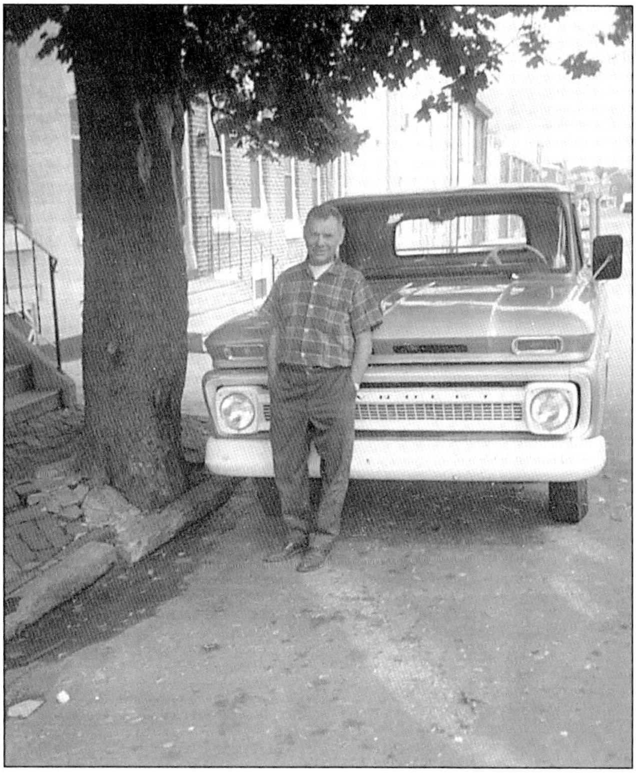

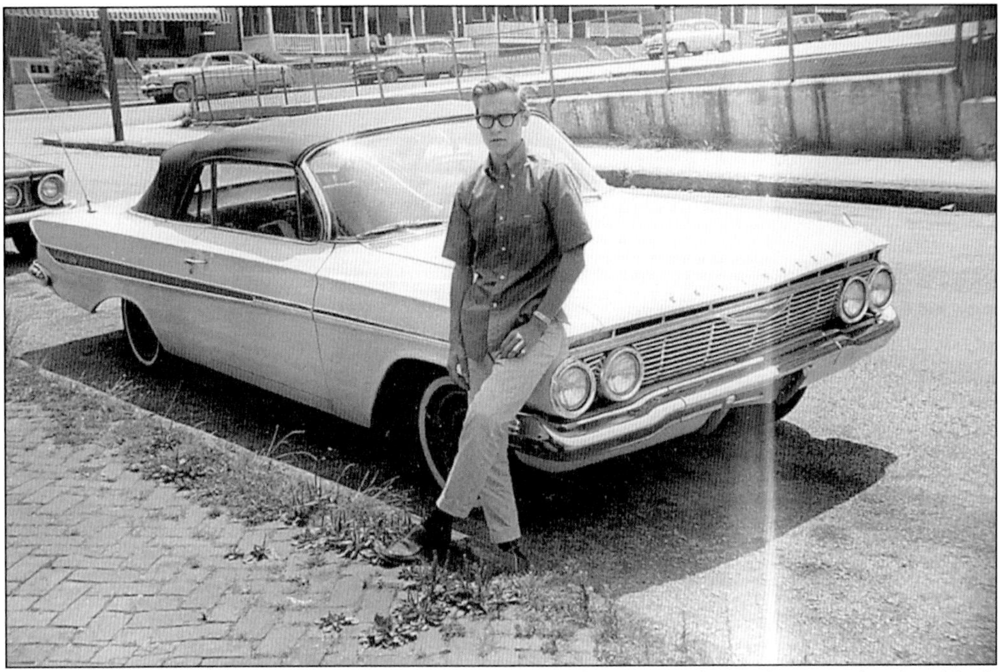

Penrose (Penny) Hall is seen leaning on the fender of his 1961 Chevy showing the 500 block of Bush Street in the background. In 1961, the average Bridgeport resident could expect to pay $2,800 for a new car and 27¢ for a gallon of gas. Bridgeport's economy was very healthy back in 1961 with nearly 80 retail establishments. (Alex Hall.)

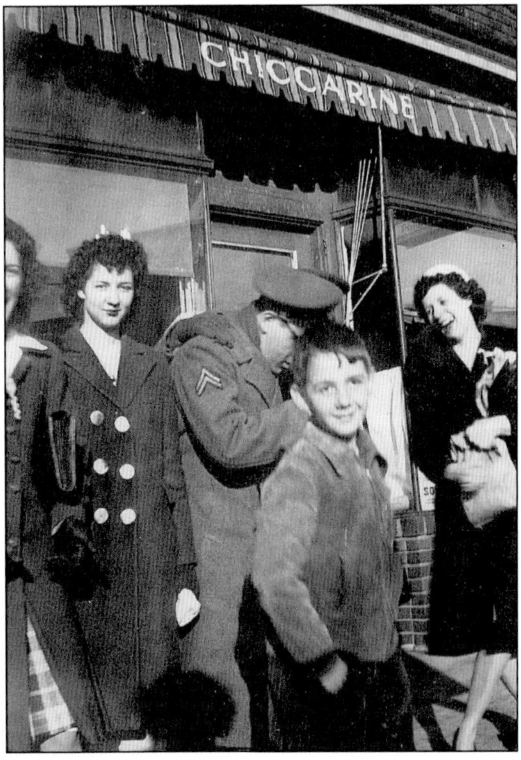

Soldiers returning home from World War II in the mid-1940s were always a welcome sight for Bridgeport residents, as was the occasion when Michael Cardamone, in the center of photograph, returned to friends and relatives standing outside Chiccarine's bar on Fourth Street. Included from left to right are Ann Chiccarine Cardamone, Millie Chiccarine Peroni, Michael Cardamone, Louis Chiccarine, and Rose Chiccarine Cicippo. (The Chiccarine family.)

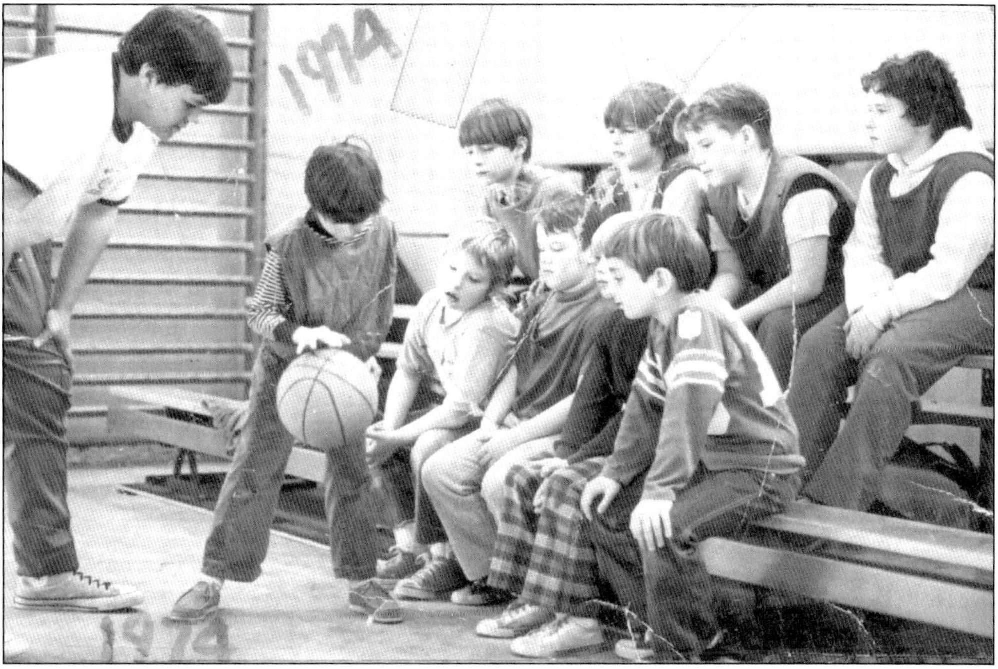

In Bridgeport every winter the winter recreation program begins for children in the borough. Events include basketball, tennis, and gymnasium programs for boys and girls. Several youngsters are seen in this photograph taken back in January 1974. From left to right are (first row) Ted Pruskowski, Brent Jones, James Rodenbaugh, and Nick Rotondo Jr.; (second row) Tim Kobrzynski, Michael Milke, Terry Jones, and George Bickert. David Santoro, on the left, was a recreation aide and watches Darren Schantz dribbling a basketball. (Bridgeport Hall of Fame.)

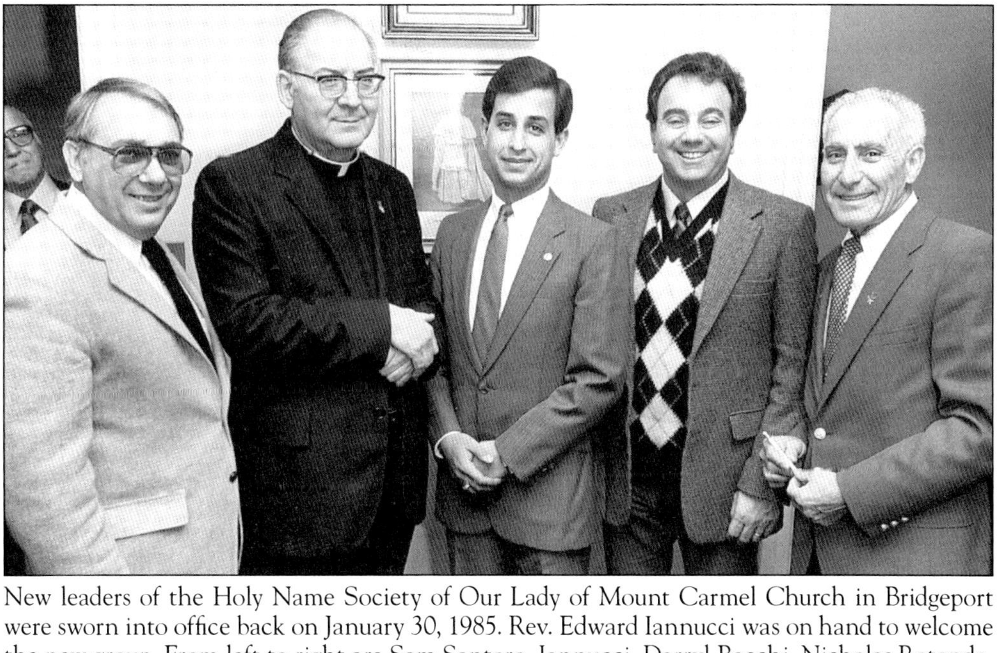

New leaders of the Holy Name Society of Our Lady of Mount Carmel Church in Bridgeport were sworn into office back on January 30, 1985. Rev. Edward Iannucci was on hand to welcome the new group. From left to right are Sam Santoro, Iannucci, Darryl Bacchi, Nicholas Rotondo, and Paul Angelilli.

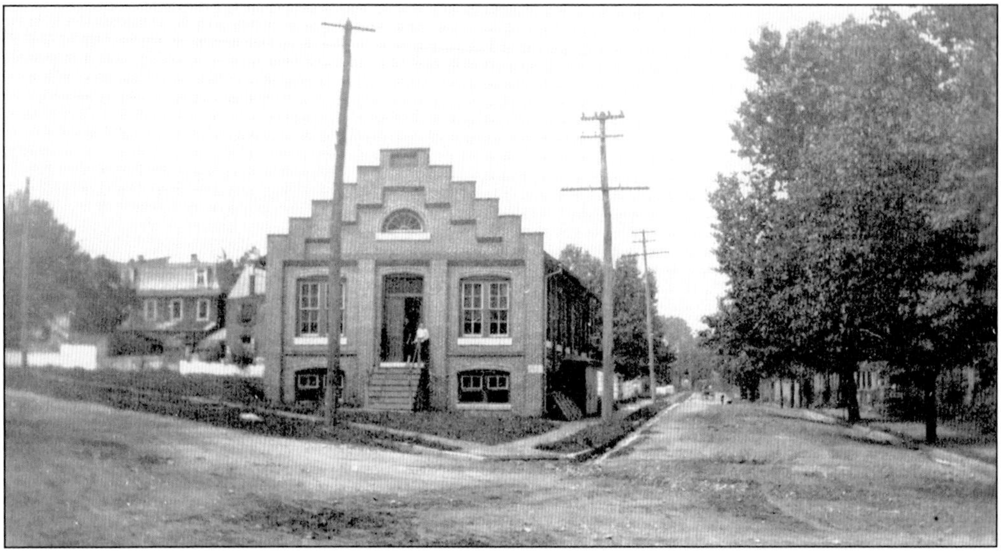

St. Augustine's Parish Hall located across the street from the church was built in 1911 by the St. Augustine's Temperance Society. The property once owned by the borough of Bridgeport was purchased by Arthur Kane for the sum of $100 in 1910, Kane later deeded the land to the temperance society for the purpose of constructing a building. This was a very popular place to be over the years as it has served as a dance hall, Boy Scout meeting hall, minstrel show hall, and in 1918, Bridgeport's only hospital. In recent years the building has been called Parish Hall, or St. Monica's Hall, but the hall built by the temperance society will always be known as Temperance Hall.

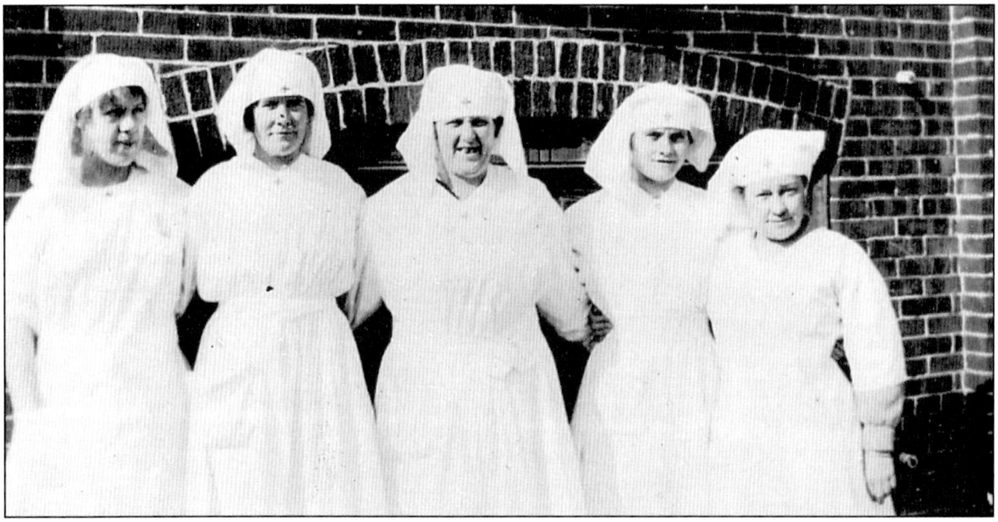

In October 1918, an epidemic of influenza raged throughout the community, there were 1,400 cases of influenza or pneumonia, one-third the population of Bridgeport was reported. Temperance Hall was set up as a hospital and from October 12 to November 1, 1918, 41 patients were cared for, with 11 fatalities. The flu of 1918 became a deadly epidemic throughout the country. Nurses from St. Augustine's Parish who helped the Red Cross Auxiliary No. 138 of Bridgeport are seen posing outside Temperance Hall in 1918. The nurses who risk their own lives to treat patients included, from left to right, Barbara Locke, Catherine Lawless, Elizabeth Cameron, Rose Finneran, and Ann Finneran.

Nine

SPORTS

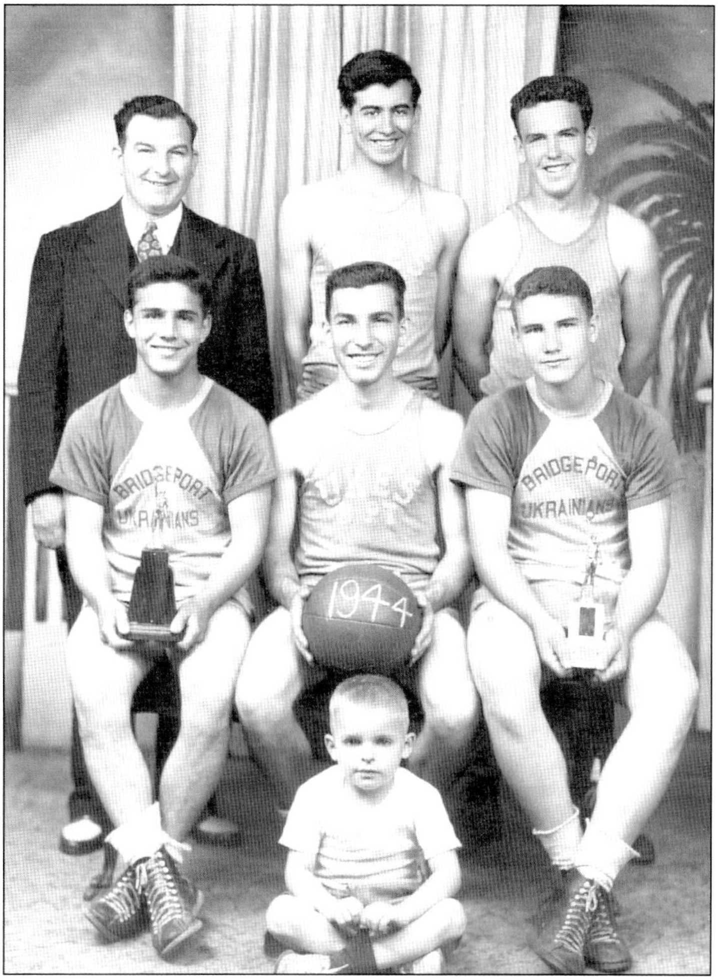

The Bridgeport Ukrainian basketball team of 1944 played in the Bridgeport Church League that included teams from other area churches. While baseball, football, and basketball dominated the borough's interest in sports, James Lees Carpets won a number of championships in the greater Montgomery County Soccer League, and Bridgeport residents were bowling in league competition following World War II. Other clubs and organizations like the Triple S Club of the St. Salvatore Society and the Triple C Club from Our Mother of Sorrows Parish competed in different sports as well. (Bridgeport Hall of Fame.)

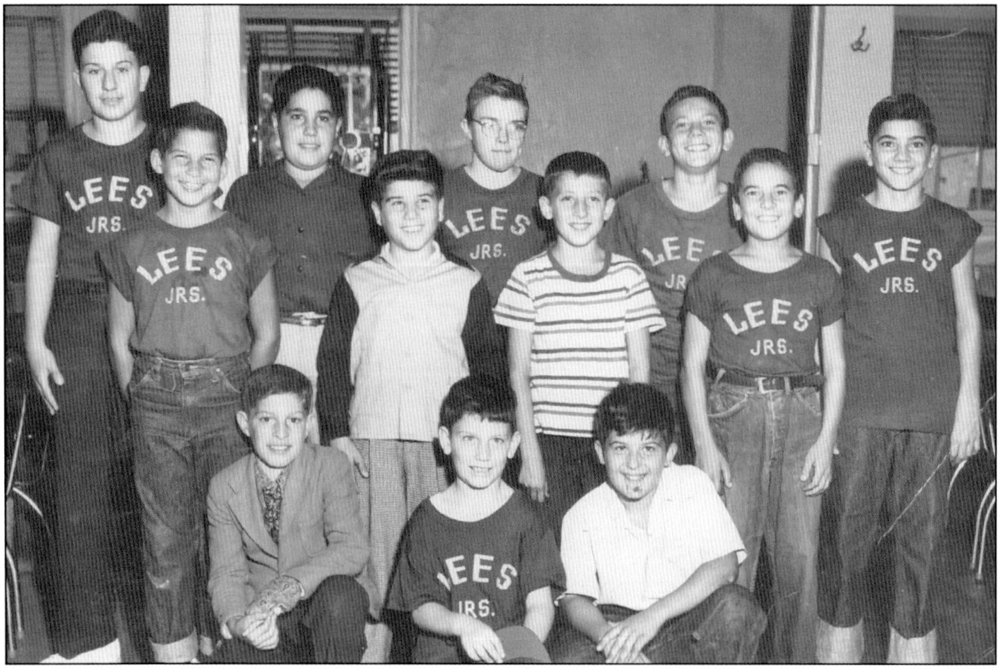

Members of the Lees Carpets junior baseball team pose for a team photograph back in 1951. The squad was part of the Bridgeport Recreation summer morning baseball league. Members of the team, from left to right, included (first row) Vince Iacovino, Jesse Frangiosa, and Al Pastino; (second row) Rick Falcone, Jim Vernase, Carmen DeStefano, and Sal Rotondo; (third row) Len Frangiosa, Mike Capaldo, Jim Keeley, Anthony DeStefano, and Nick Rotondo. Absent from the photograph was Sal Bello. (Bridgeport Hall of Fame.)

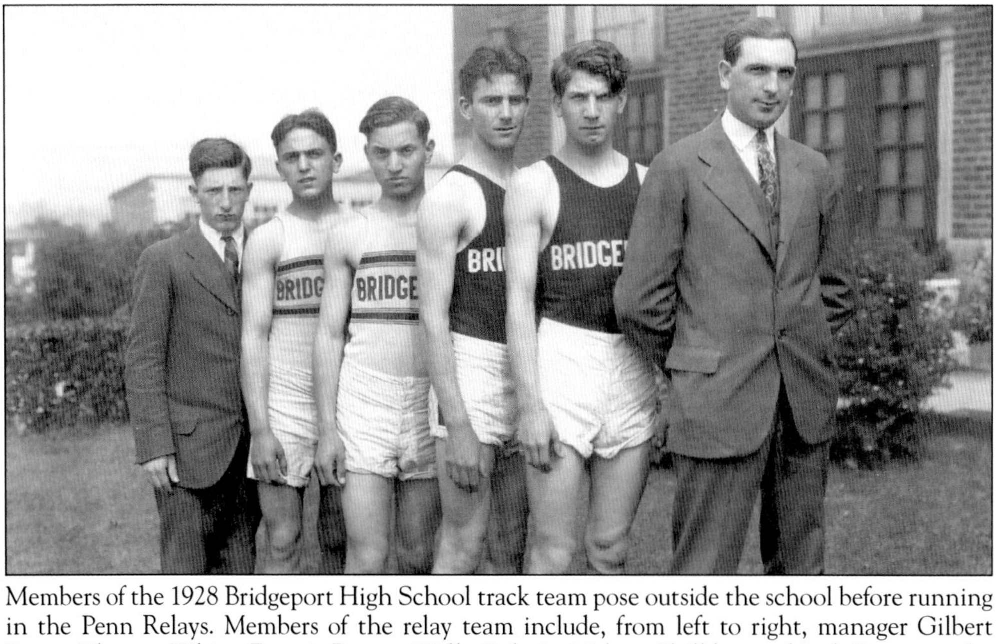

Members of the 1928 Bridgeport High School track team pose outside the school before running in the Penn Relays. Members of the relay team include, from left to right, manager Gilbert Fusco, Thomas White, Francis Bruno, Wally Dalosio, Nelson Shillday, and Jack Brennan, the track team coach and athletic director for the high school. (Bridgeport Hall of Fame.)

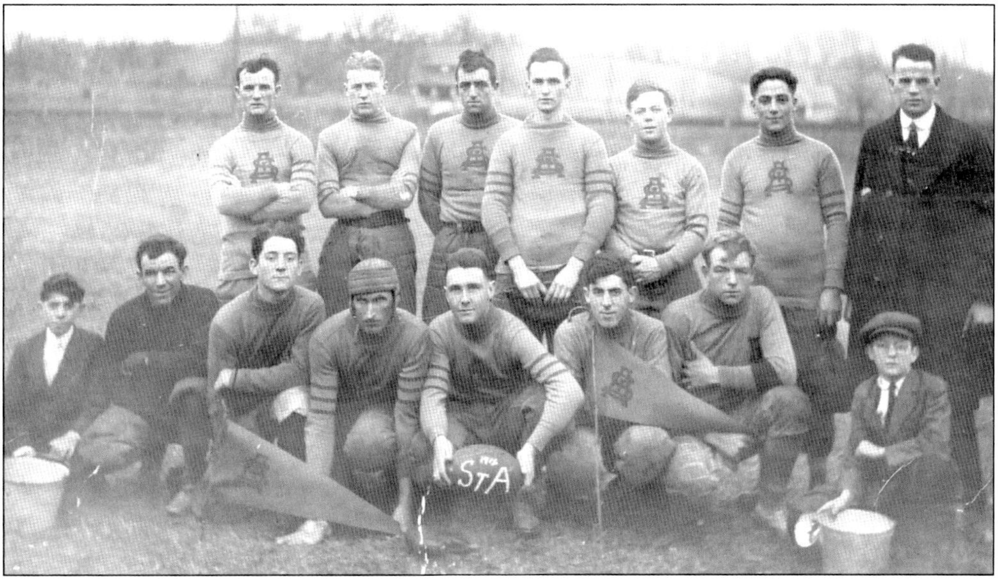

St. Augustine's football team of 1912 was one of many professional and semiprofessional teams playing in the area back in the early part of the century. These semiprofessional teams were mostly made up of clubs, churches, or areas, including Swedesburg, Conshohocken, Norristown, and Phoenixville. St. Augustine's won a league championship back in 1928, and the St. Augustine Juniors won a championship in 1929, defeating Mount Carmel 18-6. Although Charley DiNolfi ran for a 95-yard touchdown at the Dekalb Terrace Field, it was not enough as Morris, Kane, and Bilella all scored for the winners. (Bridgeport Hall of Fame.)

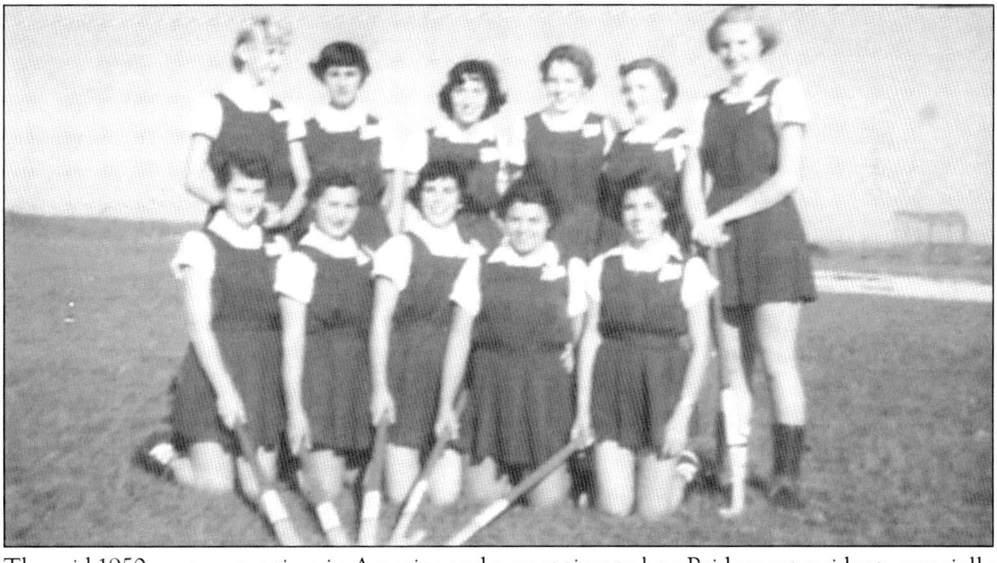

The mid-1950s was a great time in America and a great time to be a Bridgeport resident, especially a high school resident. In 1954, when this photograph was taken of the Bridgeport High School field hockey team, construction began on Disneyland out in California, and high school kids knew all about the World of Walt Disney. If one was lucky enough to own a television in 1954, one would have seen the first episode of the *Davy Crockett* television series. The music of the teenagers back in 1954 included "Mr. Sandman" by the Chordettes, "Sh-Boom" by the Crew Cuts, and "I Need You Now" by Eddie Fisher.

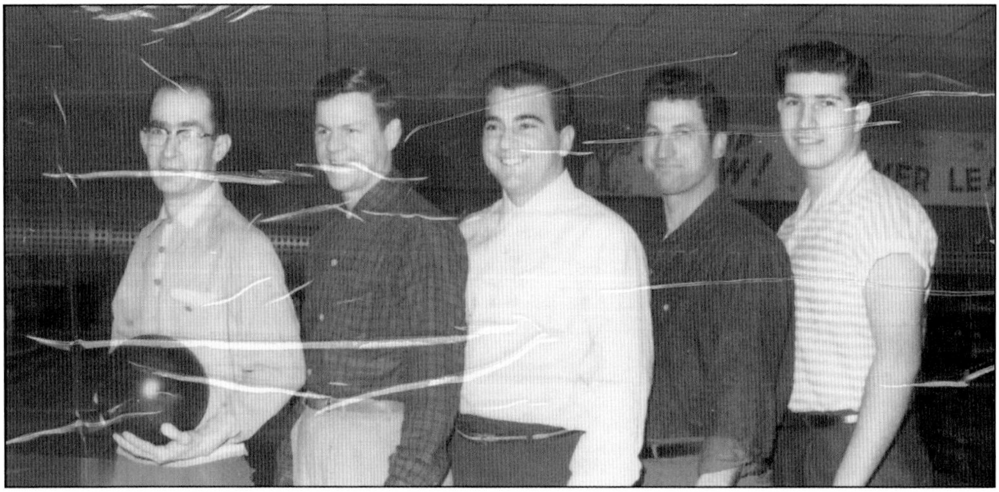

The Our Lady of Mount Carmel bowling team from 1960 competed at the King of Prussia Bowling Lanes, once located in the Valley Forge Shopping Center. Posing from left to right are Morris Amato, Lenny Bennett, Nick "Chief" Rotondo, Ralph Bruno, and Joe Mastercola. The King of Prussia Bowling Lanes have long since closed. Interesting enough, 1960 was the year that the Bridgeport Bowling Lanes opened a 10-lane bowling alley on Fourth Street, the facility has also long been closed and is currently Advent Electric.

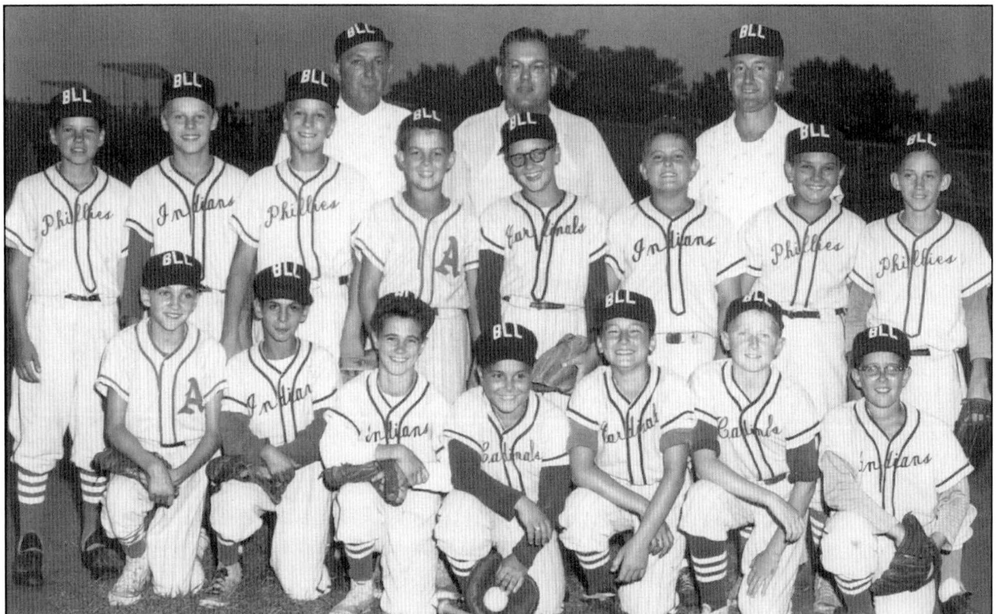

The 1950s was a great time in Bridgeport if one liked sports. The Bridgeport High School always had games going on, there were church leagues, club leagues, bowling leagues, and independent leagues. And in the heat of the summer there was Little League baseball. In 1958, this group of all-star Bridgeport Little Leaguers posed for a team picture that included, from left to right, (first row) John Colucci, Augustus Dieciedur, Rodger Rhoads, Charles DiSanto, Stan Branco, Ed Ocelus, and Ralph Pelusi; (second row) Paul Hansell, Ken Nadwodny, Ed Rakowski, Michael Nailon, Joe DiFilippo, Carl Nadwodny, Joe Cygal, and Jesse Sohoski; (third row) Ed Kobrynski, Stan Nadwodny, and Warren Eisenberger.

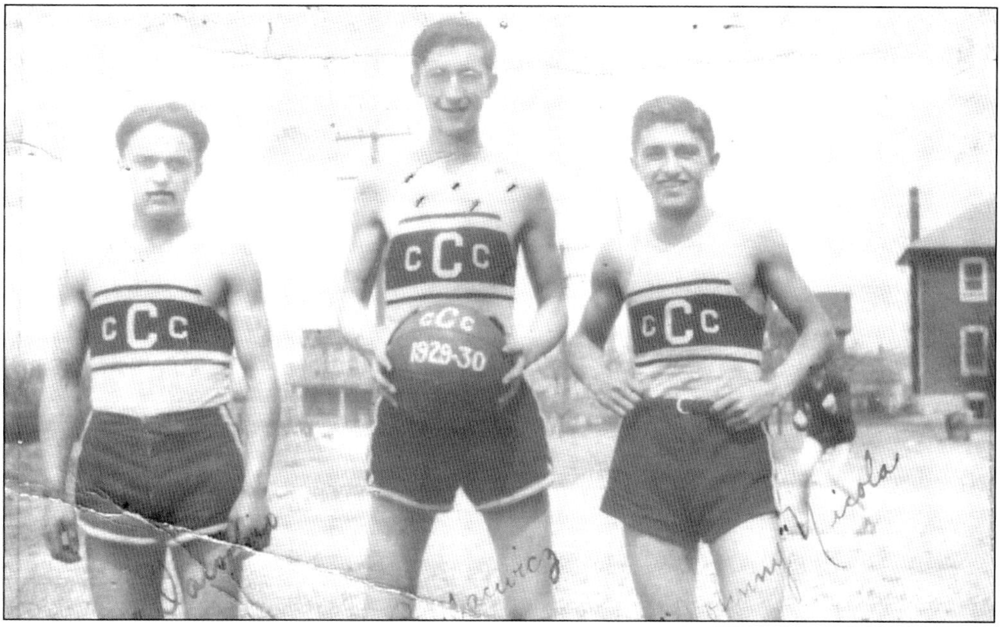

The borough of Bridgeport was a thriving mecca for sports of all kinds back in the 1920s and 1930s. Basketball leagues were plenty, and players would meet at the Good Will Fire Company "Band Box" or at James Lees and Sons Company cafeteria to play their games. One such team was the Triple "C" squad, of Our Mother of Sorrows Parish. The photograph above shows leading scorers of the team from 1930, including, from left to right, Wally Daloisio, Pete Bulawicz, and Johnny Nicola. The threesome averaged 14 points per game, with Bulawicz scoring 340 points in 40 games. While 14 points per game might not sound like many by today's standards, keep in mind that many final scores back in the 1920s and 1930s would look like 25-21 or 28-25. The photograph below shows the Triple "C" team of 1930–1931. (Bridgeport Hall of Fame.)

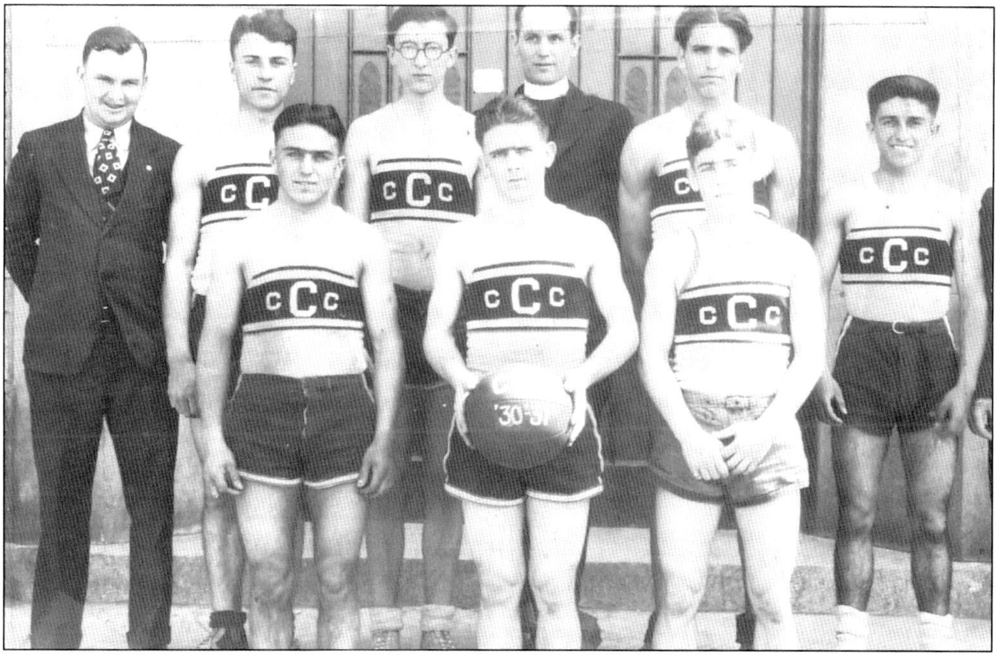

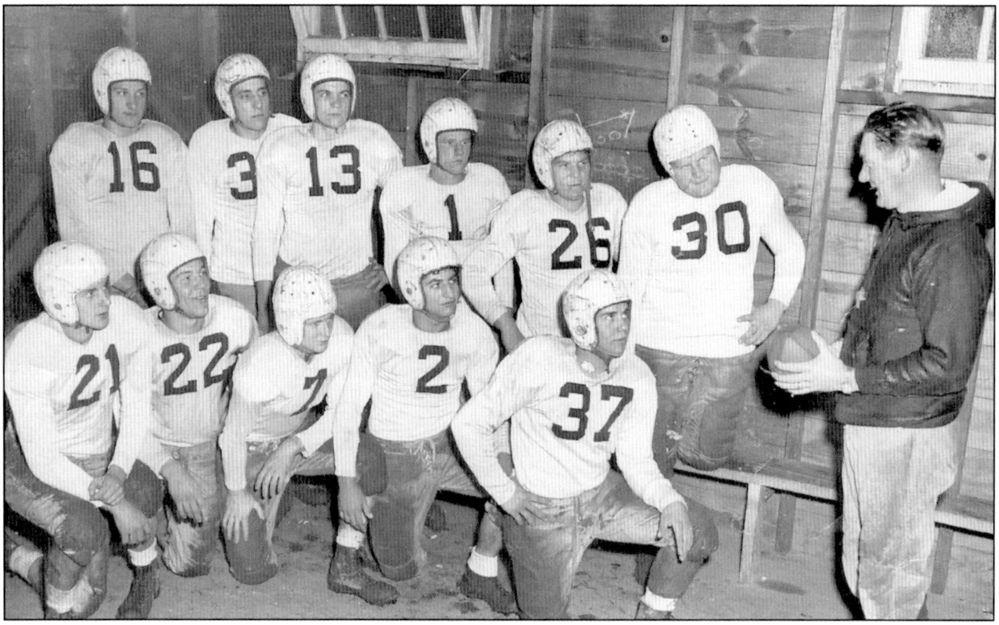

Seniors on the 1948 football squad for Bridgeport High School included, from left to right, (first row) Nick Borzillo, Steve Barzowski, Jim Pastorius, Ralph Ross, and John DeSanto; (second row) Dan Valerio, Dom Battaglio, Michael Valerio, Philip McKenna, Joe Biscotti, and John Biscotti, as head coach Ted Kershner looks on. (Bridgeport Hall of Fame.)

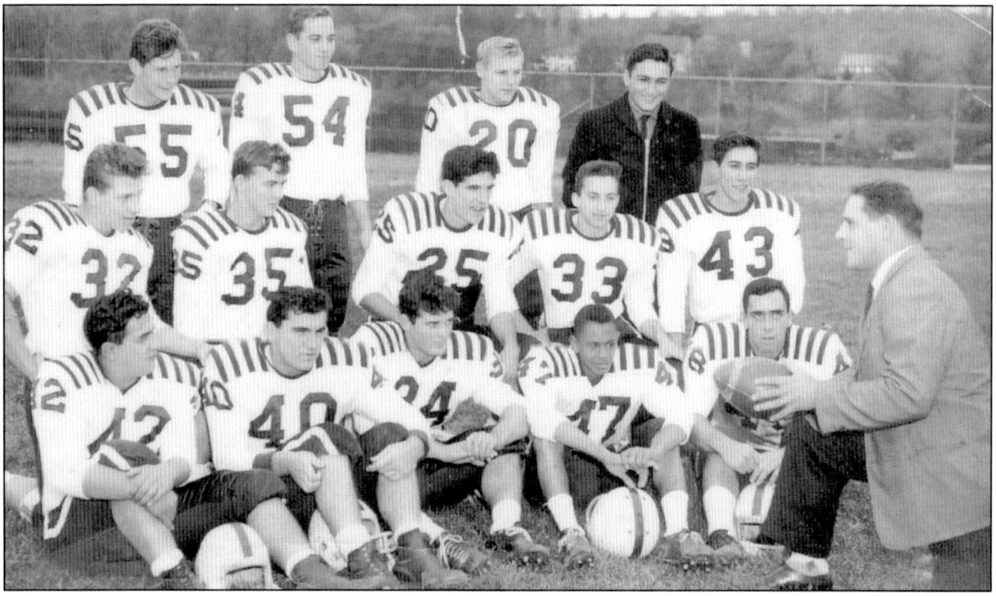

By the fall of 1962, Bridgeport High School started to see a decline in students but the high school sports teams were as competitive as ever. Senior football players relax during a practice to listen to coach Anthony Chiccino, on the far right. Senior members of the team included, from left to right, (first row) Ed Villanova, Bob Brady, Ron Pascucci, Ronald Drakeford, and Bill Bale; (second row) Chet Pietluck, Mike Nailon, Mike Puscar, Tom Debiaso, and Anthony DiDesidero; (third row) Leonard Gorski, Phil Pishock, Ken Nadwondy, and Anthony DiSanto. (Bridgeport Hall of Fame.)

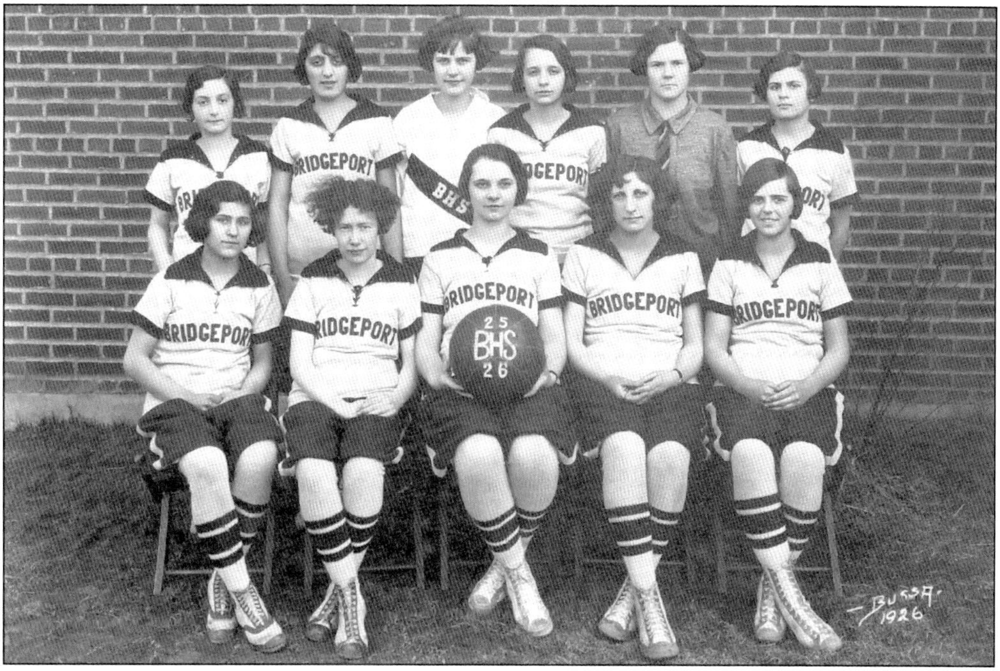

When Bridgeport built a new high school at Seventh and Ford Streets back in 1924, the school's sports programs started to expand outside baseball and football. Part of that expansion included female sports, and Bridgeport quickly introduced girls' basketball. In the fall of 1925, Bridgeport fielded its first girls team, seen in the photograph above. A year later the team claimed a championship, and while the records are not clear, it may very well have been the school's very first championship. That championship team of 1926–1927 can be seen in the photograph below. Notice the high-top running shoes, as they were called then, and the full-length stockings required as part of the uniforms back in the 1920s. (Bridgeport Hall of Fame.)

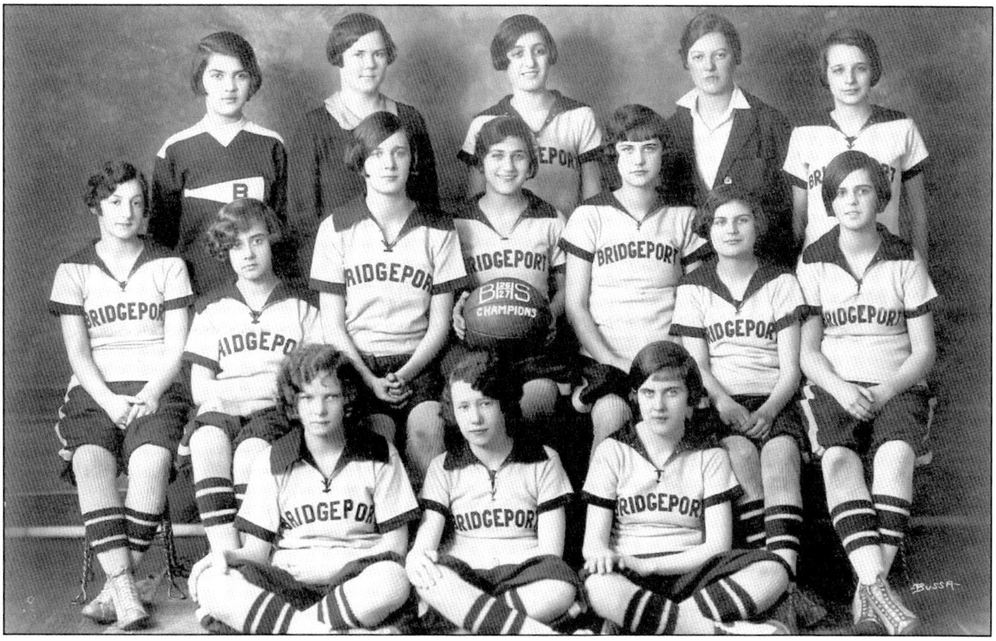

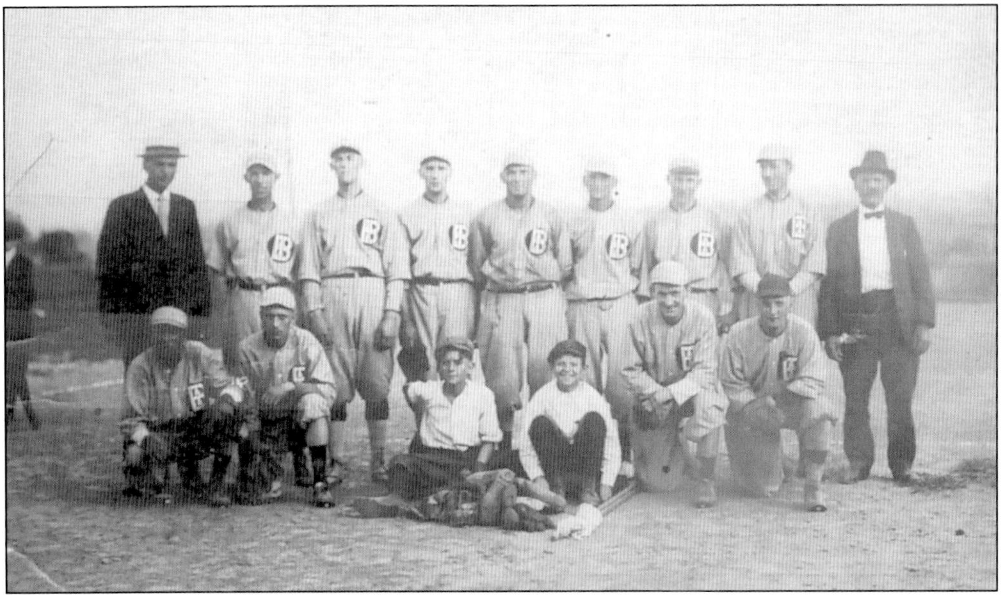

This is one of Bridgeport's many independent baseball teams from the early part of last century. From 1900 through the 1940s, Bridgeport had many independent and semiprofessional teams. These teams would play their games at Toll Gates field just south of the King Manor section of Upper Merion Township. These games in the early part of the 20th century would sometimes draw more than 1,000 spectators on a Sunday afternoon.

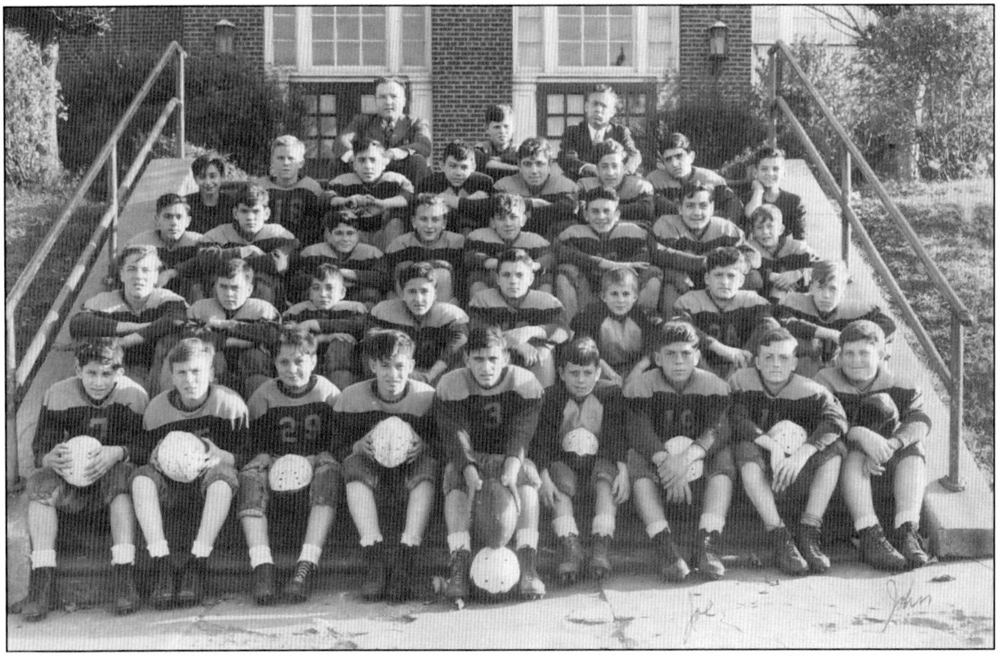

Members of the 1945 Bridgeport Junior High School football team playing for coaches Andrew Octtovario and Edward Luther in no particular order included John Biscotti, Sal Paciello, Dom Battaglio, Doug McCoy, Phil McKenna, Nick Borzillo, John DiSantis, Mickey Valenio, Joe Biscotti, Albert Donofrio, Water Gensick, John Klocko, and Angelo Borzillo, just to name a few. (Bridgeport Hall of Fame.)

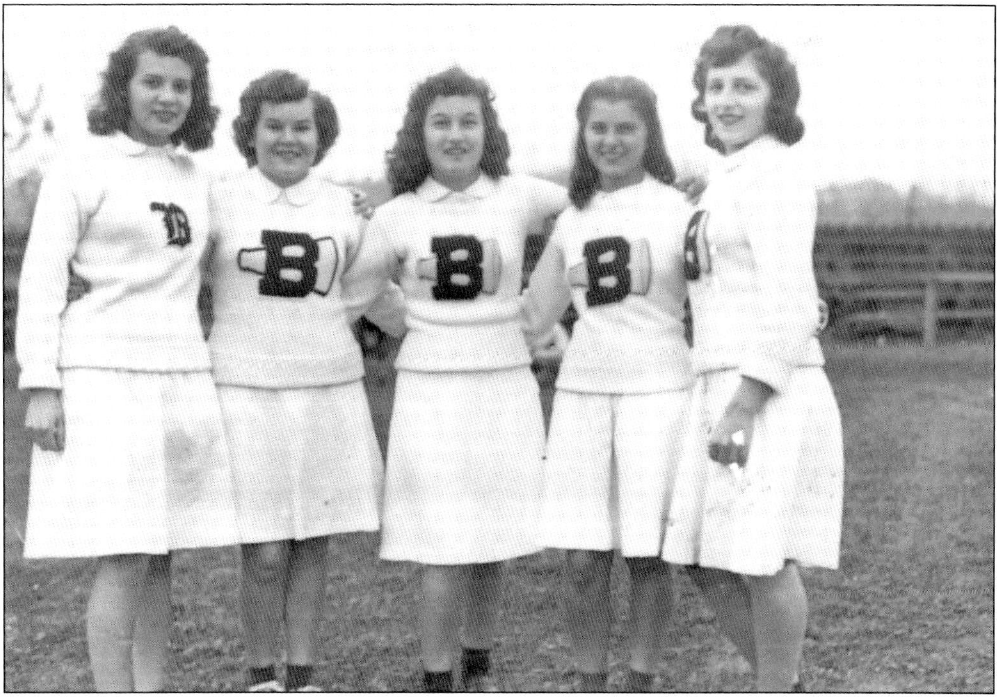

Bridgeport High School played its first football game back in 1930, also the first year cheerleaders appeared in uniform for the Dragons. Over the next 36 years, cheerleaders supported most of the high school events. While uniforms style and colors changed over the years, the spirit and enthusiasm of the school was always represented by the cheerleaders.

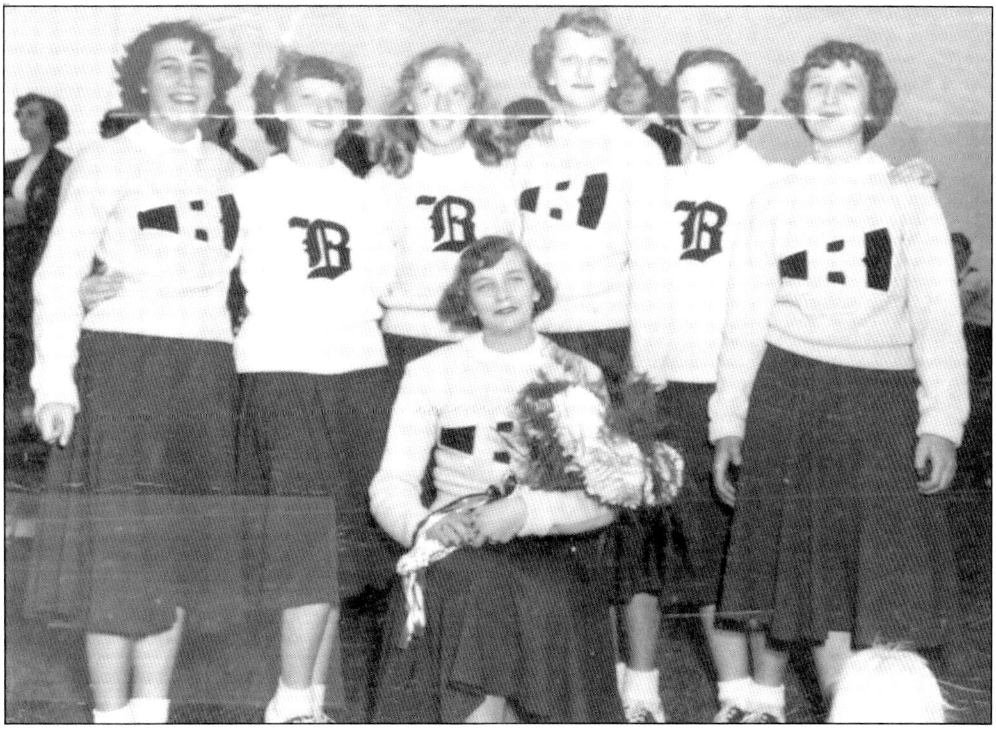

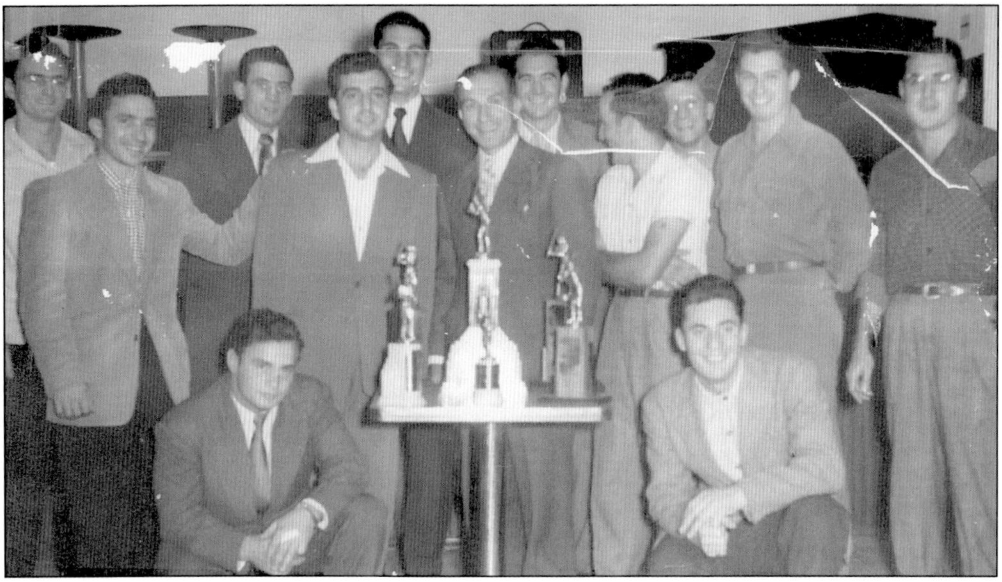

The Triple S Club of the St. Salvatore Society located on Holstein Street has long been affiliated with sports in the community. Fielding mostly softball teams over the years, the Triple S Club has won a tremendous amount of championships. In 1947, the baseball team celebrated another one of its championships. From left to right are (first row) Anthony "Spud" Della Pietro and Mike DeStefano; (second row) Richard Ritrovato, Anthony "Paynie" Diotisalvi, Joe DeStefano, Jim Fabrizio, Carmen Falcone, Tony Borzillo, Joe DeFusco, Frank Romano, Larry DeStefano, Jack Gambone, and Charley Ritrovato. (Bridgeport Hall of Fame.)

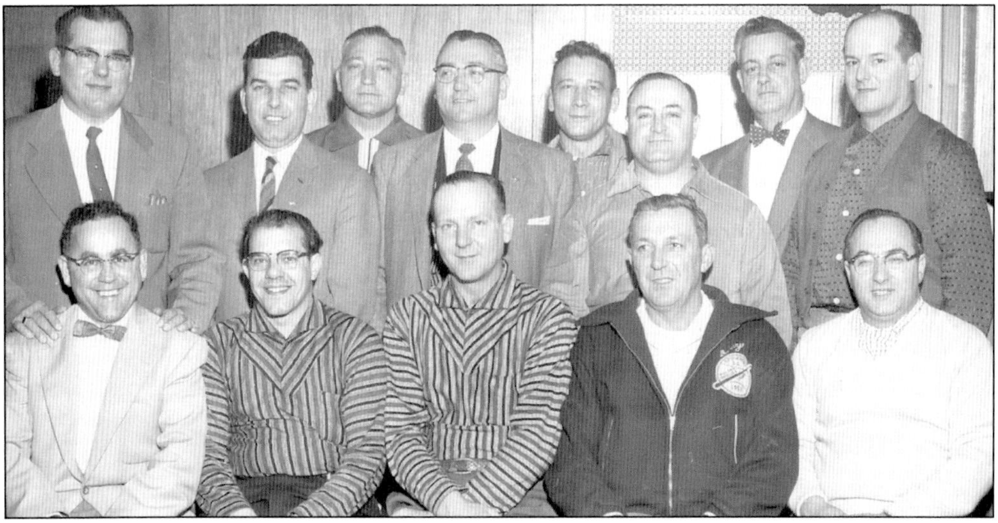

Managers and officers of the Bridgeport Little League gathered at the 1958 Little League banquet for a team photograph include, from left to right, (first row) Nick Pagano, Michael Cilio, Henry Nadwodny, Ed Kobrynski, and Sam Storti; (second row) Stan Nadwodny, George Homa, John DiFillippo, Alex DiFillippo, Joseph Cygal, Anthony Bearoff, Paul Hansell, and Stephen Nadwodny. In 1958, Bridgeport Little League had four teams playing with 15 boys on a team. No females played Little League baseball in the 1950s or 1960s, it was not until June 30, 1974, 40 years after Little League Baseball, Inc., was established, that they announced that females were permitted to play Little League baseball.

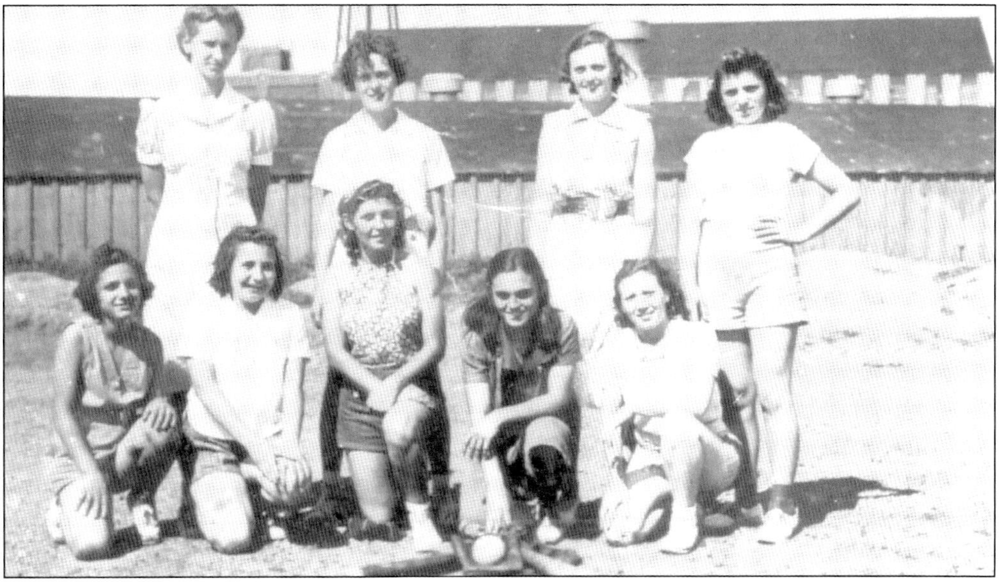

In the summer of 1943, the All-American Girls Professional Baseball League was founded to entertain baseball when most of the major-league baseball players were off to fight in World War II. The girls league played from 1943 to 1954 and inspired girls baseball teams across the country. Bridgeport had its own version of the All-American Girls Professional Baseball League when girls from the Fraley and Hurst Streets area known as the Chinatown Girls formed a team to play other area teams. Posing for the Chinatown team with the James Lees Mill in the background are, from left to right, (first row) Rita Storti, Elizabeth Carlino, Sophie O'Bare, Della Ritrovato, and Miss Dragone; (second row) Helen Makoid, Yolanda DiGiacomo, Elizabeth Kelly, and Mary Storti. (Triple S.)

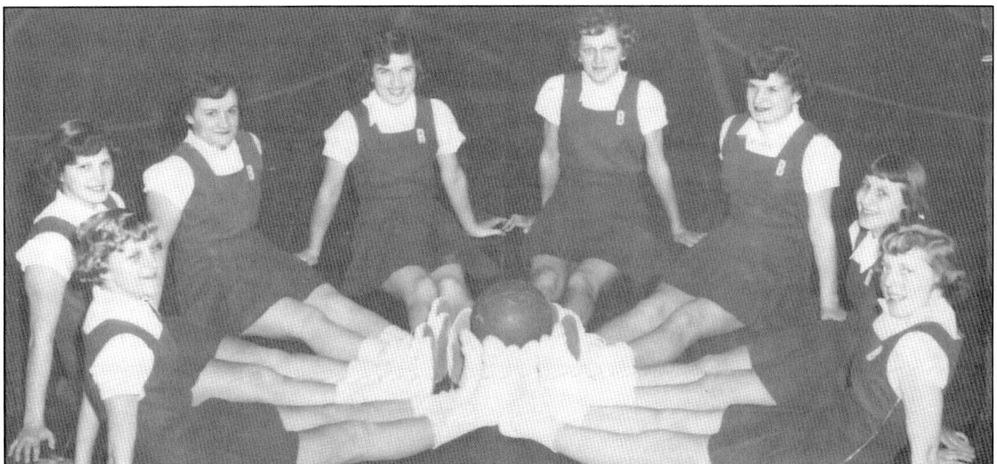

Bridgeport High School fielded some pretty good female teams in its more than 40 years of competing, but none were as perfect as the 1952 girls' basketball team. The lady hoopsters recorded a perfect 8-0 season, scoring 50 points three times that season and recording their closest victory over Norristown 43-41. The team included Mary Sokol, June Phillippy, Gloria Almeida, Vera Roberto, Kass Sokol, Tina Santoro, Louise Carfagno, and Pat Klus. In 1952, Bridgeport High School graduated 43 students, including five members of the undefeated girls' basketball team. (Bridgeport Hall of Fame.)

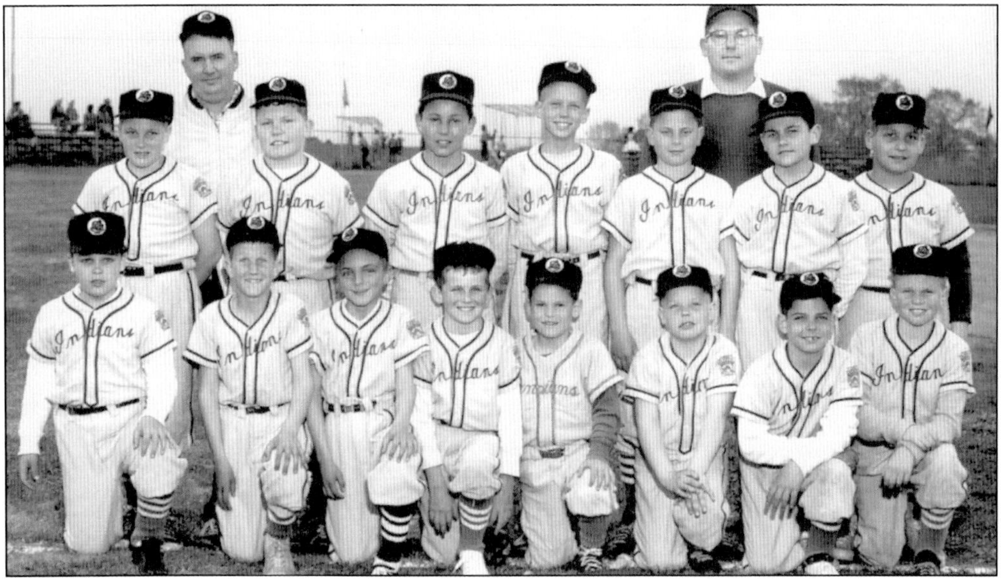

In 1961, the Indians Little League team sponsored by Coats-Wafer Post No. 840 was one of five Little League teams playing in Bridgeport at the time. Stan Nadwodny was the team's manager, and John Brady was the assistant manager. In 1961, it was reported that Little Leaguers Michael Maslayak and Joe Fabrizio of the Cardinals, Noah Jeffers of the A's, and David Nawodny of the Indains each hit grand-slam home runs. The last Little League grand slam happened three years earlier when Ken Nawodny, David's older brother, hit one for the Indians as well. (Bridgeport Hall of Fame.)

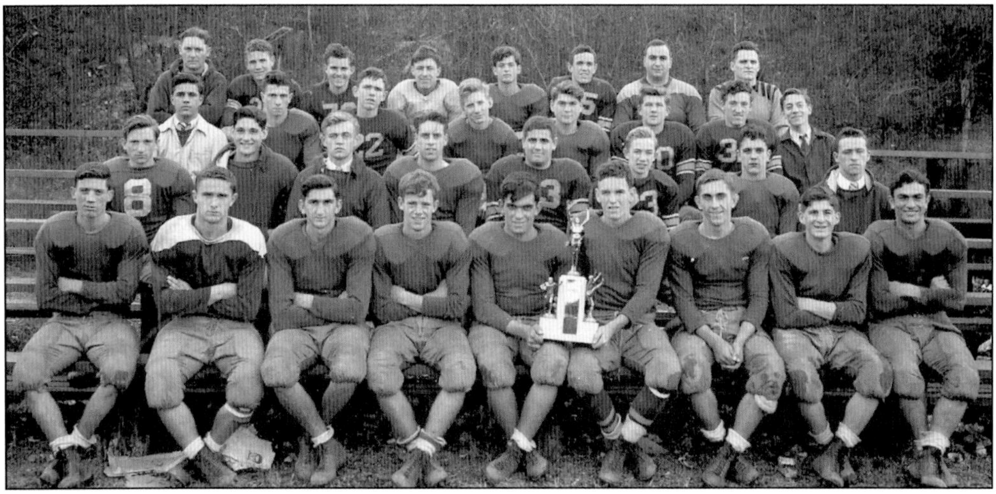

A banquet was held at the old Bungalow Inn to honor the players of the Bridgeport High School 1944 undefeated football team. All members of the team were awarded sweaters for their outstanding 9-0 season, and Tony Manilla was named to the all-state team. From left to right are (first row) Joe DeStefano, John Moletsky, Carmen Rupert, Al Wagner, John Polumbo, Frank Brady, Stan Makowski, Nick Rossi, and Charley Giambrone; (second row) Lou Piantone, Carmen Falcone, Henry Henning, Palmer Price, Lou Carfagno, Leonard Lizak, Gene Daloisio, and Tony Manilla; (third row) Raino Perone, Bill Hetrick, John Bolger, John Keller, Sam Santoro, Bill Gallagher, Frank DeFusco, and Alan Berkowitz; (fourth row) coach Ted Kershner, Joe Mardi, Jack McKenna, Nick Mattiola, Rudy DeStefano, Gerry Brady, Howard Michener, and assistant coach Harry Spangler.

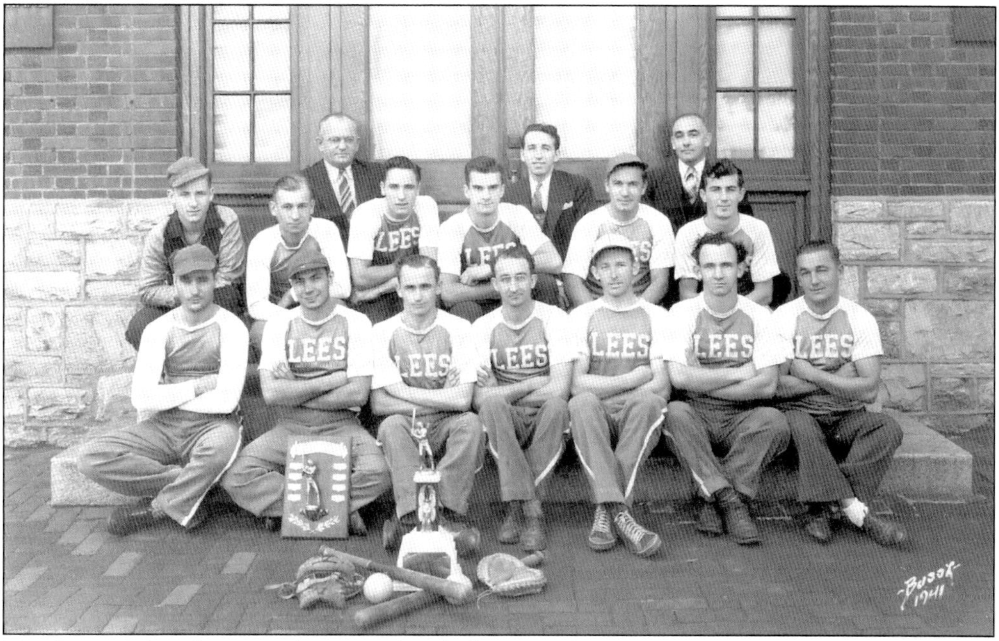

Members of the championship Lees baseball team of 1941 pose for a team photograph with company executives shortly after celebrating their undefeated season. James Lees Carpet Mill was founded in 1846 and operated in Bridgeport for more than 100 years. Ever since the early part of the 20th century, Lees baseball, soccer, bowling, and basketball teams were a major part of Bridgeport industrial leagues. (Bridgeport Hall of Fame.)

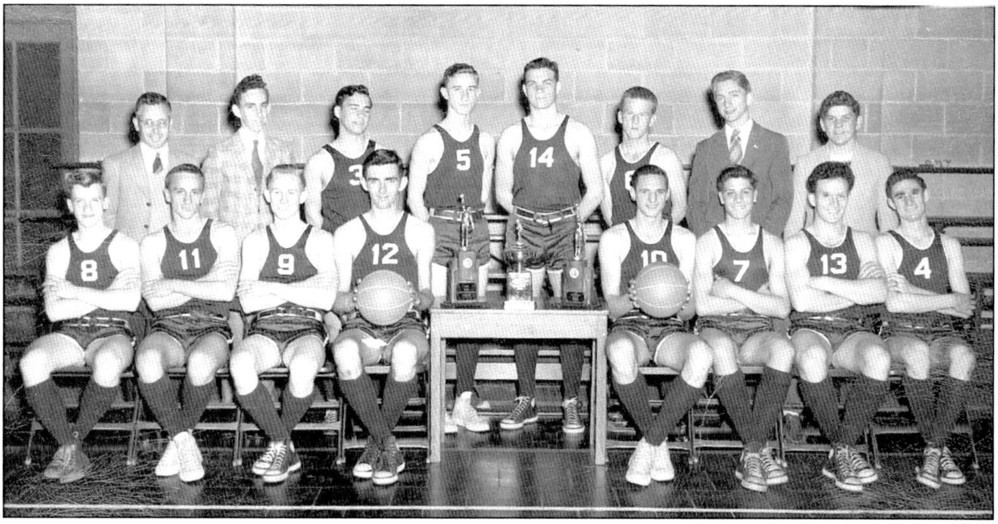

The Bridgeport High School boys' basketball team of 1947–1948 posted 19 victories with just eight setbacks to claim the Pennsylvania Class "B" State Championship. It took a couple of close playoff victories to gain the trophy, including a 39-36 victory over Prospect Park in the District 1 playoff and a nail-biting 43-41 win over Weatherly in the Pennsylvania Interscholastic Athletic Association playoffs. From left to right are (first row) Tom Nowicki, John Kudoba, Harry Lawton, Jim Burns, Norm Phillippy, Carmen Picard, Frank Picariello, and Dan DeStefano; (second row) coach Andy Otaviano, Steve Gober, John DiSanto, George Mardi, Mickey Valerio, Phil McKenna, Vincent Tancredi, and John Biscotte.

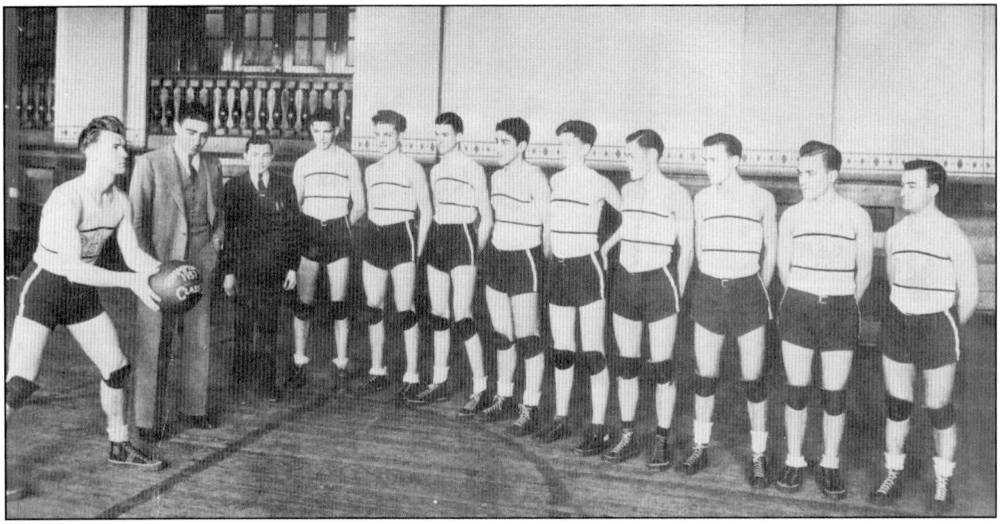

Members of the 1936–1937 boys' class "B" championship basketball team line up for a team photograph in the school gymnasium. Members of the team include, from left to right, Mike Bucha, coach Joe Daher, Ted Adams, Charlie Differ, J. Krawchuk, Mike Bellack, Vince Daher, Gene O'Hara, Jim Rath, Walt Gadzicki, Tony Palombo, and Kissy Cuomo. In 1937, the basketball players, along with the other 300 students attending Bridgeport High School, undoubtedly hung out on lower Dekalb Street where one could find McKernan's Saloon (not that any students would be drinking) or at Anthony Gambino's Billiard Room, John Kinnane Auto Dealership, Otis Rhoads Motorcycle Dealership, James Demetris Lunch Room, or the Broadway Theatre, all of which could be found on the 100 block of Dekalb Street in 1937. (Bridgeport Hall of Fame.)

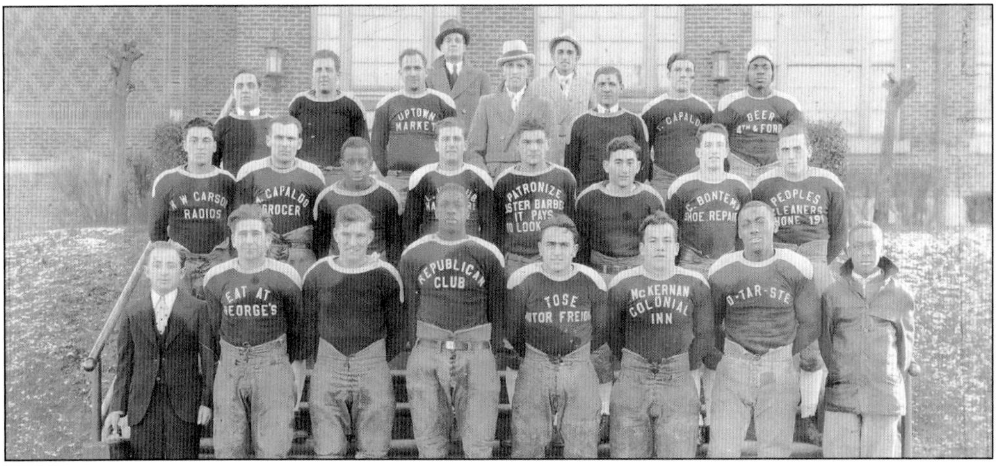

The Bridgeport Athletic Association (BAA) was one of many organizations or clubs that organized a sports team back in the 1920s through the 1950s. In 1933, the BAA recorded four victories, all were shutouts. The Bridgeport 11 also suffered four setbacks, including a one-point loss to Conshohocken. The team also played to a couple of scoreless ties with Conshohocken and Phoenixville. From left to right are (first row) Kayo DeMarco, Dom Porrecca, Joe Donohue, Bob Young, Wally Dalasio, Rabbits Barbaretta, Sylvester Young, and Joe Young; (second row) Sal Branco, Leo Logue, Charley McPherson, John Carfagno, Charley Biscotte, Footy Palmiero, Paul Fusco, and Mike Piermatteo; (third row) Lou Desimone, Tom Chondorain, Mike Santillo, Tony Benedetto, John DeSimone, Nick Salamone, and Guy Young; (fourth row) coach Ben Scirica and Johnny Nicola Sr.

Ten

IN RECENT YEARS

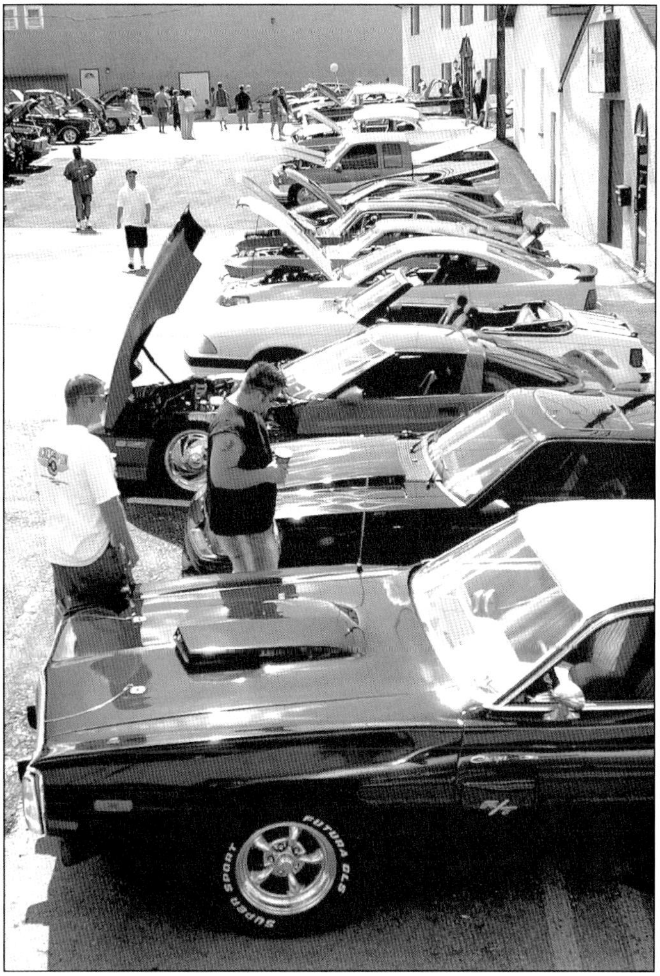

Bridgeport today is a borough of proud residents who continue to work together with programs that bring the community together, such as the classic car show, which started in 2003 and is sponsored by Delliponti's Automotive. Cars were lined up at the 2006 show, a show that now draws more than 200 cars from surrounding communities. (John Berry.)

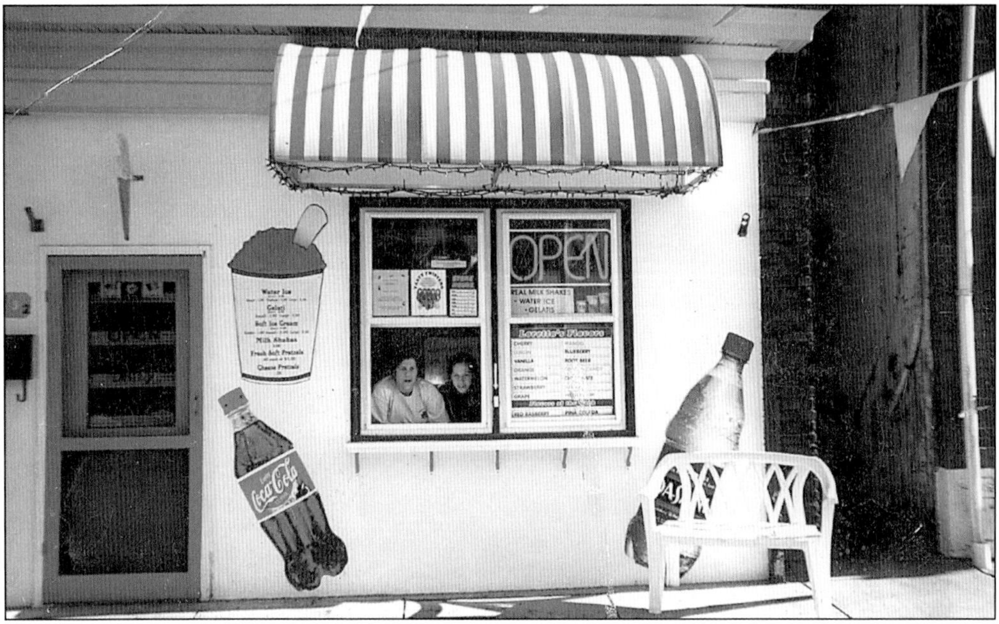

Bridgeport residents would line up at Loretta's Water Ice, once located at 134 West Fourth Street in Bridgeport, to cool off on those hot summer nights. The store was located in the Daub's Building for a number of years before owner Loretta Steffy moved the operation to bigger quarters in Conshohocken. The store is currently Los Arcos Mexican Store. Notice Loretta on the left, and her daughter Nicole peeking out the window.

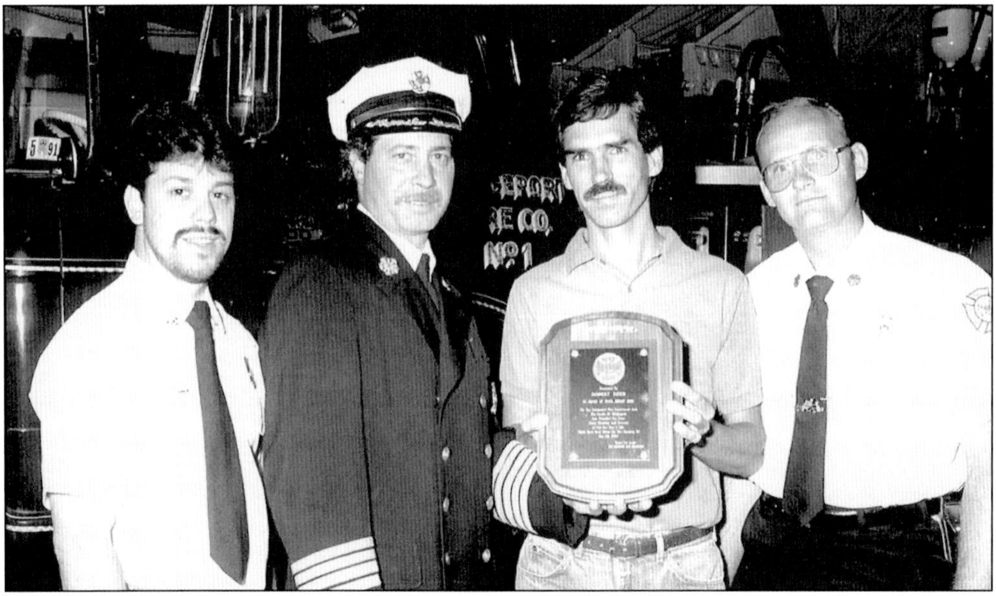

Members of the Bridgeport Fire Company present Robert Reed, a member of the George Clay Fire Company of West Conshohocken, with a plaque thanking him for his efforts along with the members of the Bridgeport squad for rescuing a woman. Members in the photograph, from left to right, include Bridgeport firefighters Steve Wanczyk, Goodwill fire chief; Joe Tomchick, department chief; Reed; and Ken Frymoyer, Bridgeport Fire Company No. 1 chief. (Bridgeport Fire Company No. 1.)

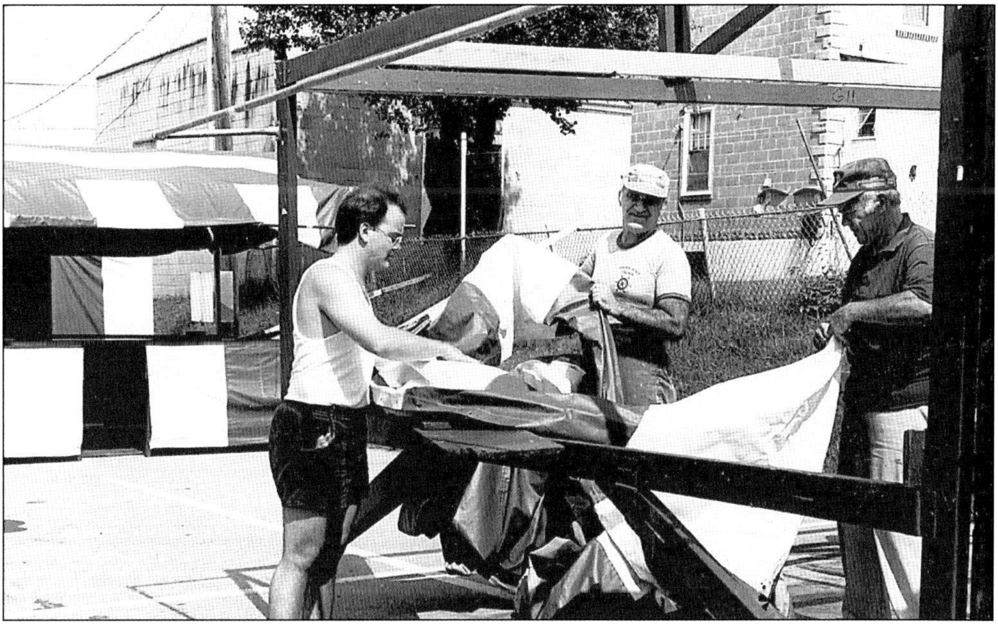

Setting up for the 63rd annual feast of Our Lady of Mount Carmel are, from left to right, Anthony Santoro, Tony Natalina, and Franny Coscia. The three men were preparing booths for the 1987 feast, a ritual that has thrived in Bridgeport for more than 80 years. The tradition in Bridgeport celebrates the feast day of its patron saint with a weekend of food, games, and music that always climaxes on a Sunday with a street procession, which attracts thousands of residents and visitors. (Our Lady of Mount Carmel Church.)

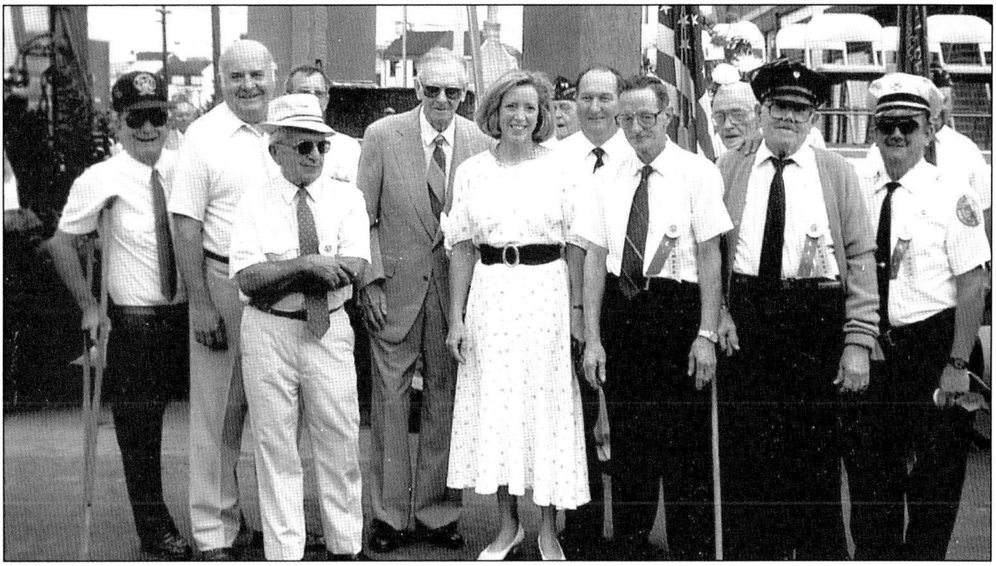

Officials gathered to celebrate Bridgeport Fire Company No. 1's centennial celebration back in 1991. Bridgeport only had 2,500 residents back in 1891 when more than 80 interested residents gathered at Sam Coats Hardware Store to form the fire company. Standing in for the celebration photograph, from left to right, are Corney Philips, Pete Grisinski, John Nicola, unidentified, Bob McCracken, Pennsylvania state representative Ellen A. Harley, unidentified, John Stanzak, Joe Fryday, John Cresco, Mike Getzik, Lester Siders, and unidentified. (Bridgeport Fire Company.)

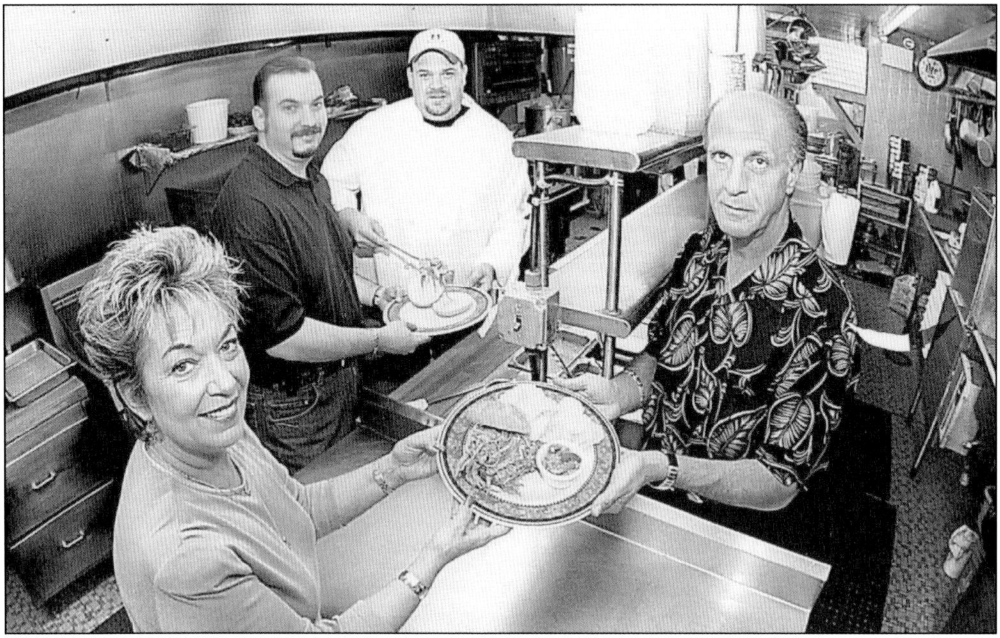

Members of the Gallo family, owners of Anthony's Tavern located at Fourth and Grove Streets in Bridgeport, show off one of their award-winning dishes. Anthony's Tavern was formerly the Friendship Grille, founded in 1933 by Joseph Granese, and a staple in the borough for more than 70 years. The name changed in July 1998 when Frank, on the far right, purchased the business with his wife, Marilyn (left), and their two sons Keith (second from left) and Frank Jr. (Anthony's Tavern.)

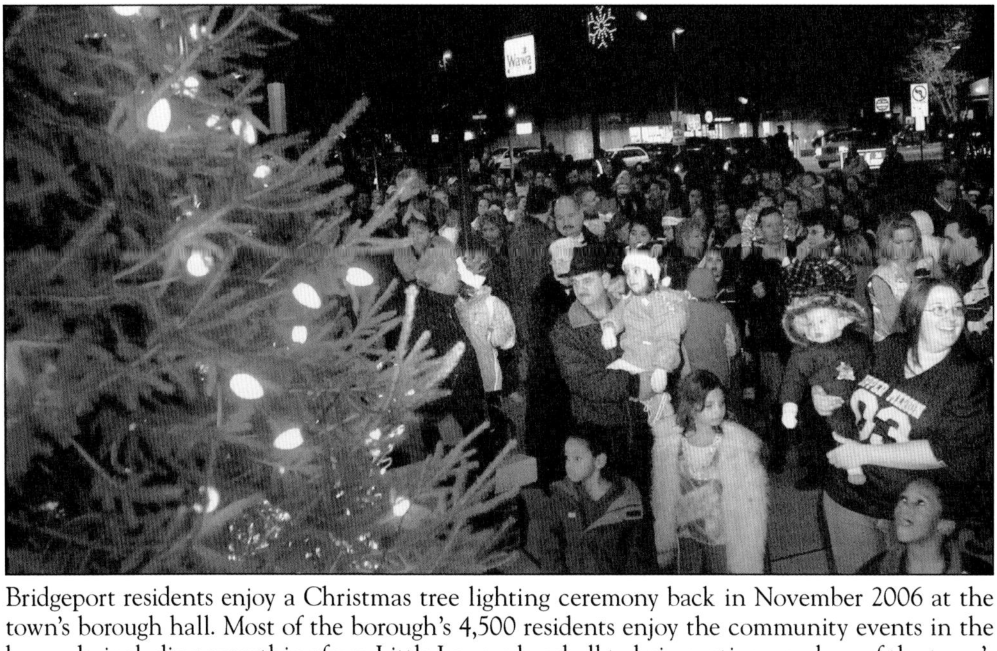

Bridgeport residents enjoy a Christmas tree lighting ceremony back in November 2006 at the town's borough hall. Most of the borough's 4,500 residents enjoy the community events in the borough, including everything from Little League baseball to being active members of the town's two fire companies. The same spirit is shared among residents as when the founding fathers incorporated the borough back in 1851. (John Berry.)

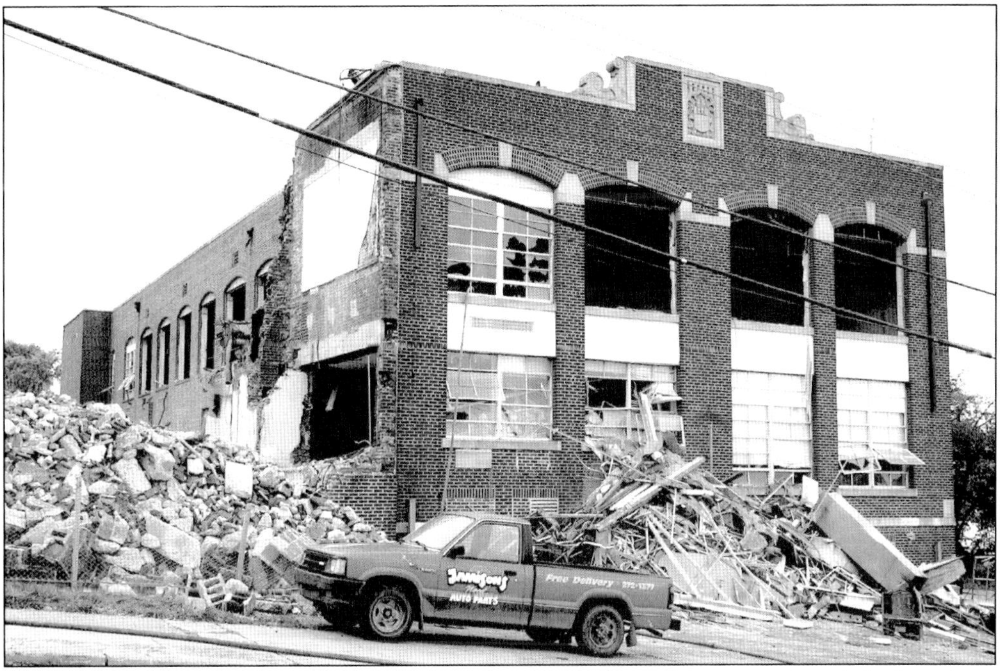

In November 2001, Bridgeport High School located on Ford Street was demolished, making way for 30 townhouses. Bridgeport High School was established in 1893, and 73 years later in the fall of 1966, Bridgeport High School merged with students in Upper Merion Township. The Pennsylvania legislature passed Act 299 in August 1963, mandating the merger of Bridgeport, West Conshohocken, and Upper Merion Township into one new district, taking effect in the fall of 1966. The high school was opened in 1924 and had 44 graduating classes before it became an elementary school. The final graduating class had 34 graduates. (Gene Walsh.)

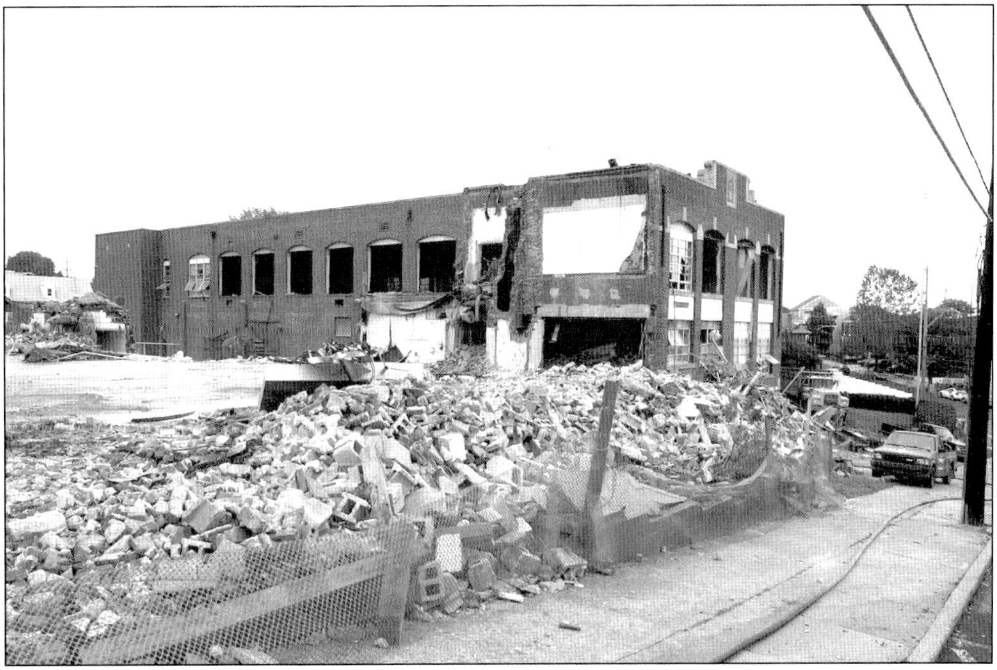

ACROSS AMERICA, PEOPLE ARE DISCOVERING SOMETHING WONDERFUL. *THEIR HERITAGE.*